ADVANCE PRAISE FOR *TRUSTING TECHNOLOGY*

"Graham Binks's book, *Trusting Technology*, is exactly what is needed for leaders today. Back in 2006, when we conducted research on the 'Leader of the Future,' being technologically savvy was identified as a needed skill set. This is a great source for adding this skill if you are in a leadership position."

—Marshall Goldsmith, *New York Times* #1 Bestselling Author of *Triggers, Mojo*, and *What Got You Here Won't Get You There*

"Technology has shifted from an operational tool running in the background to a powerful engine that generates fresh value. *Trusting Technology* brings together business, technology, and customer conversations using simple, powerful frameworks that focus on what matters most: growing your business. Take a step-by-step journey to identify real opportunities, explore meaningful alternatives, create smart solutions, and align your team to follow through on inspired solutions. These are the essential tools of modern technology strategy. They will help you cut through complexity and harness the right technologies for your business."

—Tom Wujec, Author, Technologist, and Design Thinker

"Whenever we have hired Graham, he's broken down complexity and shone a light on the simple path forward. Now he's pulled that off in a book!"

—Sean Smith, CEO, PetHealth Inc—A Fairfax Company

"Technology offers a path to building a better business. When we understand how to use it, we can find the right balance between innovation and keeping the lights on. *Trusting Technology* provides valuable insights on translating between business and technology, avoidin[illegible] pitfalls, and to finding your path to success."

—Glenn Laverty, President and C[illegible] and SV[illegible] [illegible]ca

"Technology doesn't drive change, i[illegible] [illegible]n business technology requires a rich blend [illegible] [illegible]ing buy in and oversight starting with the CEO down. In *Trusting Technology*, Graham has laid out an invaluable blueprint for change, a learning mindset, the generation of insight, and capturing intellectual property. When we put our trust in people, we usually know what we're getting. If we are to put our trust in technology, we need this depth and breadth."

—Hazel Wheldon, CEO, Multi-Health Systems Inc (MHS)

"When it comes to utilizing technology, the single most important question for companies to ask is: *'How does this help us improve our relationship with our existing customers, or enable us to serve our prospective clients better?'* Graham shows how any company can use technology to add real value, with plenty of great examples and practical applications throughout."

—Noah Fleming, Author of *Evergreen*

TRUSTING TECHNOLOGY

MASTERING TECHNOLOGY FOR NON-TECH LEADERS

GRAHAM BINKS

FOREWORD BY ALAN WEISS

A POST HILL PRESS BOOK
ISBN: 978-1-64293-272-0
ISBN (eBook): 978-1-64293-273-7

Trusting Technology:
Mastering Technology for Non-Tech Leaders

Cover art by Graham Binks

Post Hill Press
New York • Nashville
posthillpress.com

Published in the United States of America

To Ken and Nancy
Without whom…
Thank you

TABLE OF CONTENTS

FOREWORD

The Luddites, named after a fictitious Ned Ludd at the end of the 18th century, protested mechanization in English textile mills, claiming it led to deceitful and underhanded treatment of labor. A rebellion of sorts, from 1811 to 1816, resulted in fires and destruction of machinery and plants. Mill owners took to shooting the rebels on sight and the insurrection was finally put down with the use of military force and legal restrictions after half a decade.

That may sound far-fetched to you, as you sort through a thousand on-demand television options or use your smart phone to order pizza or check your stock portfolio on a tablet. Yet as you're doing that, in America and elsewhere in the world, taxi drivers and taxi companies, threatened by the advanced technology of Uber and its offspring, are in the streets, in the courts, and in a dither. We're talking 200 years after the Luddites, but we're not quite out of the fearful technological woods as yet, or so it would appear.

We're in an age of preparation for autonomous vehicles, yet many current drivers can't be bothered to use their turn signals. Hotels provide keyless entry and check in by smart phone, but many guests can't figure out how to be recognized by the elevators to choose their floor. It sometimes takes longer for the clerk to check you out in the supermarket on the computer than it would if the clerk simply used an old cash register. The infamous spell-check on the platform on which I'm writing this makes as many errant corrections as legitimate ones.

Technology has to be synergistic. It doesn't exist for its own good any more than insurance exists for its own good. We're not talking about cheetahs or tulips, which are successful by merely perpetuating the species. Insurance needs people to protect in order to provide value. Technology needs consumers and customers whose experiences need to be enhanced in a way that the improvement is appreciated and cost-effective, if it is to provide value.

In this splendid book, my colleague Graham Binks helps you to discern the nature of and uses for technology in this synergistic fashion and in a wide variety of scenarios. This book is not about learning how to use a tablet or a computer. It's about how you can improve your life and help others to improve theirs, at work and at home.

He looks at the interstitial relationships between supplier and buyer, creator and customer. He demonstrates that technology is an *enabler* of a better world if we understand it correctly and use it effectively. That is a huge "IF" and that's why we need this book.

Absorb herein how you create, control, and capitalize on technology, today and tomorrow. It's not only well worth the time, it's a terrific read, and by its end, at least, you should be reassured that technology is a powerful servant.

You needn't go around burning the technology mills, and no one will be sending the militia.

—Alan Weiss, PhD

Author, *Million Dollar Consulting* and over sixty other works in fifteen languages

INTRODUCTION

I remember the day the package arrived. About the size of a case of beer, though much lighter. It took me a day to assemble my first computer kit. When I was done, the Challenger 1P looked like a small piano with a QWERTY keyboard. The unit boasted four kilobytes of RAM, and I had to co-opt my parents' portable black-and-white TV to display its twenty-four lines of text. That was about enough memory to store this page of text and enough screen real estate to read half of it without scrolling.

The assembly was fun, like Lego for big kids. But the real rush came a week or so later, when I ran my first program. I instructed the computer to display "Hello World." And when it did, I was hooked.

Technology is about getting better. Finding new ways to do old things or discovering new things entirely. Most of the time, the new ways are better, freeing you of grunt work so you can spend more time creating, innovating, and enjoying the rush of your own version of "Hello World."

Several decades into a tech career, I've had the great pleasure to guide hundreds of businesses in their quests to improve the way they generate insights for their customers and employees, the way they automate much of their work, and the way they grow. In that time, I've had the opportunity to impact how people commute, enhance their health and safety, dress, entertain themselves, prepare for their retirement, and take care of their families.

Technology is great when it works. But that takes persistence to meld the tech with its context—the people who will use it and the jobs they need to get done.

From developer to consumer, we all struggle to get this stuff to work. Every day, the tech news media reports the breakthroughs and missteps of the big tech brands. While Google, Facebook and Tesla may lead the charge, technology remains a confusing, risky, and under-used tool for most business leaders.

We know success in technology requires expertise—there are over a hundred distinct career paths that budding technologists can follow today—but this is an industry with a proclivity for complicating matters. After all, it's much harder to simplify.

Trusting Technology is written for the business leader who pines to get beyond this nonsense. Whether you love tech or hate it with a passion, this book will help you navigate the waters of change and achieve value for your customers and colleagues.

Too many business technology conversations begin with the solution. That's fine if the goal is to inspire ideas but dead wrong if the solution is seen as the silver bullet. Some say "we always begin with the problem" but that's also flawed thinking. The first step to success lies somewhere else, and technology isn't even step two.

To get there, you have to take a short journey back in time, place our current environment in context, and follow a simple path to understanding.

WHY "TRUSTING TECHNOLOGY"?

I hate waste.

And I love overcoming challenges.

Since you've picked up this book, I sense you may feel the same way.

My own path began in software, then business systems, and ultimately tools that help leaders turbocharge their businesses and help people enrich their work lives. If that sounds grandiose, I think of this as helping people to avoid the dull work and make the interesting decisions faster.

I like to understand how things come to pass. For this reason, I find history to be a great informer. Fact is, there are way more stories in history than we could ever make up. As my early career developed, it became apparent that technology was a lot harder for most people than it was for me. And those challenges created barriers. If my mission was to help people use tech to create opportunities and realize higher goals, it was clear that my focus had to go beyond the nuts and bolts of technology.

As the technology industry developed through the latter years of the twentieth century, I began to see what was missing—translation between the world of business and the laboratory of technology.

Technology offered the promise that we could re-imagine business, but it was all a tease. The fact is that technology alone could do none of this. It simply provides a platform for our ideas. One glance (well, more than a glance) back at history bore this out. The platform only promised potential.

With an oncoming tide of new tech ideas—some proven, most not—it's easy to get carried away by the tech hype cycle and pick the wrong goals. Too ambitious and you burn credibility. Too conservative and, well, what's the point?

If I had to pick one piece of advice after five hundred career projects across three hundred diverse businesses, it would be this—*think big and act small.* Lofty goals fuel worthy breakthroughs, but they're best achieved in a spirit of learning, one step at a time.

In the course of reading these pages, you'll gain a new perspective on how you can achieve the promise that technology offers your customers, employees and, thereby, your shareholders. If you stick with me to the end, I hope you'll be inspired.

This is a book, and books are the first technology that allowed humankind to communicate stories beyond the verbal. In so doing, books carried stories and knowledge through the barriers of time and distance. A book is a tactile object that offers the wonder of secrets within—assuming we find the topic to be stimulating. But I'm walking the walk by offering information in other, complementary media. Please take a few minutes to refer to the *Trusting Technology* companion website where you'll find tools, videos, and other useful material. Long after this book has gone to press, the site will remain topical. The booksite is here: *www.trustingtechnologybook.com.*

WHAT'S IN THIS BOOK FOR YOU?

Time is our most precious resource. The minute that it takes you to read this section is one you'll never get back. If you're going to read the rest of the book, you'll need good reasons. I hope you find at least one below.

If you are a CEO and don't consider yourself technical, I hope *Trusting Technology* becomes your best friend. Because while you'll find hundreds of mentions of technology, you won't find a single technical detail.

Promise. This book is about building success with technology by looking at the *whys* and the ways it can be used, but not the techie *hows*. It's my experience that the *whys* and the ways are where business struggles. Get those right and we can figure out the techie parts. I hope this book will give you the confidence to do more and move faster with technology in your business.

If you are an ambitious technology leader, *Trusting Technology* offers some ways to connect your stakeholders with the brilliant technology that you provide. What you do is complex. Explaining it in terms that 95 percent of the business population understands is tough. My goal is that such translation will become your superpower after reading this book.

If you are a business leader trying to figure out how to use technology in your part of the business, *Trusting Technology* strips away the aura of mystery that surrounds the tech-god headlines you read every day. Who cares what Google, Facebook, and Amazon do? Let's discover what's possible for *your* business.

If you are a technology vendor trying to better understand your customers, *Trusting Technology* offers a language of change that you can borrow to bridge the gap between your customers' needs and the service you currently provide. Understand their context and you'll be a prized partner.

And if you work with any of the above, *Trusting Technology* offers a common vocabulary to help you help each other do better work and build better businesses. By focusing every effort on the simplest core challenges, on minimalist change, and by designing and discovering together, the sky is the only limit to your success.

A word on the examples given.

This book presents dozens of examples, mini case studies that illustrate success and failure with technology. I've had the pleasure of being involved in many of these cases. Some examples are already in the public domain. Some must remain confidential for reasons of trade secrets or, in some cases, a reluctance to attribute hard-won lessons. For these reasons, you'll note that some of the names have been hidden to protect the innocent. Rest assured that the examples are all real.

Whether you are a technophobe or tech guru, I hope you'll find riches in the pages that follow.

HOW TO READ THIS BOOK

Here's your roadmap for *Trusting Technology*. You'll see that each chapter builds on the previous one. However, if your goal is to develop a roadmap based on your business needs, you may want to jump ahead to Chapter Nine.

Chapter One: Making Ideas Happen Technology is a platform for your ideas. Chapter One examines the ideas process—where ideas come from and where they go. We'll look at how you can turn ideas into reality and whose opinion really matters when you judge success. You'll find the first in a series of exercises that place these lessons in the context of your own business and the six steps to mastering technology as your platform.

Chapter Two: Forming an Opinion Your first step to technology mastery is to form an opinion on the technology potential for your business and where you should play next. The second step is to refresh that opinion. Tech is such a massive field, and "keeping up" is a daunting task—more so if tech is anathema to you. Chapter Two provides guidance and tools that will help you to develop an informed business opinion without becoming a technology expert.

Chapter Three: Setting Your Sights Sometimes the hardest step is the first one. Chapter Three provides techniques designed to help you to set your sights on the big goals worthy of your attention. You'll clarify what's good and bad about your business today, what needs to be better, and why you may think that's a challenge. (Spoiler alert—you'll revisit those same challenges at the end of the book to see how far you've come.) Someplace, somehow, someone has already done what you need to do. You can follow their lead if you think big and act small.

Chapter Four: Changing with Your Customer Impact begins on the outside with your customers. Understanding the relationship you have with your customers is vital if you are to make it better. What role does the customer play in your business, and what exactly do you do for them? What journey do you offer your customers, and what impression do you leave? The answers will determine how you should partner with your customers—are they leading you, are you leading them, or do you take turns?

Chapter Five: Building Confidence When you change your business, you're messing with the comfort zones of your customers and colleagues. For many businesses, the promised outcome is not realized. The customer may or may not benefit, the work may get easier for a few, but may get harder for most. You don't have to be one of those businesses. In this chapter, we'll explore the secret of successful change—building confident teams.

Chapter Six: Getting It Right by Doing the Quickstep It takes courage to admit to what you don't know. After all, we're all hired as experts. But when you set big goals, you're setting out on a unique journey—no one has ever done what you are about to do in your exact context. Your big journey truly starts with a single step, and that step is recognizing what your business needs to know and planning to learn as you go. Proceed with caution but move quickly.

Chapter Seven: Inspiring Insight Every business is a machine for turning raw materials into useful products. People are great at making decisions. Technology is great at directing the flow of information to support those decisions. Digital strategy—quite simply—means rendering information in a way that can be directed by technology. In this chapter, you'll identify the information that currently exists in your business—and the information that could exist. With this in hand, you'll paint a picture of how that information can be delivered to whomever needs it, whenever they need it—to make the best-informed decisions. This chapter also includes everything a business leader needs to know about security—on one page.

Chapter Eight: Bottling Innovation Your business has a secret sauce, your recipe for making or doing something new that your customers value. The best technology will help you convert this recipe into assets that deliver this value to your customers faster and cheaper. In Chapter Eight, you'll identify these crown jewels and begin to understand the ways that technology can help you create and deliver more. So your smart innovators can focus on what you need them to focus on—creating more secret sauce.

Chapter Nine: Mastering Technology Chapter Nine provides a master plan for bringing together the components of technology-enabled innovation in your business. Your needs are unique, and you'll lay out a roadmap here. When done, you'll have a vision, ambition, and a place to begin your journey to becoming a better tech company.

You *could* begin your read of *Trusting Technology* here and refer back to the previous chapters as you explore this chapter. Your call.

Chapter Ten: Your Next Business ...in which you'll envision your business boldly going where others have gone before. The goal of this book is to broaden your horizons and engender confidence and ambition. In Chapter Ten, we'll fast forward to the day when you've mastered these ideas. Dream big.

Oh, and One Last Thing ...Enough about your business—what about you?

— Graham Binks
Toronto, Ontario
May 2019

PART I

MAKING FRIENDS WITH TECHNOLOGY

HUMANKIND'S LOVE/HATE RELATIONSHIP

CHAPTER ONE
MAKING IDEAS HAPPEN

Technology Is Your Platform for Innovation

In which we examine where ideas come from, where they go, and how they get there and what that has to do with your business.

Technology is a platform for your ideas.

Every one of us has ideas every day. Many are fleeting—they emerge from our subconscious, maybe prompt a chuckle, and disappear like gossamer on the breeze. Other ideas stick. Something about them prompts us to pursue. Maybe we take a note, sketch an outline, or hum a new tune.

This is how every human endeavor begins. Great art originated upon waking from a dream; scientific breakthroughs in a moment of realization, business plans inspired in the shower.

If ideas are to last and make a contribution to the world, they must be made real. Having the idea is the easy part. Humans are idea machines. Success lies in the manifestation—the sharing, the compromise, and the conviction that this one counts. That it's worth the hard work needed to convince others.

Technology is one way to make this happen.

In this chapter we'll look at how you can turn ideas into reality and whose opinion really matters when you judge success. You'll find the first in a series of exercises that place these lessons in context of your own business and the six steps to mastering technology as your platform.

ESTABLISHED TEN MILLION YEARS BC—A BRIEF HISTORY OF ALMOST EVERY TECHNOLOGY

Technology gives us tools. The earliest tools have been dated to around ten million years BC, well before Raquel Welch roamed the earth: axes and hammers made from stone and antlers. Alas, we'll never know how our ancestors used these tools—because the first technology for recording events came much later.

Some cave guy or gal struck a flint against a stone and set a fire around eight million years later, and with that came warmth and the ability to inhabit cooler climates. They say clothing arrived fifty thousand years ago, further expanding the regions where humans could reside.

In his landmark TV series *Connections*, James Burke shares ten stories of the history of technology, with tales linking riding stirrups to telecommunications and tracing computing back to the Black Death. It's the best kind of history-telling because he doesn't stop at the present. Leaning on historical patterns and his knowledge of contemporary technology, Burke predicted the smartphone and free, universal, instantaneous, global communication. Hard to believe there was ever a time when such concepts weren't obvious.

Connections was first broadcast in 1978. Find a copy and binge.

That kind of foresight is a superpower—imagine the bets you could place!

This book is about applying those same principles to your business. About having an opinion on where things are going, what that could mean for your business, and putting yourself in a position to reap the benefits.

On the shoulders of giants

The history of technology is a history of building on the work of others. Burke illustrates this with examples from Lady Hamilton to Edison, from artillery to the loom. Where art frowns on plagiarism, technology—and its close friend science—embraces the concept. In Chapter

Two, you'll discover *the stack*—tech's way of building something new with components that others invented.

Building on others' shoulders

Sportsmen in France form a human pyramid, 1919.
(Photo: M. Rol/Ullstein Bild/Getty Images)

Apple built the world's biggest business on the back of a small package containing technologies invented by others. Steve Jobs's genius was simply to package that with a great user experience and call it the iPhone. Don't you wish the guys that invented the TV remote had had one tenth of his foresight? In the case of the iPhone, the breakthrough was not the technology, but the ease of use, fit for purpose, and plain sexiness of the product.

Likewise, Google, Microsoft, and Facebook were not first in their space. Their big idea was not the thing itself, it was how to make that thing attractive to the buyer. That's where they applied first-mover advantage.

For the rest of us, the lesson is simple—you don't have to be the pioneer (with all the attendant risk) to win. Much easier to know what's going on elsewhere, what market risk others have addressed, and how to blend innovations to create your own special brew. You simply have to master the practice of rapid experimentation to learn your way to market success.

The one theme common to all technologies since those stone-and-antler axes is that success builds on success. Technologies allow ideas to evolve. When new things become possible, and eventually easy, they advance the platform for further ideas. No technology lasts forever, but every successful one advances our game.

More recently, the convergence of several technologies provides you with a pocket device that converts your unique speech patterns into text—at no charge. Actually, your pocket device provides only a piece of the puzzle. Speech recognition was the holy grail of AI for many years (our thanks to IBM for sinking billions to solve the software problem).

But speech recognition software requires computing power way beyond that of your phone. That's when smartphone developers had an *aha* moment—why don't we send the audio file over the wireless data network to massive computing resources, run the conversion there, and send the text back? We call that cloud computing these days, but it's the exact same model we used to call client/server and our ancestors used to call bureau computing.

Technology has always provided the platform for entertainment. If it ain't live, entertainment needs a medium to transmit what we now rather blandly call content. Do you think Shakespeare and Billy Wilder thought of their work as content? Marshall McLuhan described content as the message rather than the medium, and technology has always provided the medium. In Shakespeare's time it was pen and paper, and in Billy Wilder's time it was film. Today the medium is digital—TV, movies, music, books, and games. Same genius, only now it's instant.

Technology's essence, relentless advancement, and fundamental value lies in the way it enshrines the building on the "shoulders of giants" concept. And that's what can make technology your launchpad for success.

WHERE IDEAS COME FROM

Ideas are born of impatience: dissatisfaction with the way things are that inspires the dissatisfied to conceive of a better way and drives their determination to make the change work.

We can sit on the couch all day long and ask why no one's invented a better way to control the TV. That may be an interesting parlor game for the couch-potato genius, but it doesn't get stuff done.

Don't underestimate the role of adversity on the pace of innovation. Look around your office or living room right now and consider how many objects can be traced back to the wave of innovation driven by the panic of World War II. Write them down and make James Burke proud.

The classic image of inspiration is the eureka moment—Archimedes leaping from his bathtub in excitement at recognizing the concept of displacement. A sudden lightning strike of complete understanding. Ironic, isn't it, that Archimedes may never have had that epiphany if the shower had been invented.

The danger with such icons as Edison, Jobs, and Einstein is that they suggest that the true source of ideas is largely a property of individual inspiration. Without question, the determination of these individuals—and countless other less famous talents—made a difference. But we need to bust this myth by recognizing that ideas never succeed until they are placed in the hands of the community they best serve. Until they are allowed to evolve, live, and die.

Experience

When we experience something we like, something that works well for us, we feel joy. The thirst for this joy influences how we react to things we don't like, things that bug us, cause significant inconvenience, and that just don't work for us.

If we're so inclined, we might spend the time to think up ways to improve bad experiences. Quite possibly, we may not give it another thought until an idea pops. Whether new ways arise from a deliberate process or happenstance, we've had an idea.

The next question is whether anyone else cares.

Insight

When any of us are new to a field, it's not uncommon for us to rethink what we see. As a new leader in a team, you get to "ask the dumb questions" as you assimilate. It's important to do this with two aims in mind: to further your learning of the status quo and to prompt new thinking amongst those already familiar with the situation. Do so in a way that respects what has gone before and that applies new insight, and you have a chance of influencing everybody to change.

The application of insight helps an idea mature. Writing it down is a great way to start. I don't mean just adding a few words to a list. I'm talking about thinking it through as you write. Getting the idea out of your head, sharing it with yourself, fleshing things out, and reading it back. Sometimes it makes sense, other times it fails the test.

If the idea evolves to a point where you're convinced it's worth pursuing, that's what you will do. (If you never find the time to pursue it, you were never convinced in the first place.)

Conviction

It's that conviction that fuels your effort, that inspires you to spend time, and to stand up for the idea in the face of resistance. And there is always resistance. Without this gusto, your idea will fade away. Without vigor, you won't share the idea and convince others that it's a thing worth pursuing.

Gusto is what separates Edison, Jobs, and their ilk from the couch potato genius.

Gusto and two other things....

Sharing

None of us is smarter than all of us. You can probably prove that with math.

An idea that we keep to ourselves is fine for self-satisfaction. We all do that, and I hope we all get pleasure from our inner thoughts. But that's not the kind of idea this book is about.

Ideas build on ideas and are improved by group participation. New concepts are stitched together by groups in the retrospectives, at the conference table, or by the water cooler. The advent of the coffee shop drove remarkable innovation in eighteenth-century Britain. Coffee and tea are stimulants and replaced alcohol as the clean drink of choice in these environments. Is it any wonder that exchanges of ideas flowered? Chance favors the connected mind.

Ideas that are shared and given over to a team for critical discourse, for testing, and for enrichment are ideas that live. Whether you display a piece of your art or suggest a new way to process customer orders, you are raising a topic, suggesting that we shouldn't be satisfied with the status quo, and offering a better way. When a group decides to pursue an idea, ownership shifts from an individual to the team. As a leader, you can set parameters, encourage experimentation and refinement, contribute to the process, and accept the outcome.

Perspective

How can you notice something new when you've been looking at the same thing through the same eyes year after year? Introducing new perspectives and welcoming outside opinions will generate new ideas and fresh takes.

Drucker's sources of innovation[1]

The first four sources lie within the business, or within an industry or service sector. They are basically symptoms:

- The unexpected—the unexpected success, the unexpected failure, the unexpected outside event.
- The incongruity—between reality as it actually is and reality as it is assumed to be or as it "ought to be."
- Innovation based on process need.
- Changes in industry structure or market structure that catch everyone unawares.

The second set of sources for innovative opportunity, a set of three, involves changes outside the enterprise or industry:

- Demographics (population changes).
- Changes in perception, mood, and meaning.
- New knowledge, both scientific and nonscientific.

1 Peter Drucker, "Purposeful Innovation and the Seven Sources for Innovative Opportunity," chap. 2 in *Innovation and Entrepreneurship* (New York: Harper & Row, 1985).

You can also help your team—and yourself—to see things in a new way by recognizing sources of new thinking. Check out management expert Peter Drucker's sources of innovation in the sidebar.

Spend some time reflecting on these and ask yourself:

- Where is your industry headed?
- Who's best today? Why do you pick them, and how would you respond?
- Ask someone in your front line (support or sales) to share a summary of customer requests. Are you tapped in to all of these?
- Have someone (else) trawl through your customer support tickets. These tickets are a goldmine of information that many companies overlook.

WHERE IDEAS GO

Innovations are ideas—implemented.

Ideas arise and prosper through a process of creation and curation. Divergent ideation followed by a rigorous process of culling. Success is born of failure—the trick is to achieve the right mix.

When innovation fails, it's not for lack of ideas—it's in the transfer of those ideas to the field. When any idea is shared, it becomes an experiment. Could this new approach work? How will it benefit others? Is this business worth building?

I don't hold with the trope that business leaders should encourage failure. Encourage informed experimentation for the purpose of learning, and recognize that no experiment fails as long as it answers a question. This process works if it reaches a series of conclusions that advance the work. (Repeated failure to achieve the same goal simply suggests incompetence.)

> *"Failure is the best medicine—as long as you learn something."*
>
> *—James Dyson*

James Dyson walked the walk of learning through failures, creating 5,127 prototypes before he learned how to create and control a cyclone (more on Dyson in Chapter Ten).

They say Edison prototyped over a thousand light bulbs before he put a product on the market.

How competent was he? If he'd had an impatient boss, would we still be reading by candlelight? The question of when to give up is a vexed one. If you (or your boss) believe that success is just around the corner, you could eventually hit on the right idea at last, or you could drive your business into the ground.

When PayPal co-founder Peter Thiel was considering investing in an early social media startup, he noted that Friendster—a rival—was tanking and their website was failing. A natural conclusion might have been that there was no future in this business. To test that theory, Thiel got hold of Friendster's visitor retention data and noted that the site's few users were extremely persistent, spending hours at a time on the site even though it was crashing around them. If Thiel had canned the idea at first glance, he wouldn't have invested in Facebook. By looking deeper, Thiel avoided the trap of the false fail—a failure that's due to a flaw in the experiment rather than the idea.

The moral is to design your experiments as thoroughly as you designed the idea you're testing.

But the biggest concern for business today is quite the opposite. Any lack of support for testing ideas puts a business at disadvantage. It discourages colleagues from trying and encourages would-be Edisons to move elsewhere. Be thorough and be smart, but also be free—and to heck with constraints!

What does success mean? Steve Jobs wanted to ship a computer that spoke human better than anything that had gone before. He practically killed the Mac team in getting the best product out to market. Twenty years later, he wanted to put a thousand songs in everyone's pocket, to make music more accessible.

Each time he had a goal. As a peerless perfectionist, Jobs was probably never completely happy, but he put his creations out into the world when they were ready. And he made compromises in the process—the first iPhones didn't support copy/paste—because he needed the market's feedback to decide where to go next.

You should take ideas so far—until you've achieved success—then stop. The notion that a product does everything it was designed to do allows us to move on to new areas. In Apple's case, it was iPod, iPhone, iPad, and so forth. Measures of success allow us to curate out ideas, know when they're winners or losers, and stop when we're done.

There's an evolution to any innovation that can be summed up as:

1. Idea
2. Innovation
3. Experiment
4. Adoption
5. Differentiator
6. Commodity
7. Redundancy

Version One, if you will. We'll look at what happens next in Chapter Two. For now, let's look at the bridge between steps one and two—making ideas real.

TURNING IDEAS INTO REALITY

Having the ideas is one thing, curating them another. But the rubber hits the road when you begin to make those ideas real in the eyes of your colleagues and, very soon after that, in the eyes of early-adopter customers. And since we're all into rubber hitting the road, most of this book is dedicated to making ideas real.

In Chapter Two, we'll look at the way innovations are adopted by their interest groups—your market—from the early fanatics to the later kicking-and-screaming adopters. This provides you with a context for deciding where your ideas can play in the innovation stack.

Since pioneers often face the greatest risks and losses, we'll spend some of Chapter Three developing a new habit—looking at businesses that have already turned ideas into reality in the manner you are considering and asking, "What if we could do that?"

When you present your customers with anything new—high tech, low tech or no tech—you're offering them a change, a new way of doing something that is important for them to do. They will test your ideas and inform your next steps. You change them, they change you. Chapter Four looks at this notion of changing with your customers.

> *If you want an easy life, stand still.*

And as we all know, implementation of new ideas means change, and that can mean havoc for your colleagues. Important to ask whether your business is embarking on a one-off change or becoming a serial-change outfit.

The pace of change, and the mode of change is another muscle you'll need to build up. Chapter Six lays bare the options for change cadence handling a loss of predictability.

Innovation can provide the greatest achievements of our career, but it ain't simple. Chapter Nine pulls it all together to make tech mastery *easier.*

THE ONLY OPINION THAT REALLY MATTERS

Every idea should be respected, but the buyer's opinion is the only one that really matters. Steve Blank says that "no plan survives first contact with customer."[2] This begs the question—how soon can you get customer feedback on your ideas?

Your business is a machine that serves your community of customers and colleagues. We'll look at this notion in Chapter Four.

This book is about building a better machine to better serve your community.

Better Service Test[3]

List three ways that you think your customers could be better served.

Then list three ways that you think your colleagues could be better served.

3 *This is the first of many tests that I offer with the intent of helping you generate and capture your ideas. These exercises build on each other, so I implore you to spend the few minutes that each will take as you go along.*

Now that you think about it, you probably have an idea of what "better serve" means for your community. This is important, so I want you

2 Steve Blank, "No Plan Survives First Contact with Customers—Business Plans versus Business Models," April 8, 2010, *https://steveblank.com/2010/04/08/no-plan-survives-first-contact-with-customers-%E2%80%93-business-plans-versus-business-models/.*

Every one of your colleagues, every one of your customers has ideas.

to note what you're thinking right now. Take the Better Service Test so we can build on this later.

There's an illusion that ideas come from special places—science labs, innovation teams, think tanks—anywhere but here. Allow me to disavow that notion.

They won't all be natural communicators or have the courage to step forward and suggest change. The job of the leader is to encourage everyone to submit their ideas, to curate the list for focused action, and to communicate rationale and results back to the originators. If you didn't act on my idea, I'll keep trying as long as you tell me why.

Going public

Ideas propagate with exposure. The trick is to continually refine the manifestation of your ideas and reach a growing audience of relevance. If the audience doesn't grow, you need to change the idea. If the idea doesn't take hold, try another.

There's nothing wrong with killing an idea when the evidence dictates. If it helps your process, consider that you're setting it aside for later rather than killing it entirely.

The question is how you share, how you manifest the idea in public, and with whom. There's a tendency to polish the implementation before sharing, but shininess won't dictate the basic appeal. Rough-and-ready prototypes boil ideas down to their essence, and it's the essential value that you are interested in testing. Better still, such prototypes can be created quickly, tweaked easily, and killed with less concern for sunk cost.

Let me be clear: sunk cost should never dictate a decision, but that doesn't change the fact that it's easier to cancel a project when the cost is low.

There's an irony that most businesses have been running a prototype of something for many years. Built as a proof of concept, it turned out to be good enough. As an engineer, I'm familiar with the visceral need to build a better version of everything, but I'd rather spend time on the best thing. You should too.

When you put ideas out into your market, into your customer community, you're demonstrating leadership. Sometimes you'll be responding to customer requests, other times you'll be offering a new way.

> *The customer's always right.*
> *—H.G. Selfridge*
>
> *It's not the customer's job to know what they want.*
> *—Steve Jobs*

Customer requests tend to be tactical—fix this instance of this problem, do this thing for me or I'll take my business elsewhere. But if you ask this question often enough, speak to enough people with similar needs, you'll have insights that could lead to bigger change—ubiquitous, global communication devices in every pocket and purse, for example.

It's hard to say no, but you can at least think twice and strike the right balance. If you want to build a customer following, you need to lead.

EXACTLY HOW MANY IDEAS AN INNOVATOR NEEDS

Fifteen.

Or sixty-four.

Heck, the more the merrier, as long as enough good ones make it to reality. If you like numbers, I suggest you spend 10 percent of your innovation time on idea creation and 90 percent on curation and testing. If you're struggling to bring good ideas to reality, consider involving customers at the outset of your curation process.

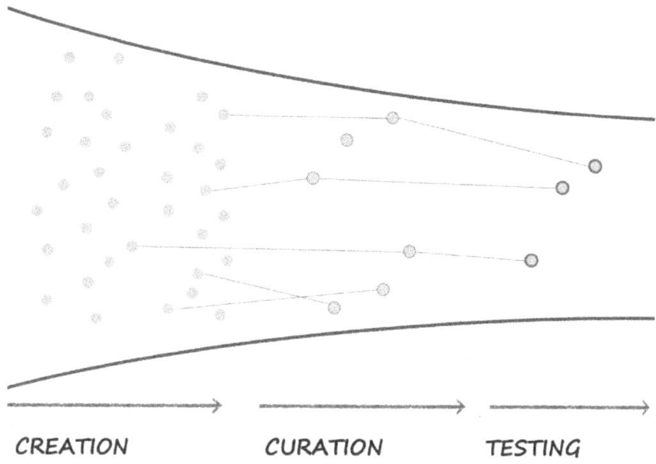

Ideas made real

Idea creation is a divergent process. You encourage wild and crazy thinking by ignoring constraints and focusing on the *what.*

Idea curation is a convergent process; deciding which ideas make the most sense here and now. Some questions for your curation of each idea:

- How much value could this create for the customer? How much for the business?
- Has this been done before? If so, what were the results? Could that apply here?
- If not, what's the risk of failure? Is the potential value worth the risk?
- Are we blowing up an existing approach or just tweaking it?
- How do we test this with our esteemed customers?
- How quickly will we see results—positive or negative?
- Where does this fit in our innovation portfolio?

We go deep into innovation portfolios in Chapter Eight. For the time being, just note…

The first step on your journey to technology mastery is to forget the technology.

Instead, consider the value of the thing you're considering. Tech is part of the *how.* You may find inspiration in the tech others have used to do something similar. You may need to spitball some implementation approach to get comfortable with risk and timeline.

But don't pick a specific solution and base your plans on that until you've created and curated ideas that lead you in that direction. Sounds obvious, but you'd be surprised how many times leaders put the proverbial cart before the horse.

No sense having ideas if you can't make them real. The role of technology at this stage, beyond inspiration, is to provide you with the means to rapidly prototype and test curated ideas. It's this capability that has driven much of the thinking around innovation over recent decades. This may have been born in tech, but every business is a tech business now, right?

For further inspiration, Chapter Seven examines the role of tech in generating insights. Chapter Eight covers tech's role in automation, enshrining intellectual property, and creating assets for your business.

And Chapter Ten offers the rosiest of futures for your tech mastery business.

AVOIDING THAT NIGHTMARE NEWS

Imagine waking one morning, turning to your favorite news source, and reading that your biggest competitor has announced a revolutionary new product that could eat your market share for breakfast. Now imagine that didn't happen, and you arrive at work to hear a proposal from your team that could eat your competitor's breakfast.

Where would you rather find out about a new innovation: (a) in a competitor's press release, or (b) from your own people?

If you answered (b), process more ideas. When you ensure the best rise to the top, you'll astound your market with the pace of change you offer. Consider this six-step process:

1. Turn your business into an idea machine.
2. Be aware of the shoulders you can build on—spread the word.
3. Have an opinion on the future of technology in your field.
4. Grow with your customers.
5. Turn the havoc of change into confidence for your colleagues.
6. Think big and act small.

Technology provides your means for building out these ideas. In the course of this book, we'll examine these steps in detail.

MAKING IDEAS HAPPEN—IN A NUTSHELL

Technology is your platform for ideas...

- Along with art and including science
- Technology makes ideas real

- Leverage serial innovation by building new ideas on existing technologies

Ideas come about when…

- We get impatient with the way things are.
- You apply experiences, insight, and conviction.
- New perspectives are introduced.
- You share ideas and give groups time to think.
- You allow for happenstance.

Ideas die or thrive…

- Failures demonstrate…
- Successes demonstrate…
- Curation—relevance, timeliness, dependencies, *thank you*s keep the ideas flowing
- Understand what success means for you
- Ask the right opinions

Making ideas real requires mastery of…

- Changing customers
- Leveraging the havoc of change
- Pace and uncertainty
- Blood, sweat, and tears—it ain't easy
- Thinking big and acting small

Who gets to decide?

- The opinions that matter
- How do *you* think things could be better? How do they?
- Going public
- Change *with* your customers—lead and follow each other

Creating an idea machine:

- Tech is a friend—a key pillar of your business
- First steps to tech mastery

Booksite extras at www.trustingtechnologybook.com/chapter1 include an intro to the booksite and the workbook for all tests, including a template for the Better Service test.

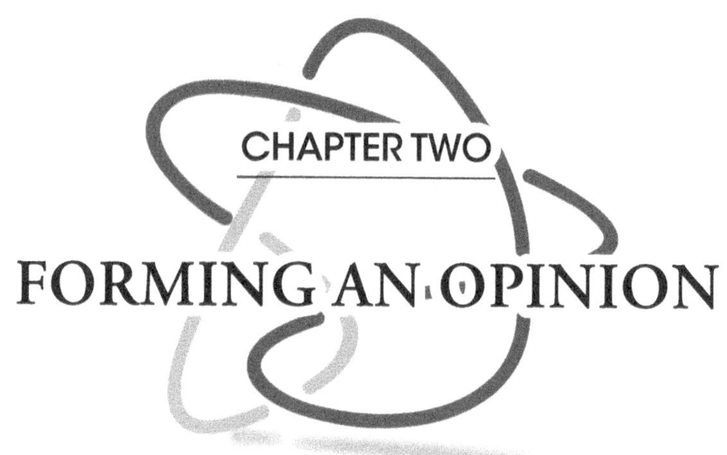

CHAPTER TWO

FORMING AN OPINION

Setting Your Expectations for Technology

In which you'll challenge your opinion of technology and begin to shape a new perspective.

Technology is more accessible today than it's ever been.

Whether you're building it, buying, or partnering, the options available are unprecedented. That's both boon and bane. The boon is that somehow, some way, technology can propel any business—including yours. The bane is that you'll have to sort through a bewildering assortment of options to find that flame.

Unlimited hardware, a vast array of software components—both of which we can consider bricks to build complex systems—and abundant entrepreneurial enthusiasm have driven the tech industry to new heights since the dot-com bubble burst at the beginning of the century. Though that tumultuous event has been lost in the mists of time, hard lessons were learned about commercialization, innovation, and idea validation.

While there's nothing new about innovation, the rebirth of tech has accelerated the pace at which ideas can be implemented. It's never been easier to launch a new business. It's so easy that many businesses still launch before they have a viable product—then take the inevitable nosedive. It's evolution on steroids, a world teeming with upstarts, startups, and established businesses.

Somewhere in this frenzy, consumer technology has leaped ahead of commercial tech in terms of design and customer experience. In the process, our expectations of technology have increased. We're all consumers, and we all use our phones for everything from staying in touch with everyone we know (and many we don't) to managing health plans, bank accounts, and those angry birds.

Why, then, when we get to work in the morning, are we faced with systems that frustrate us, give us migraines, and seem to slow us down more often than speed us up?

Expectations.

Hands up if you remember the days before spreadsheets allowed we laypeople to run quantitative risk assessments at the push of a button. (You still can't do that? Well, the days when you had to manage your budget with a calculator.) Before you could run what-if scenarios, produce endless tables and reports, then present professional-looking slide decks to sell your concept. Receive a message in the middle of the meeting that your client's stock just tanked and adjust on the fly. Debrief over video with your colleagues Ben in London and Ignatius in Hong Kong. Then turn around the revised proposal before close of business.

We get a lot more done these days. Sometimes it seems like too much. Over the last generation, we have slowly been trained to expect more and more from technology. We've developed a low tolerance when it fails to deliver, when it's hard to learn, or when it simply doesn't perform as expected.

That's the lot of your consumer persona. Now leap across your desk and put on your supplier hat. Everything your business does to sell, deliver, and support your products is judged by the same standard. Your product may deliver on the features in the brochure, but does the experience you provide exceed your customer's expectations?

The bar today is set by form as much as function.

EVERYDAY JOBS—WHAT TECH CAN DO FOR US

So we get a lot more done today than we used to. You'd think that would mean lots more time in the day to do other stuff, more recreation

> *"The trouble is, you think you have time."*
>
> *—Buddha*

or downtime. But that's not the way things roll. The ability to do more creates an even greater appetite for speed and productivity.

Not to mention that "more" includes handling a deluge of incoming information. Emails from colleagues at 9:45 p.m., social network updates from everyone with a cat, it seems, and more news-tertainment than anyone can handle.

This all makes it harder to know what we should get done, let alone when we can find the time can do it.

The tech we like helps us get everyday jobs done with more ease, or perhaps even does the job for us. Too tired to pick up groceries tonight? No problem—pop open that app, order in dinner, and pick up your fridge replenishments at the door.

Tired of scheduling your own appointments? Easy—there's an app for that too.

Let's play a game—what little tech things have made a big difference in your life over the last decade? I'll go first:

There's nothing quite like the tactile feel of a good book. An exciting subject has so much potential. Much as I love this, I do most of my reading on a tablet now. It's a different experience. I can preview many books for free so I know that I'm reading the ones I want. When I've bought the book, I can look up an unfamiliar word and fill out the experience by researching a related topic. Within a few seconds, I'm back with the author. Digital books are just one of Amazon's several user interfaces.

I spend a fair amount of time on the road. Nowadays, I can make this time useful by listening to podcasts and asking my phone—hands free and eyes on the road—to play any music as the fancy takes me. I can ask my phone to call or text anyone as easily and safely as speaking to a passenger.

Time was, it used to take a couple hours a day to work out and a ton of time picking healthy meals. Now with my handy-dandy 8fit app, I can get a great workout in twenty minutes a day and prepare simple, delicious meals without the research. I'm in the best shape I've been in for years.

Now it's your turn—write out a few ways that tech has changed your life over the last few years.

Where has tech helped you?

What has it been worth?

While these examples may seem like trivial consumer things, you can be forgiven for underestimating the technology behind them. That's because of the stack, a concept you'll read about in a few pages.

Sure, making business easier with technology is on a different level of complexity. But it doesn't need to be. Technology function is the same—to make ideas real, deliver information to create insight, and automate any process we can describe.

If you haven't already done so, ask your customer where tech has helped them and what it's been worth. Then think on what their answer could mean to you.

It's time to challenge your technology opinion.

HOW TECHNOLOGY MATURES—FORECASTING TOOLS

I don't hold with the idea of crystal balls and predicting the future. Then again, it's fun to guess, test your theory, and iterate to the target. We may not know what technologies will emerge over the next five or ten years, but we know most of the ideas that will impact that window of opportunity have already been invented. And we *can* trace their potential paths with some confidence by following a couple of patterns that have proven reliable in the past.

If you combine these perspectives with the ideas of giant shoulders and consider potential combinations, you can begin to form some opinions about what this could mean in your business.

Recall the evolutionary path of innovation from Chapter One:

1. Idea
2. Innovation
3. Experiment
4. Adoption
5. Differentiator
6. Commodity
7. Redundancy

An idea passes the curation test and is implemented—Version One, if you will. The concept either passes or fails its first exposure to customers. If it passes, it's adopted. If Version Three or Four is unique in the market at that time, it is differentiated and prospers with the customer segment that cares. But eventually, a product will reach commodity status, and then it's a race to the bottom. Finally, some new innovation disrupts the market and the product fades away. You may notice four critical decision points in the cycle:

A. Idea to Innovation: do you place your bets on this idea?

B. Experiment to Adoption: what level of adoption merits investment?

C. Differentiator to Commodity: how do you sustain differentiation?

D. Commodity to Redundancy: how and when should you exit?

You may have a great idea, but you still need to formulate your theory on how it will evolve. Truth is, of course, that any plan is a theory, but there are some tools that can help you reduce the uncertainty.

The Gartner Hype Cycle and the Rogers curve

All nascent technologies have their ups and downs—AI being a topical example. That's entirely consistent with the way we adopt new things. If you're at all interested in innovation, you should know how this works.

Everett Rogers published his Rogers curve in 1962. It's the best model I know for understanding how successful innovation hits the mainstream. Rogers drew a bell curve, then represented early adopters on the left, mainstream in the middle, and late adopters on the right. His theory of the diffusion of innovation states that success begins with the intrigue of early adopters[4]—visionaries, techies, and the curious. When the value becomes evident to the majority, they will adopt. Eventually, even Luddite late adopters will jump on board.

Rogers's theory has borne out countless times.

4 Interestingly, 'adapter' works as well 'adopter' in this context. Take your pick.

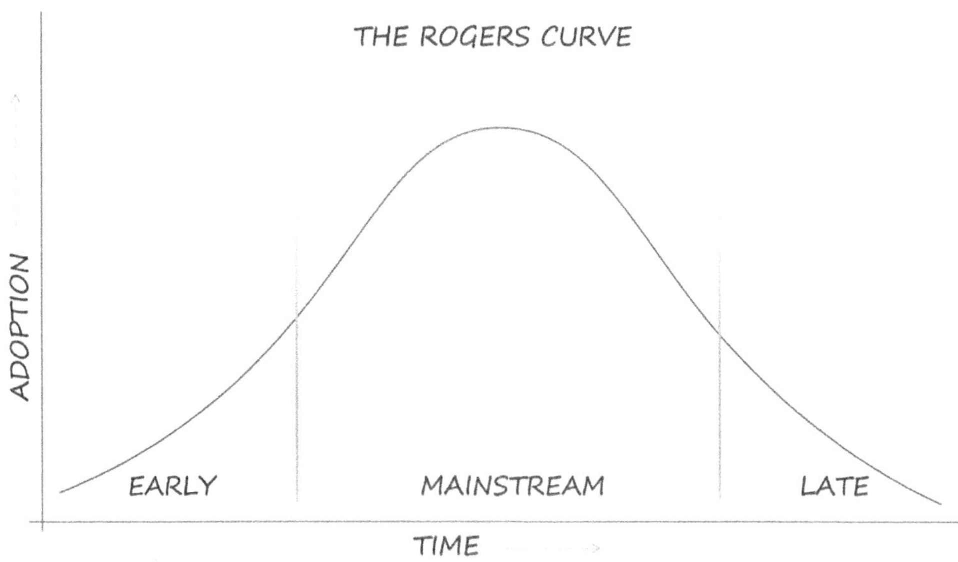

The Rogers Curve

The secret sauce, of course, is the early detection of winners—innovations that make it all the way to the right of the curve. Success takes a combination of factors:

- The recognition of technology potential
- A matching problem or opportunity
- The zeal of a pioneer

If you have tech potential alone, stay in the research lab. If you can match that with opportunity, you may be on to something. And if you have zeal, you have a shot at commercial success.[5]

There's a fourth element, a kind of karma. Being in the right place at the right time, combining the right technologies and customer needs.

It's this fourth element that can cause many innovations to flounder for decades. Artificial intelligence (AI) may be all the buzz today, but it was conceived in the 1950s. After tons of successful science projects and some minor commercial successes, the right circumstances have finally

5 What's a good scale for your Mainstream? Commercial success may only require a peak of a handful of big customers

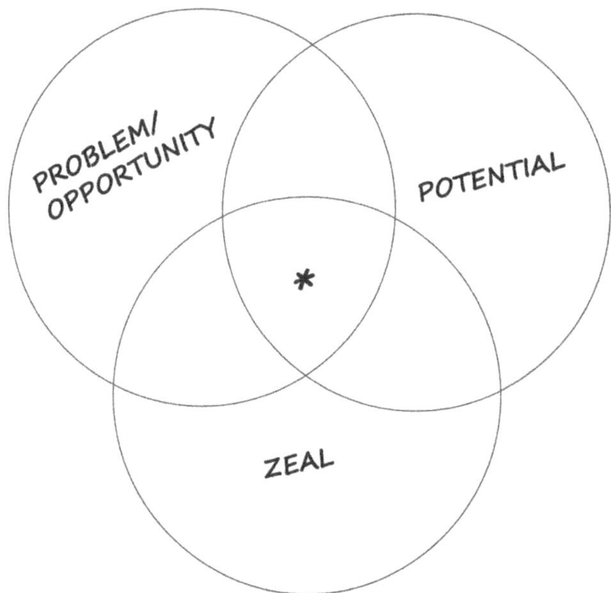

The Venn Diagram of Innovation

arrived for AI to hit the limelight. It's taken massive affordable computing power and a glut of data to spark commercial success, but we're still left of center on Rogers's curve.

You can apply zeal when you recognize potential and opportunity. But being mindful of karma will save a lot of false starts.

Which of these best describes your ambitions?

1. Go big or go home
2. Consistent, steady progress

If you're on the *go big* team, be extra mindful of the critical success factors. You're seeking a revolution—like Steve Jobs and Elon Musk. When you reach for the stars, you may not get there.

If you're more concerned with steady progress, you'll take a more measured approach, test ideas every day, and quickly reject those that fail. That's evolution—if the work has merit, it will succeed.

Perhaps AI can help you find the answer....

The FOMO effect

When a new technology emerges, Rogers's early adopters get excited. They tell all their friends and start dreaming up possibilities. Blockchain evangelists see their beloved technology as offering an Internet of Truth—an incorruptible information store that could revolutionize the tainted finance system, disrupt four hundred-year-old accounting practices, and end electoral corruption. The trigger in this case was a quite brilliant white paper that was released anonymously (under a pseudonym, which is the same thing) in 2008. The paper proposed solutions to a set of problems that combined to enable a shared ledger of events that might address these issues and deliver that internet of truth.

In order for technology to succeed, it must meet the needs of enough paying customers to sustain a product, business, or industry. Your business might efficiently solve an expensive problem for a small group of customers—many businesses can win with a low peak on the Rogers curve—or it might offer a free solution to billions, like Facebook, and monetize that reach.

Either way, I believe the path to reaching those customers will sketch an arc of expectation. I used to dislike the notion that hype, specifically over-hype, would drive the success of a technology. That was, until I realized that this is evolution in real time—tech investment is driven by the anticipation of potential. The concept of the Hype Cycle[6] isn't new, but I believe it's been neatly captured by Gartner, a respected research and advisory company.

Over a decade later, it is clear to me that blockchain has not lived up to this promise, stymied by a combination of suspect markets and technical challenges—the current technical solution consumes enough power to run a small country with a relatively small deployment.

I think we may be somewhere in the slope of enlightenment, but there's enough value to convince some big investments from Walmart, IBM, and J.P. Morgan. You, too, can experiment with public or private blockchain—there are many services available that you can subscribe to.

Time will tell, but I believe that it's the promise of what could happen—factual, unimpeachable information stores—that will inspire

6 Gartner, Inc., "Hype Cycle Methodology," 2019. *https://www.gartner.com/en/research/methodologies/gartner-hype-cycle*.

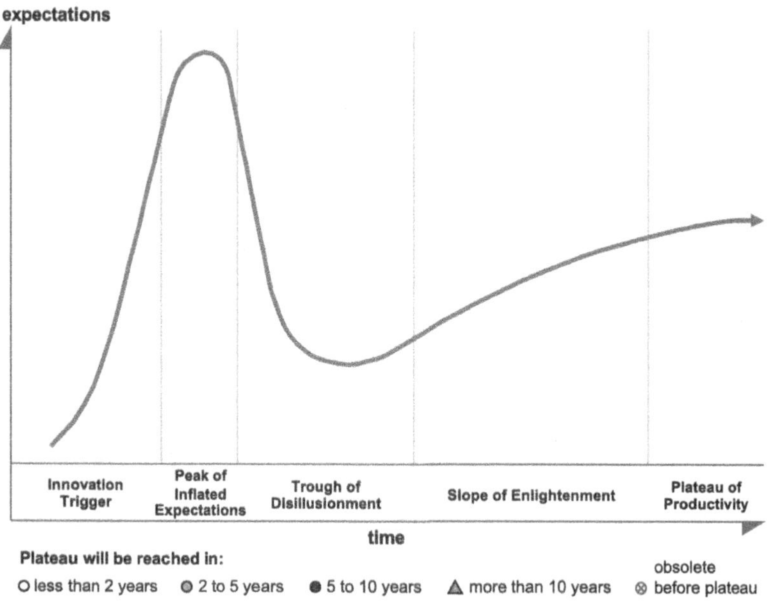

Gartner's Hype Cycle[7]

enough people to find a way. Whether it's blockchain or some other technology, this is just too great a prospect to ignore.

Every major technology you can think of has gone through the same thing, just at different paces. AI (seventy years and counting), the internet (twenty-five years to mass acceptance), the smartphone (seven years to reach a billion users); you name it, I think they've all inspired inflated expectations, plumbed the trough of disillusionment, and approached or reached the plateau of productivity.

I believe that the Hype Cycle provides a useful tool when you are forming your technology opinion because it tells us two things:

1. How the burgeoning technology has fared so far
2. Where and when it is likely to plateau

If your opinion says you should be ahead of the game, take a gamble on adopting new tech during its trough. In my view, if you gain little

7 Gartner, Inc., "Hype Cycle Methodology," 2019. *https://www.gartner.com/en/research/methodologies/gartner-hype-cycle*

from taking such risks, wait till the slope of enlightenment. There seems little point in buying in to inflated expectations, and you'll be in catch-up mode if you wait until the plateau.

Innovation horizons

We all know there are no true overnight successes in the business of innovation. Ideas become real over time as they progress through distinct horizons of innovation. You need to decide which horizons you will play in.

Basic research is the process of discovery, making the scientific breakthroughs that make new things possible. This work is generally done by people in white coats, beavering away in academic, commercial, or government laboratories. Basic research offers breakthrough solutions. The question is, solutions to what? The transistor was invented by researchers at Bell Labs while they were looking for ways to improve the phone switch. But the transistors they developed were expensive and unreliable, not suited to replace switches. Bell had no idea what to do with their invention.

Applied research is the process of moving ideas out of the laboratory and into specific problem domains. It's an experiment to find problems for the solution to solve. After years of applied research, Bell Labs decided that transistors could be used to shrink the contemporary hearing aid. The transistor went on to enable the miniaturization—and therefore the portability—of electronic devices.

Pioneers are people who are passionate about a problem and determined to create a better way. Founders live here, dine on applied research, and mortgage their homes to fund the hard slog to success.

And when they find that success, fast followers jump in. This is where the giants of tech began—Apple, Facebook, Google, and Microsoft all followed the pioneers and created successful applications. In many cases, theirs were not the best technical solutions, but that matters not. What counts is that adopters adopted. Could have been time and place (Bill Gates won the IBM PC operating system deal, bought the MS-DOS technology, ring-fenced the market, and Microsoft never looked back). Could have been a passionate fan base (Apple's customer experience appealed to creatives), network effects (Facebook) or simple elegance (Google).

The highest horizon is the simple adoption and adaptation of someone else's solution. Buying a system for your business and adapting it for purpose.

Horizon	**Plays**
Buy solution	Someone's built what you need
Mainstream	Build something better for the plateau of productivity
Fast follow	Build something new to climb the slope of enlightenment
Pioneer	Be first to market and ride the rollercoaster past the peak of expectations
Applied research	Launch a hype cycle—maybe
Basic research	Science project—long term speculation

Innovation horizons

As you cross each horizon, technical risk diminishes. Every business is a tech business today, but the vast majority play at the top level—they buy solutions from application vendors.

When forming your tech opinion, consider where you will play. As you develop your innovation portfolio in the coming chapters, it may make sense for you to place most bets at the custom layer and some at the pioneer layer.

To a large extent, where you play with an innovation depends on the degree of differentiation you are seeking. If you see no differentiation from having a better payments process, you'll place it at the customer layer, buy a system and be done. If you seek to change the way that money moves, you'll innovate new ways like Jack Dorsey did at Square, the Collison brothers at Stripe, or Thiel and others at PayPal.

Consider when you should buy, build, or partner to get the tech you need. Which trends do you watch and which do you ignore?

The stack—a big pile of tech power

I suggested in Chapter One that technology's essence lies in the way it enshrines the building-on-the-shoulders-of-giants concept. The idea that every piece of technology that has gone before is there for you to build on, and if you build something on solid foundations that has value to others, you'll have a business asset which others, in turn, can build on. Isn't that a thing of beauty?

The technology stack is the principle way that this concept is embodied today. Every time you use a piece of tech, you're using the top of a stack. Your phone has a touch screen user interface that allows you to access applications—software you can see, touch, and use—which runs on an operating system—software that controls your phone's hardware—that commands hardware to do your bidding and move information across a network to your TV, your printer, or any other device connected to the internet.

And every one of those devices operates in a stack.

A Technology Stack

When the app vendor changes their app, that part of your phone's stack is updated without breaking any other layer—assuming they've done their quality assurance. When your phone manufacturer improves their operating system, that layer is refreshed. When they convince you to spend on their latest hardware, your new phone can be set up with the existing software and data, and it just works—assuming they've done their QA.

In the same way, your business systems run on top of a complex array of software and hardware. Depending on your preferences, this may all happen in the closet next to your office or in the cloud. The stack can be spread around the world.

Most importantly, you only have to understand one layer—the top layer right in front of you—to take advantage of the enormous technical power at your fingertips.

It's easy to take that for granted and to grumble when part of that stack fails inexplicably. There's always an explanation, of course, and it's usually poor QA or the network. But that's not our point here.

Our point is that you can replace parts of the stack if you're in the tech industry—or build on it in any other industry.

Skip ahead to my piece on Cloud Services (**p. 269**) for more on what this could mean for your business. For the time being, consider your opinion on where the stack might play in to your industry.

TECHNOLOGY BY DESIGN—HOW YOU CONTROL IT

What You're Actually Doing When You Apply Tech To Your Business

If you've lived through a major technology project, you'll recognize the high of expectation, the trough of disillusionment, and the plateau of productivity. As you'll see in Chapter Five, the emotional ride of any big change bears a remarkable similarity to the hype cycle. There's a reason why these curves are so similar, and it's not because of the technology.

When a new technology comes to market, lots of enthusiasts pitch in and contribute to the experiments that result in the solid, mature solution adopted by the mainstream.

Your business is a machine that delivers value to those it serves—your business community of customers and employees.

When you apply technology to your business, you are redesigning the way that machine works. Changing the way you interact with customers, altering the way you manage manufacturing and distribution, and enriching the information you monitor to provide better insights. When you apply technology to your business, you are placing your customer at the top of a stack.

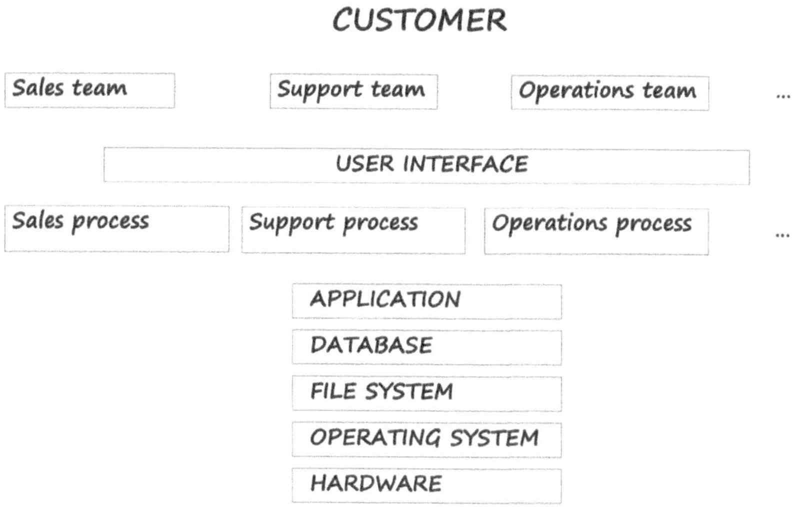

CUSTOMER

Sales team | Support team | Operations team | ...

USER INTERFACE

Sales process | Support process | Operations process | ...

APPLICATION

DATABASE

FILE SYSTEM

OPERATING SYSTEM

HARDWARE

Your business stack

Too often, I've heard buyers justify new systems projects because they "needed a new process." Maybe their sales and marketing teams need to collaborate better across the sales funnel, or manufacturing and shipping are miscommunicating. Systems as canned processes come with a warning on the can. To the extent that your chosen business system has matured in the market, it will provide processes out of the box. And yes, only change those processes where it's worthwhile. But please make sure you understand the way this system works, are happy that 90 percent is valid for your business, and have identified the 10 percent that must be customized. Valid, here, should not mean that the system behaves the way you're used to. Valid means that the new process is good enough. It may be better than you're used to, but you should not over-engineer. Save your energy for the areas that your customers will notice.

Use the out-of-box system as a blueprint by all means, but understand the overall design of this part of your business. Once you have that down, the technology is the easy part.

Designing your business

Every business has been designed. Everything that happens is done the way it is for a reason. The question is whether that reason was considered in isolation or holistically. Whether that reason was considered years ago or in context of today's needs. Do you know whether…

- Product development has addressed those defects that support reported last year?
- Your accounting system can report the data that is now required by services?
- The IT team that just came off that project could help the new software team?
- Your onboarding is efficient for all your customers or just the big ones?
- The support system has the FAQs for last quarter's new product?
- You could wind down those unprofitable product lines?

Get busy changing or get busy dying
—Paraphrased from Stephen King's Shawshank Redemption[8]

8 Stephen King, "Rita Hayworth and Shawshank Redemption," in *Different Seasons: Four Novellas* (New York: Viking Press, 1982).

Things change in any business. We get smarter, new technology becomes viable, customer expectations change, and competitors turn heads. Any business that cannot keep up with their environment is slowly dying.

Take the Blueprint Refresh Test and tally up your score.

There's no right or wrong answer with this one. It's merely a measure of how often your company challenges the way you operate. Any answer that you're happy with is a good answer.

The next time you embark on such a redesign, be sure to pick the process before you pick the system. And be bold.

Tomorrow's opportunity may be today's problem

We're driven to change by two forces:

1. We spot an opportunity that's worth pursuing.
2. We tire of a problem that's worth fixing.

While this book is mostly about pursuing opportunities, you will have to divide your focus between fixing problems—to keep the lights on—and innovating to grow.

A few words, then, on fixing problems.

Problem vs. symptom

Businesses are complex entities, and the technology we use to support them is rarely simple when you get past email and file systems at the top of the stack.

When something breaks, it's always tempting to fix the symptom—most often there's no time to do more. But consider the cost of fixing the symptoms a dozen times before you get to the root cause. If your bedroom ceiling drips water, do you patch up the drywall or re-tile the roof?

If you're to master technology, you'll want to focus as many of your efforts as you can on building the future and creating innovations that attract customers. But if you have a leaky roof, you'll be pouring resources into drywall forever. Take a position on root-cause fixes that you're reasonably certain won't slow you down in the long run.

Blueprint Refresh Test

Check the box for each area of your business that's been (re) designed in the last five years.

- ☐ Customer journey
- ☐ Order to cash
- ☐ Product validation
- ☐ New product launch
- ☐ Manufacturing
- ☐ Financial reporting
- ☐ Change management
- ☐ Customer on-boarding
- ☐ Others? Add to the list....

Tally up your score by counting the check marks.

Solving vs. moving problems

When you're solving a problem, it's all too easy to obsess on the issue at hand and ignore the overall context. It's important keep in mind the distinction between fixing a problem and simply moving it someplace else. In the long run, out of sight is not out of mind.

We're all familiar with the Value Chain concept, the notion that customers receive the value that results from a series of steps completed by your organization (production), their organization (onboarding), and perhaps your suppliers (raw materials and supporting systems). Since every business has a supply chain of some sort, let's consider this example.

If you've identified a problem in your value chain, there are three things you can do about it—live with it, fix it, or move it. If you choose to fix the problem, your solution must consider the downstream consequences of the change you make for customers, and the upstream demands that change may impose on suppliers. Absent this, you could:

- Add a component that reduces manufacturability and reduces margins.
- Create a complex solution that dramatically increases customer onboarding costs, has your support center phones ringing off their hooks, and brings customer adoption to a standstill.
- Place unreasonable demands on your suppliers and damage your partnership.

...and so forth.

To be clear, the overall health of your value chain can be improved by moving a problem to a less costly part of the chain—provided you anticipate this move and bolster the impacted area.

Consider a solution that you have implemented in the last year, but that failed to meet your goals the first time around. Who was unhappy with the outcome, and why were they unhappy? Who had more work, not less, as a result of the fix? What did you do about it?

How can you apply these lessons to your next problem-fixing exercise?

Simplify, simplify, simplify—the secret to making tech easy

Techniques go stale. An approach that's new today will age over time. Workarounds and add-ons will be stuck to the side, new needs will be accommodated by compromise fixes, and the whole thing eventually turns to spaghetti. Glass half-empty, you say, but I guarantee this is happening in business today.

When a problem rises to the top of your fix-it pile, you have an opportunity to step back. We'll look at a spectacular example in Chapter Nine that improved turnaround by ten times, but here's a preview of the three magic steps that make tech easy:

1) **Understand the big picture**—how does this problem impact the whole system? How important is it and why? Is there an opportunity to obviate the problem with a new approach?
2) **Simplify the problem**—Strip out unnecessary steps. Challenge the need for exceptions. Understand constraints and ask how you can lift them. Run manual tests to check that the outcomes are as good or better.
3) **Apply technology to fix**—automate what you can. If some steps cannot be automated, see if you can change the rules to make this possible.

Simplification isn't natural to most of us. We see a challenge, rush to judgment, and implement the first solution that comes to mind. Practice the habit of writing down at least three approaches before you move. You'll be on your way to a simpler life.

The beautiful thing is—the simplification skill applies as much to opportunities as it does to problems.

Your business laboratory

I've referred to the revolution in technology practices that have made it possible to build, launch, and test new ideas as quickly as you can find a customer. Since the turn of the century, much time and energy has been spent on the practice of testing innovations.

Steve Blank was a serial entrepreneur before the first internet bubble burst in 2000. Since then, he's become an academic authority on entrepreneurialism. Blank advocates customer development over product development—in other words, you can't have products without customers, so you'd better seek the latter as you're testing the former.

There are lots of further reading opportunities here, including the work of Steve Blank, Eric Ries, Alexander Osterwalder, and Ash Maurya. See the "Permission to think bigger" section (**p. 67**) later in the book for more on these guys.

For our immediate purposes, consider three approaches to testing new ideas:

1. Roulette—launch it and they will come.
2. Find friends—recruit and launch to early adopters and seek advocates.
3. Fast pivot—partner with early adopters and build with them.

Your odds of success increase as you progress from one to three. Most failures occur with option one, often after significant investment in scaling the business. The fastest failures—and most winners—arise from option three. That way, you only invest in the sales and marketing required to scale when you're confident.

No opinion on technology can be complete without an opinion on how you will establish demand for your innovations.

FORMING YOUR OPINION

You are the boss.

Ultimately, your success will be driven by your opinion. This chapter has provided you with the ingredients to consider while forming and refining your opinion on the role that technology can play in your business.

We'll wrap this segment up with some simple questions.

1. What do your customers expect of your business over the next five years?
2. Where do you expect your business to be in five years?
3. What opportunities exist to:

    - Differentiate—build on what's special about your business?
    - Accelerate—do more and do it faster?
    - Streamline—do more with less?
    - Inform—educate your customers, colleagues, and yourself?

As you read the rest of *Trusting Technology*, I ask that you consider ways that technology can impact all of the above.

I have one more question—can you do it?

But wait! Don't answer till you've read the rest of the book.

FORMING AN OPINION—IN A NUTSHELL

Challenge your opinion of technology with these perspectives:

Technology is more abundant than it's ever been, making it easier for consumers and business to:

- Generate insights by capturing and directing information
- Enshrine our knowledge of how to do things, converting IP into assets

Predictable patterns help you decide where to play and when to jump in:

- The Rogers curve predicts how successful ideas will be adopted
- The hype cycle lays bare the expectations we should and shouldn't have
- Innovation horizons and the stack

Make technology easy by addressing ground rules before you deploy technology:

- Think of your business as a machine at the top of your stack
- Refreshing the designing of your business
- Distinguishing between opportunities, problems, and symptoms
- Understanding and simplifying the problem or opportunity

Consider ways that technology can help you answer these questions:

1. What do your customers expect of your business over the next five years?
2. Where do you expect your business to be in five years?
3. What opportunities exist to:
    a) Differentiate—build on what's special about your business

b) Accelerate—do more faster
c) Streamline—do more with less
d) Inform—educate your customers, colleagues, and yourself?

The rest of this book will help you answer the biggest question:

<u>Can you do it?</u>

Booksite extras at www.trustingtechnologybook.com/chapter2 include the workbook for all tests.

CHAPTER THREE

SETTING YOUR SIGHTS

Why Incremental Thinking Will Kill Your Business

In which we'll talk about placing bets on technology by thinking big and acting small.

As you form your opinion on the potential of technology in your industry, you do so against a backdrop of ambitions for your business. All leaders talk up a big future, but all have different definitions of *big*. Are you going for a profitable exit or all-in on a long-term vision to change your piece of the world? Is your back against the wall, or do you need to stay ahead of the competition?

Whether you're thriving or surviving, technology can play a role. If you're to make the best decisions, you need the best information. Too often, great opportunities are missed because of outdated information or bias.

Assuming that you're reading this book because you've decided to improve something, the next question is why? What's wrong with what you've got?

WHAT'S WRONG WITH YOUR BUSINESS?

Since you're a leader, the odds are that you have that impatience with the status quo that defines an ideas person. And if you're inherently restless, you probably have a long list of things you'd like to improve about your business.

It's time to park your bias for action.

If you have a well-formed vision of what "great" means for your business, jump to the next step. If not, or if you fancy pondering that one again, allow me to ask a question.

Ingredients of your great business

What's wrong with your business today? Or if you prefer, what's left over when you note down the things that are good? Take the What's Wrong Test, grab a cup of tea, and meet me back here in eight minutes.

Great—you've just completed an exercise in incremental thinking: starting where you are today and listing what you need to change to move forward. The question is, where do you need to be?

That's a question of strategic thinking. Since you're on a roll, let's answer it now. Take the Great to Good Test. See you in ten minutes.

Done? Good—you'll have a list that looks something like this…

Consider this list as a set of priorities for your business design, areas to be upgraded—or not—over the coming year or

What's Wrong Test

Write down the ten best things about your business. Rank them if you think that will help.

Now write down the ten worst things, or areas that are holding you back, losing business, running at a loss, degrading your customer experience, or causing your colleagues to be inefficient in their work. Rank these from most worse (#1) to least worse (#10).

Later, make the time for your management team to take the same test. They each get five minutes. Then compile the results and review together.

*	Customer purchase process	8th worst
*	Call center service	Best
*	Product learning curve	3rd worst
*	Manufacturing costs	Worst
*	Agility	5th worst
/	Access to new skills	Meh
/	Shipping times	Best
/	Partner relationships	Meh
/	Decision making information and insights	9th worst
	...	
	Website	10th worst
	Accounts payable process	Best
	Legacy products	Best

Great to Good

Great to Good Test

Merge your right and wrong lists into a single list of twenty items. Imagine we're in one of those whiteboard group-vote sessions, and I've given you five star stickers and seven checks. Place a '*' against the five items that will impact your business the most over the next five years, then place a '/' against the next seven that could weaken your position.

When you're done, you'll have eight items with no * or /.

two. If you look at the starred items as areas of differentiation, do they all feel like areas you should excel at—be the best in your industry? If so, circle the starred items that are not best in your industry—they may be on your best list, but are they good enough?

Now review the seven checked items. Do these look like areas that you should be great at to avoid risk of weakening your strategy? Circle the ones in the "need to be great" category.

Next, check through the items left uncircled. Would you be happy if none of these received any attention over the next two years—in other words, that they're all good enough today?

Finally, ask yourself whether any of the uncircled items could be canned, cancelled, discontinued? If so, strike them out and plan to shut them down to free up resources that'll make the upgrade work a whole lot easier.

*	Customer purchase process	8th worst	Invest
*	Call center service	Best	Maintain
*	Product learning curve	3rd worst	Invest
*	Manufacturing costs	Worst	Invest big
*	Agility	5th worst	Culture
/	Access to new skills	Meh	Recruit/Develop
/	Shipping times	Best	Maintain
/	Partner relationships	Meh	Recruit
/	Decision making information and insights	9th worst	Invest
	...		
	Website	10th worst	Maintain
	Accounts payable process	Best	Maintain
	~~Legacy products~~	~~Best~~	Retire

Great and Good To-Do List

You're left with a list that defines the work required to make your business great, and the work that can be left in maintenance mode, parked, or cancelled.

Isn't *that* great?

Recipe—a design for your business

Frank Lloyd Wright was the greatest architect of his time. When you view one of his 532 buildings today, they look interesting, but not breakthrough. That's because, like any great pioneer, he set the standard. His ideas have become the norm. Visit any of his buildings and you'll see that they are so much more than a striking exterior. Walk through the Guggenheim or Taliesin West and experience the way the light plays in each room. Wright invented the uplight and placed windows in novel ways for better illumination. His designs were holistic.

Your Great and Good to-do list is a list of ingredients for your business that line up with your medium-term goals. But there's one more step before you can get to work. For a holistic recipe, you need to step back and consider the parts as a whole.

From the customer's perspective.

For instance, you know what they say about first impressions. Consider a new customer's first exposure to your business and your products—their out-of-box experience. What will that be between their first two critical assessments—their decision to buy through their first use of your stuff? In our example list, the customer purchase process is at the top and the product learning curve is third—both are areas for investment. If you conduct these initiatives in the order of priority this suggests, you run the risk of designing point solutions and overlooking synergies. Perhaps they could download your product for free, overcome a reduced learning barrier, and order the license from within the product. Or maybe your purchase process could ship a pre-configured product and remove the setup process from the customer's to-do list.

Consider your recipe through a few different lenses to gain perspective. For example, draw out the customer's journey in the ninety days that follow their decision to buy your product, and put a blue dot against any ingredient that will have impact during this time.

Other useful lenses include your business's process from order to cash, the experience of the community that your business serves, and your front-line employees' experience in selling, delivering, or supporting your product. Simply pick a stakeholder, walk a mile in their shoes, and capture their victories and setbacks on the whiteboard.

Your holistic vision gathers your strategic and incremental objectives into bundles designed to deliver upgrades next, soon, and later. This is aligned with the agile approaches we discuss in Chapter Six.

Add up the sum of all the components on your Great and Good list, and you have your business design.

Designing business is a broad topic that provides a vital perspective for the mastery of technology. If you'd like to research this more, I recommend Roger Martin's work, particularly *Design of Business*.[9]

WHAT'S HOLDING YOU BACK?

Talk is cheap. It's one thing to decide what needs to be done, quite another to do the job.

Change is tough work. Unless your team was built for continuous improvement, everyone will be busy in their day job, content with the way their world works right now. How can you inspire or challenge them to leave their comfort zones and embark on this journey with you? Perhaps some are up for a change, but even where there's a will, they may not see a way to keep the wheels turning while changing the tires.

9 Roger Martin, *Design of Business: Why Design Thinking is the Next Competitive Advantage* (Boston: Harvard Business Press, 2009).

Reservations Test

Re-read your Great and Good to-do list. Now make a list of reasons why you're reluctant to start.

We can't make this work because...

____

____

____

____

Feel better? Now that they're written down, you can begin to address your reservations.

Start by marking the biggest three concerns with an X.

Upgrading your business requires a specific mindset, one that must be embedded in your culture. We talked about idea generation in Chapter One. An effective machine for soliciting ideas from *everyone*, filtering those ideas through your strategic lens, and acting on—or justifying inaction for—each idea is a way to begin.

Ultimately, technology mastery requires excellence in acting on ideas, making the right ideas real with the minimum work required, testing and quickly pivoting or killing ideas that don't fly, and moving on when the solution is good enough.

This approach is neither natural nor easy. Like any new habit, it takes determination, practice, and patience. With time, change will become easier and more natural.

Your alternative is to struggle with change and probably put off big upgrades for fear of pain. That makes those upgrades much bigger, more complicated, and hurried. Which makes change harder. And round and round it goes.

Now that I've sown some seeds of doubt, it's only fair that I give you a chance to get any concerns off your chest. You'll feel better after you complete the Reservations Test.

If I was a magician, I'd know what you wrote down, and we could talk it through. Alas, I'm not, so I'll have to take a guess until we actually get a chance to meet. I've asked these questions of hundreds of leaders. Here are the top reservations:

We've never done anything like this before.

Everyone's too busy running the business to take this on.

We don't have any budget for that.

Where do we start?

We won't be able to find the right skills.

We tried that once and it didn't work.

We got started, but then we stalled.

We're not a tech company.

Does that list look familiar? Well great—because the next few chapters will provide you with plenty of ideas to overcome these challenges. In fact, you'll have a chance to repeat the test before you reach the end of the book.

If you're up for developing the change habit, then throw off the shackles, roll up your sleeves, and add your own cliché here. In Chapter Five, we'll talk about confidence being your secret weapon in this endeavor—confidence built on overcoming challenges as a team.

In the spirit of different perspectives, let's pivot from *what if we couldn't* to *what if we could.*

WHAT IF YOU COULD?

One way I set my sights is by following the achievements of people I admire. A lot of these folks have written a book, and that's one reason I wrote this book. The prospect intrigued me, and I wanted to try the experience and, in some way, emulate a few of my idols.

The technology press constantly bombards you with stories of the same old companies—paragons and pariahs of the industry doing something great. Again. Or behaving badly. Again.

I get that news has largely become entertainment. The battle for eyeballs is easier won by rolling out the same familiar names. But it also speaks to journalistic laziness. Inspiring things are happening in lesser-known businesses all the time—just scan any trade magazine for companies that are revolutionizing their supply chains, their payment process, and any number of other examples.

Of course, you can only keep up with your own industry (there's no time to scan *all* the trade papers). But knowing what the leaders are doing both inside and outside your market provides insights that could inspire new thinking for you and your market.

It prompts the *What if I could* question. What if I could capture customer data like Google; what if I could run my supply chain like Walmart; what if I could manage my inventory like Dell (they keep two hours of inventory on hand and don't miss an order)?[10]

There was a time when you had to be Walmart, Google, or Dell to do these things. Not anymore. The practices they follow are largely within reach of every business today.

Thank you, technology.

And you can't fully form your technology opinion without knowing what's going on elsewhere.

Take the What if We Could Test now to make a start.

This is, of course, a simple and expedient exercise to dip your toes into global research. You may want to share interesting links with colleagues for further work. You might even assign someone to stay on top of this stuff for every topic in your top twelve.

What If We Could Test

Flip back through your notes to your Great and Good to-do list.

Google the best in class for each of the top five (for instance, "best in class customer purchase process") and see what's going on. Page down past the inevitable sponsored links and pull up any news articles and see what's going down.

If you see anything of interest, scribble "if I could *X* like *Y*" against that to-do item.

Mastering the trends

Sooner or later, ambitions are constrained by resources—budget, effort hours, skillsets.

Or so we think. How is it that an entrepreneur can spark a business idea with nothing more

10 "Dells Just In Time Inventory Management System," UKEssays.com, November 2018, All Answers Ltd. June 2019, https://www.ukessays.com/essays/information-technology/dells-just-in-time-inventory-management-system-business-essay.php.

than their passion and an internet connection? If you're running an established business, you *must* have more resources at your disposal. It's simply a matter of isolating less-productive activities to make the time for someone to do this. If they have to learn how, give them 50 percent more time for starters—they'll figure it out pretty quickly.

What is less productive than seeking ideas to skyrocket your business? Lots, right—you don't need to list them.

Here are the questions to answer:

1. For each of our priority initiatives, who does this best in the world? And who's best in our industry?
2. When did they start doing this the way that works, and what impact has it had?
3. How did they go about doing it?

And for bonus points:

1. What could this mean for our business?
2. How might we replicate their success?
3. Keep tabs on all of these companies every week—stock price, press releases, make contact if appropriate.

The internet is resplendent with research sources (I keep a bibliography of the best at the booksite).

Keep your finger on the pulse and include an update on all your planning agendas.

PERMISSION TO THINK BIGGER

Startups do not represent the model way to run every business—too much chaos, a pile of uncertainty, maybe a lack of discipline. But the startup model has evolved around the ability to try a lot of ideas very quickly, supported by the venture capital funding model that embraces the stakes—roughly one in twenty startups achieve profitability—and are staffed by folks who are experimenting with workaholism.

You might reproduce some of that in your business, but the odds are that the folks you hired into a more conventional business may prefer to skip the hard parts. Pretty much every business will have its innovators—Steve Blank reckons around 10 percent of staff that signed on to a traditional business are likely innovators[11]—and anyone with a pulse will have ideas on making their work better.

But elements of the startup culture are worth considering when it comes to setting big goals. After all, startups live or die by their ability to think bigger, and the best take small and rapid steps towards their goals. Since they can't afford to go down too many blind alleys, the industry has given rise to many techniques that you might find useful for your innovation activities.

Here's a sampling of references; you'll find more on the booksite.

Jobs to Be Done. The human mind is conditioned to jump to solution mode when a challenge arises. The survival instinct tells us we need to act, that we don't have time to think. JTBD helps us focus on the challenge—problem or opportunity—as an example of an unmet need. If we consider five ways to meet that need, it's likely that the best way won't be our first—instinctual—answer. Pioneered by Harvard Professor Clayton Christensen, also author of the excellent *Innovator's Dilemma*, JTBD is slowly establishing itself as a tool for the design of experiences and businesses. Start your research at *https://jtbd.info.*

Business Model Canvas. Every business has the same components. BMC provides a one-page template with which to map out different approaches to each of nine common areas—Customer Segments, Value Proposition, Channels, Customer Relationships, Revenue Streams, Key Resources, Key Activities, Key Partnerships, and Cost Structure. Invented by Alexander Osterwalder in 2006, the canvas has fulfilled a remarkable range of applications including startup, new business within a business, and re-planning a mature business. I urge you to read more beginning here *https://www.strategyzer.com/canvas.*

11 Kaitlin Milliken, "Startup Culture in Big Companies," *Innovation Answered,* Podcast *audio*, November 27, 2018, *https://www.stitcher.com/podcast/innovation-leader/innovation-answered/e/57425031.*

Value Proposition Canvas. Not content with the Business Model Canvas, Osterwalder went on to develop the Value Prop Canvas as a way to better understand customer needs and design products and services they want. Extra powerful when combined with JTBD. Further details available back at Osterwalder's Strategyzer site *https://www.strategyzer.com/canvas/value-proposition-canvas.*

Lean Stack. Ash Maurya's been around startups for many years. His Lean Stack blends the work of Blank and Osterwalder and is particularly helpful in the design and monitoring of the experiments you conduct when validating your ideas with customers. More information here *https://leanstack.com.*

Agile Methodology. Agile is kind of the granddaddy of tech innovation methodologies. Lots more on this in Chapters Six and Nine!

CX. Customers have always had experiences, but it seems no one ever thought of them as such until the early '80s, around the time that poorly designed computing solutions began creating migraines. Coincidence? Whatever, if you already focus on customer experience, focus more. If you don't, you better start now because CX is becoming table stakes in many industries. If yours isn't one of them, CX can be your differentiator, at least for a while. For more information, set aside an hour, Google "customer experience resources" and start reading.

Think big, act small.

That just about scratches the surface. Think of these as tools to help you set aside your habitual viewpoint and consider your topic from a different perspective.

When you set your sights on what constitutes *good enough*, let me encourage you to think big and act small. I could quote Neil Armstrong here, but I won't.

What does that mean? It means:

- Think 10x before you think incremental.
- Find giants on whose shoulders you can stand.

- Treat your business community as your canvas.
- Take small steps towards your goals and test often with the opinions that matter.

We'll cover these areas in detail later. For now, just know that thinking big happens when you ignore your constraints, and acting small allows you to progress within constraints.

Just ask Bezos, Schultz, Zuckerberg, Edison, and Dell. Unlike those guys, you don't have to become famous to win. You just have to delight your minimum viable market.

SETTING YOUR SIGHTS—IN A NUTSHELL

Having formed your opinion on tech, it's time to set your sights.

Your first step is to sum up what's wrong with your business today.

- What needs to be great?
- What's bad that needs to be good?
- What can you ditch?
- Your answers supply the ingredients in your Great and Good to-do list, a list of upgrades for your business to focus on.
- When you consider these ingredients from different perspectives, you group outcomes and complete your recipe.

We all have reservations before we set our sights on big goals:

- You got these off your chest with the Reservations Test.
- You'll address these concerns as you read through the rest of the book.
- In fact, you'll repeat the exercise when you're done to find out where you stand.

Then you did a 180 and asked yourself "What if we could?"

- What if you could become best-in-class for your top five upgrades?

- Someone, somewhere, has done this before. You're finding out who that is and will stay on top of trends in this area.

Think big, act small:

- Startups are great at this—in fact, they don't have any choice.
- You now have a toolkit of techniques to help you set aside your habitual viewpoint and consider your topic from a different perspective.

❏❏

With ideas, opinions, and ambitions in hand, you're ready to begin the work of changing lives. But before we leap into making change, we'll take a short interlude to discuss the scope of your efforts.

Booksite extras at www.trustingtechnologybook.com/chapter3 include a bibliography, more innovation tools and techniques and the workbook for all tests.

INTERLUDE

YOUR BUSINESS COMMUNITY

Throughout this book, I'm encouraging you to see your business as a machine that serves a community of customers, colleagues, partners, and suppliers. If your business operates within a system, it is one that connects this community.

Your business operates within the system that encompasses your community.

THE BIG-O MODEL

"What does that look like?" you ask. The simplest model—and we like simple models around here—is a box for your business contained within the ellipse of your community, so let's run with that.

Your colleagues operate within the box. Your market—which is comprised of your customers (both current and potential), suppliers, and partners—operates outside your box and within the ellipse. This model is all we'll need to consider the potential for technology in your business and, most importantly, your market.

Part II is about effecting change across this community. Great companies impact, and are impacted by, their customers. Chapter Four discusses changing with your customer. Chapter Five covers navigating the

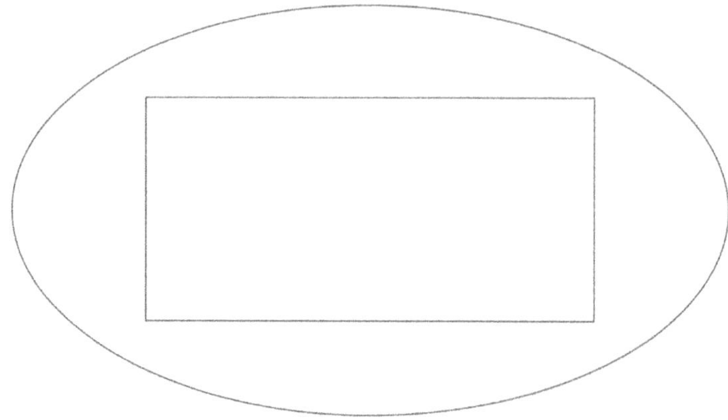

The Big-O model

transitions that will face your colleagues. The final chapter in this section looks at the cadence, the pacing, and the execution of change.

You'll see the model again in Part III.

Information moves around your business community whenever a customer discovers your product, places an order, discusses you with a friend, and any number of other transactions occur. We'll use the Big-O model in Chapter Seven to consider how you can better participate in these discussions.

Work occurs across the whole community. Your customer's process begins outside your box, flows through every time they deal with you, and ends back outside again. In Chapter Eight, we'll look at the way tech can help you grease the wheels to everyone's benefit.

Think outside the box of your business.

The whole point is simple—when considering how best to build your business on technology, opportunities will arise within your business. Some will be incremental, others substantial. But the big ideas, the 10x thinking, comes when you consider the full context—that your business exists to serve the community you've chosen (and that has chosen you). Drawing artificial boundaries at the perimeter of your business simply confines your potential.

So let's not do that.

PART II

ONE CANNOT LIVE BY TECH ALONE

PEOPLE MAKE CHANGE, CHANGE MAKES PEOPLE

CHAPTER FOUR

CHANGING WITH YOUR CUSTOMER

Following and Leading Your Customer

In which we examine the importance of being—or becoming—close to your customer, influencing their futures, and how technology has helped businesses address the opportunities and challenges most relevant to their markets.

WHAT ROLE DOES YOUR CUSTOMER PLAY IN YOUR BUSINESS?

Seriously, how do they fit in? Obviously, they pay the rent with some profit left over. But do they come and go or are they long-term partners? Are they names or numbers?

A world of inconveniences

There's no CEO alive that'll say their customer doesn't matter, but there are plenty of businesses that act that way. If that sounds harsh, consider the insurance company that bumps their premiums after a big payout, or the food store that hides unhealthy produce behind attractive labels (30 percent less sugar can still be harmful—just depends where you started). And how about the companies that offer no channels to address questions and complaints, just an email address that never actually responds to queries.

The world is full of lousy customer experiences. That isn't to say that these businesses set out to create a poor interface for their buyers. They just never thought to do a better job.

So, the first question you need to answer is: how much does your customer experience matter to your customers? Would a better experience move the needle on your business? Does a weak one set you back? How long would it take for either change to hit? Six months? Five years?

And the answer to that depends on how your customers see you and your business. Do you keep the promise that your marketing trumpets? Do your customers care how much effort it takes to order and receive your products? If your goods or services don't perform as advertised, will they go elsewhere or keep coming back?

Do they know any better? Does your competition make you look good or bad?

Because every company's bad customer experience is another competitor's opportunity.

If you work in a field that's constantly evolving, being propelled forward by a changing market and sharp competition, your more discerning custom-

Customer Cares Test

If you expect customers to buy your stuff over and over:

1. Take a stab at how many only buy once or—if you offer a recurring service—do not renew.
2. Every business has natural churn, but if this is higher than you would like, there's reason to investigate why so you can understand and adjust.
3. A better measure is customer lifetime value—the profit you make from a customer between first and last sale. If you can calculate this, use that measurement instead. If you can't, read on and you'll be able to soon.

If you're in the one-and-done business, how many of your customers were referred to you? If that's under 10 percent, your customer experience may be in need of repair.

ers may appreciate the opportunity to be engaged in your innovation, to share their vision for what they do, and to benefit from your combined thought leadership.

Take the Customer Cares Test now to establish the impact of customer experience on your business.

Whatever you say publicly about your customer's experience, this test provides one simple objective measure for how you're doing. If you want to do a better job—or would like to scale the same job at lower cost—read on.

What customer experience really means—and what tech has to do with it

Customer experience is not an event, a department, or a philosophy. It's simply a commitment to viewing your business from the perspective of the customers who fund it and taking appropriate actions to improve what you see.

What does this have to do with trusting technology? Hasn't customer experience been a thing for centuries? Well, actually, customer experience—the term and the practice—was created by the tech industry only twenty years ago. Technology had defined a new interface for business, and some of those interfaces were built to be lousy, without appropriate care and attention. Hence the concepts of customer experience design, the customer journey, usability, and the like.

In this context, technology helps you design and monitor the experience. And tech gives you the means to move information between customer and colleague, to redistribute control of what gets done, and to continually adjust these channels as you learn more and your needs evolve. Of course, tech alone doesn't guarantee that the results will be stellar. That's up to you to determine, and this chapter will provide some guidance and set the stage for the rest of the book.

From here on in, we are customer-focused. Let's begin by walking a mile in their shoes.

WHAT EXACTLY DO YOU DO FOR YOUR CUSTOMER?

I know you know this, but I don't. So please explain…

Why do your customers care about your business? What role do you play in their life or their business?

I'm serious. What do you do that they couldn't live without? If "live without" is too strong a phrase, then what do you provide that they would miss? If you ask this question of any customer—and I hope you ask lots of them all the time—they're likely to say one of three things....

1. **We need you.** We may not admit to this, but we couldn't live without your product. It's removed major pain and if we lost your product, we'd face huge challenges.
2. **It's OK**. We have your stuff and we're using it, but we've been thinking about alternative products that could replace yours. We just haven't had the time to look at this yet.
3. **Who are you**? Oh, that's right. In fact, my boss (or spouse or parent) was asking whether we could cut some costs. Let me check with my team to determine whether we really need to keep paying for your product.

This is too important to skip over. Take the Miss You Test, and set your list aside for later.

Miss You Test

Write a sentence to describe the thing your customer would miss if you shut up shop tonight. If you have more than one, keep writing till you run out.

Most robust businesses are still around because enough people are happy to pay them good money for what they provide.

Let's think about how your customers use your "sauce." Odds are they have some job they want to get done—share baby photos with the grandparents, talk about last night's party, run payroll, grow their investment portfolio, take just-in-time delivery on supplies, and so on. These are all jobs that people feel the *need* to get done. As we saw in Chapter Two, we've always been accustomed to using better tools to get more things done in a day. (Or to get the same things done and have more time to chill. Whatever.)

You and your business are part of your customer's process.

So you and your business are part of your customer's process.

You're fortunate to be part of your customer's journey

Everything you do before, during, and after you've delivered your thing will have an impact on your customer's day. If you do something simple, you'd better make the job easier for them. Why is it so hard to renew your driver's license, submit an insurance claim, or correspond with a lawyer ("sorry—email not accepted")?

If you do something difficult, you should still make it easy. Imagine seeing these thank-yous on Twitter, Facebook or Reddit:

> *"You've diagnosed my IBS—I feel like a new person. That was so easy, I love you."*
>
> *"It used to take us five days to process payroll, but now it takes an hour. I'm off to the golf course."*
>
> *"We were distraught when our house burned down, but your claims department made it fun."*

Maybe that last one is a stretch, but you get the point. What's your version of the above?

I don't ask this question to prompt you to create a new vision and mission. I ask because I'm assuming you want to define the best way to serve your customers, and you can't do that by looking at the many steps that takes in isolation. If you design your business that way, you'll simply end up with a bunch of more efficient silos.

Mapping customer journeys provides a way of visualizing the steps that your customer has to take to in order to do business with you. This includes finding, choosing, purchasing, and using your product. The best customer journeys provide you with a full picture of your customer's situation and context when they need you. Are they happy or frustrated when they need you? Healthy or sick? Are they in a hurry or looking to slow down? Do they resent your fees, or do they pay up with glee? To thoroughly track the customer journey, you need to go beyond the touch points that you know—the phone calls or emails you receive, the delivery of the package. But the more you know about your customer's process, the better equipped you are to provide them with a great experience.

And we all know how Disney, Apple, and Amazon experiences generally lure us back.

When you track your customer's mood through the course of their experience with your business, you'll uncover hints as to why they stick around or desert you for the competition. And you'll uncover ways you can influence those outcomes.

The customer journey is a simple tool to help you do this. It's a model that allows you to map each step that customers take between seeking a solution and satisfying (or not satisfying) their need. You are then able to identify their sentiment at each stage, recognize what's working well and take the necessary action to fix things that aren't.

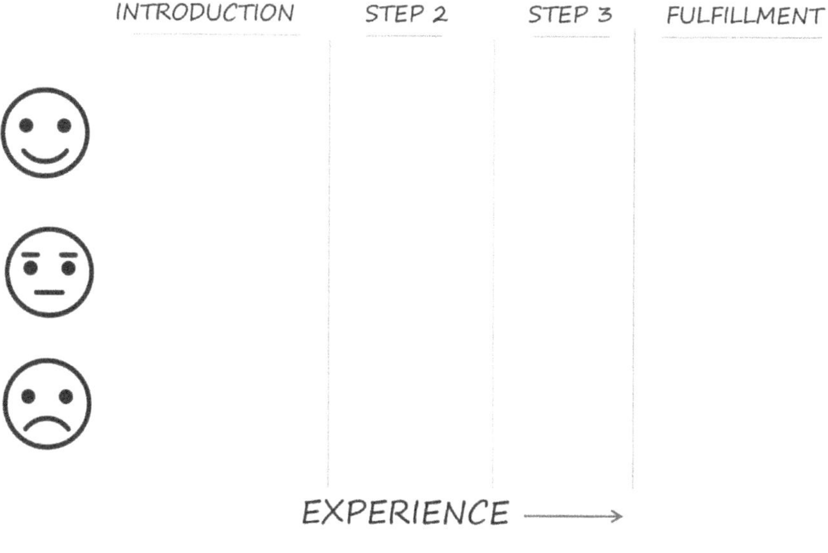

The Customer Journey Model

A good way to connect customer satisfaction to your business is to map whether you've given the customer what you said you would—whether you've kept your brand promise.

Here's the template that does just that…

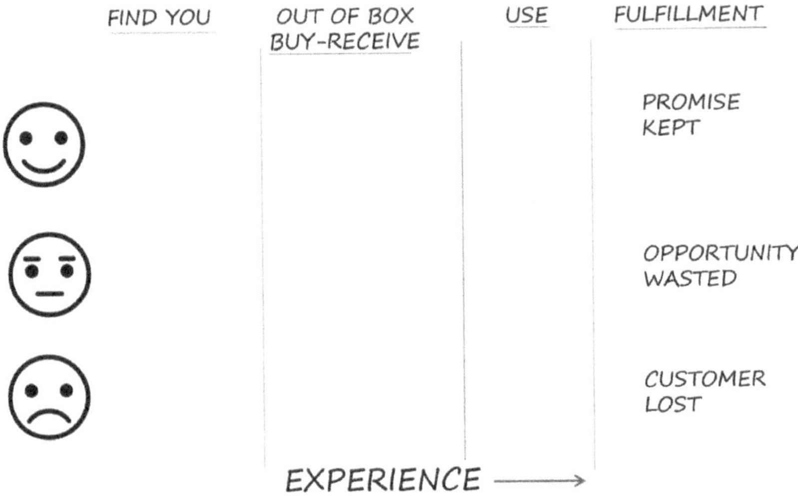

The Customer's Journey to your promise

Not every journey will be the same, of course, but when you plot some examples, your typical customer's journey might look something like this.

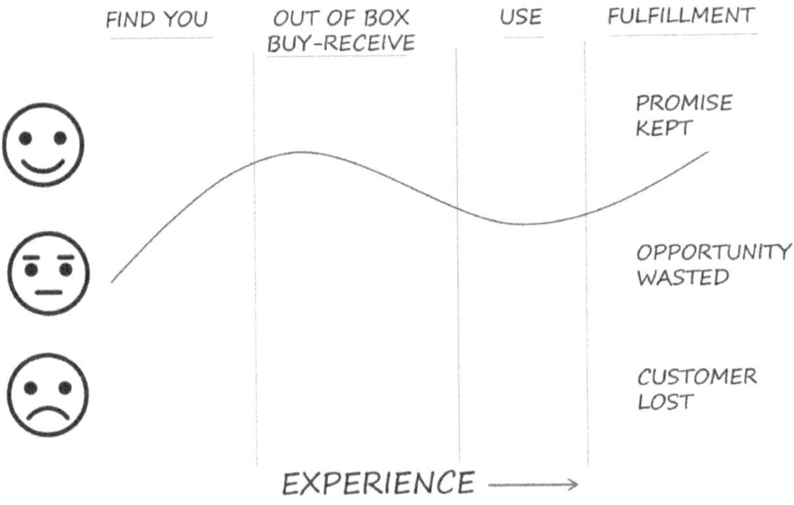

Your typical Customer's Journey?

Up and to the right is always good—it's a business cliché—and the end justifies the means. Be aware, though, that any dip towards the bottom right makes the next step a little harder.

How do you know how your customers—in aggregate—feel about each step of their experience?

Simplistic answer—you ask them.

But simplistic is not easy. We'll look at ways that you can ask later, including tech tools to help at scale.

For now, let's start at the beginning of the scene—how is the customer feeling when they walk in the door?

Take Your Customer's Mood Test to illuminate the context that you deliver in. For fun and bonus points, ask five of your customers to answer the same questions. Then ask them how you could make their lives easier.

Done? Great. Since you only get one chance at a first impression, let's focus there next....

Your Customer's Mood Test

When your customer decides to buy your stuff, what mood are they likely to be in?

- Excited in retail therapy
- Frustrated because something isn't working like it should
- Hurried because the need is urgent.
- Desperate because something broke...or may break
- Some other mood

How do you help them feel better?

First impressions—out of the box

Apple is so often cited as a paragon that I'm being very careful about using them in this book. But Steve Jobs's legendary obsession with the out-of-the-box experience is one I can't overlook. Apple products give a slick first impression, from the design of Apple's packaging, the smooth slide as you lift the lid, and the easy setup—as simple as any technology could be—is best-in-class.

Usability is the art and science of designing products that don't put anything in the way of your doing whatever it is you bought them for. Google's simple user interface, Amazon's 1-Click buy button, Disney's

FastPass jump-the-line tickets. In a perfect world, these would be a given, and every experience would be hindrance-free.

Louis Sullivan was known as the father of the skyscraper, having designed some of the earliest examples in Chicago. As mentor to Frank Lloyd Wright, he was one of the few architects that that FLW deferred to.

Sullivan's axiom—that form follows function—was half-adopted by the software industry for many decades. We got the function part, but largely overlooked form. Why else would we create software that dumps the contents of the database on screen without consideration to the user's needs?

Sad, then, that so many products are designed with function in mind but not form. Five calls and three attempts to buy, present frustration and delayed gratification; missing features and workarounds deplete the value the customer seeks, and built-in obsolescence abbreviates the life of the product. Every one of these hindrances is a barrier to pleasure and an encouragement to buy from someone else.

"Every business has an out-of-box experience, but many don't fully think them through, never mind optimize them. I'm on a crusade to change that.

How can you assess whether you're making the right first impression? Start by taking your Out-of-Box Test now.

Your Out-of-Box Test

How does your customer receive your product?

How much work do they have to do between deciding to buy and receiving the value they seek?

What does a great experience look like for your customer?

What can you do to make this happen?

What more should you do to help them feel better?

Lasting impressions—keeping your promise

You make a promise to every customer before they buy. You may not use that word, but regard your sale as anything less than a promise and you'll lose followers.

Are you solving a pain for them? Making something easier to do or ending an unpleasant situation?

Or are you helping them gain? Making the impossible possible, bringing something they need or want within reach?

Either way, how do you know they're happy? Does your product report usage so you know they're actually receiving the value they bought? Can they reach you easily to ask for help or report a defect? Do you contact them to find out if they're happy? Or confused?

Do they tell their friends and colleagues about you? Is their message to buy now or steer clear?

Your customer's journey might take many paths, but it will always end in one of three places, which determines the lasting impression you leave. The message of this chapter is to see through the cloud of your customer experience in order to better manage the outcomes, whether good, bad, or ugly.

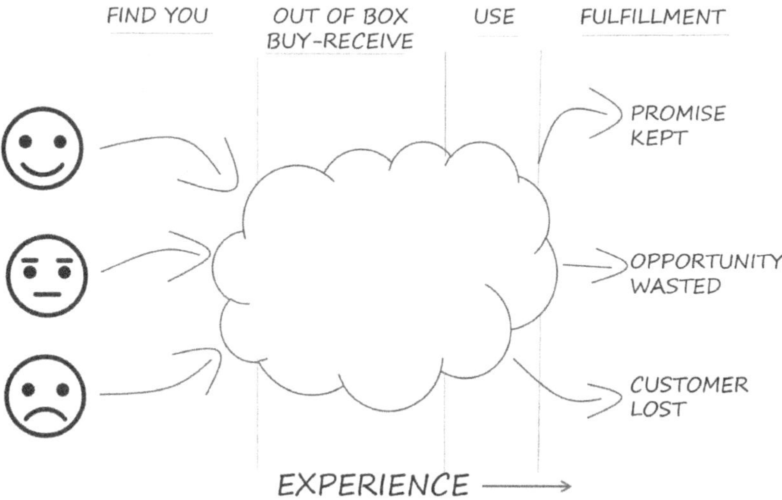

The Customer Journey—Good, Bad, and Ugly

If you've kept your brand promise, customers are apt to buy again, maybe even refer business. Giving the customer a neutral experience leaves them ambivalent about their experience and leaves you gambling with their repeat business. And a marked failure to deliver on your promise just makes next year's sales a lot harder.

FROM CUSTOMER ENGAGEMENT TO MARRIAGE

I said earlier that customer experience is not an event, a department, or a philosophy—it's simply a commitment to viewing your business from the perspective of the customers who fund it and acting appropriately to improve what you see.

In this context, technology helps you design and monitor the experience, create insight at scale with your customers, and do what you do for them more efficiently and effectively.

We can all come up with experiences that delight or frustrate us. But what is it about each that makes the difference? Let me suggest three stages of a good experience:

1. Frictionless transactions
2. Remarkably good service
3. Partnership

Frictionless transactions

If anyone actually enjoys placing an order, it's probably down to anticipation of receiving something wonderful in the mail, in your inbox, or at the counter—some form of retail therapy.

But for most transactions, ordering is a chore, and your happiest customer experience should begin with the simplest order and payment process you can provide.

Whenever you interact with your customer, you are moving information around and/or following steps to get something done. Mundane as that sounds, that's really all there is to it.

It so happens that the technologies we use today were built around the creation, storage, and transportation of information and around the streamlining and automation of work. But technology isn't smart enough to make the right information flow to the right people at the right time or to do all the work you may expect it to do. Nor is it smart enough to make mistakes. It's only smart enough to do exactly what you tell it to do.

Technology isn't smart enough to make mistakes. It's only smart enough to do exactly what you tell it to do.

It's up to you to figure out what you need and how to get it done.

If I order the same product from you over and over for instance, how about you remind me when my stock needs replenishing? If I usually order the same color, you can remember that for me, can't you? All I have to do is say the word, and you'll ship and bill my next order AEAP. (Can you guess what that stands for?)

Frictionless business is about avoiding unnecessary hurdles in the process between customer need and customer satisfaction. Given our higher expectations, many take this for granted. But frictionless transactions are far from the norm and are appreciated by customers who have lived through messy processes and the associated migraine work and delayed fulfillment. They're also great for your employee experience.

But ultimately, As Easily As Possible is table stakes. Necessary for a customer-focused business, but not sufficient.

Remarkably good service

We live in a world of expectations. Most of the things we do we've done before, and previous experience leads us to anticipate certain outcomes. When we see a different result, we are surprised. If it's a significant surprise, we tend to tell our friends. There are bad surprises, of course, but we're concerned with the pleasant ones here—good enough that we will remark on them.

There's a counterintuitive opportunity for competitive advantage here. The fact that I hate calling the cable company, for instance, means that it's easier for them to impress me. When an average call lasts forty-five minutes, I'm delighted when my concern is addressed in a quarter of that time. Their stock price hasn't moved, but I'm less likely to switch to an alternative. If they do that for ten thousand customers, the cable company really is impacting their market cap.

Once you get customers talking about your (good) service, your stature has been elevated above the competition. With rising expectations, that service will become expected—frictionless—so you'll have to find new ways to impress. And that'll keep you on your toes.

The best way I know to keep improving is to partner with your keenest customers.

Partners adapt together

Some of your customers care about you more than others. The best way I know to increase loyalty is to embrace your fans by partnering with them on innovation. Done right, it's a strategy for leading your market to new places.

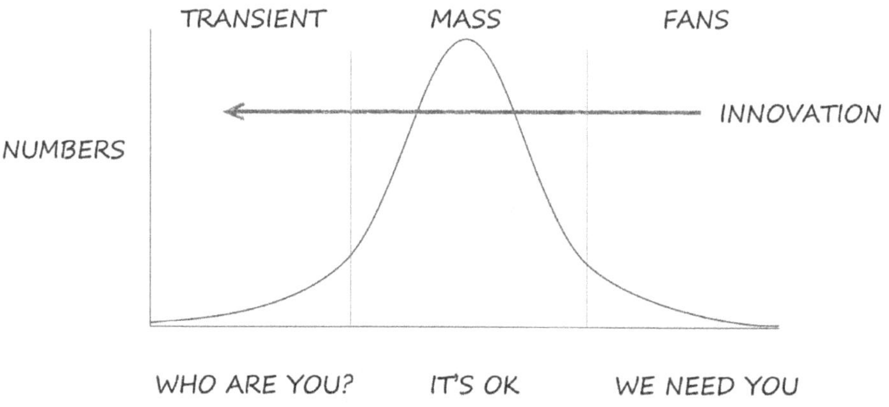

Some customers care more than others

At Alias, we owned Maya, the technology that has driven the movie special effects business for decades. Every movie that has been nominated for a special effects academy award since 1997 used Alias technology. Our company was itself honored with an academy award in 2003. Credit for this success goes to the best 3-D developers in the world—and a close partnership with the industry-leading studios that were constantly pushing the boundaries of computer realism. Maya Unlimited, the premier edition for our closest partners, was fueled by IP developed by this partnership. When new features had been released and on the market for a year or two, they made it into Maya Complete, the mass-market version. This version was used by hundreds of thousands of computer graphics gurus, professionals, and students. In this way, we were able to ship groundbreaking 3-D animation tools to the mass market within two years.

And your car was designed with Alias technology. Alias was able to carry off a similar trick in automotive design with our Studio line of products—tools that were used by Porsche, BMW, and similar marquee brands were later used to design the vehicles that we all drive.

Spend a few minutes to translate this model to your business with the Customer Partner Test.

A customer that wants to partner with you is a golden opportunity—as good as it gets in business.

Adapting *with* your customers is a process of recruiting partners and having a strategy for taking the resulting innovation to the rest of your market.

That second part is critical. Ultimately, your goal is to change your customers.

Customer Partner Test

List ten close customers. People you could call up today.

Now note down any innovations in your product set that these customers have contributed to. Then brainstorm new contributions they could make. How will you engage to close this gap?

List fifty other customers. Regular buyers but not as close as those above. What value would they find in the innovations above?

CHANGING YOUR CUSTOMERS

We've talked about the journey your customers take while doing business with you. But you have an even greater impact when your products change the way they work or live.

And you do that by treating your best customers as partners.

Pains and gains

Your business does two things for your customers—you solve pains and provide gains. It's rare that you just do one of those. Painkillers also provide relief. Investment managers avoid poverty with every fund growth. Since we know that decisions, including buying decisions, are largely emotional, it's important to be very clear on what the customer will decide upon.

What pain are they seeking to relieve? Do the associated gains provide a bonus that may swing the deal your way? Just as important: what happens when you've salved their wounds? Do they have to keep on taking your medicine? Can you pivot from problem solution to opportunity gain?

If you are selling a painkiller and your competition is selling a cure, you're all the weaker for it.

They say you make a friend for life when you pull the thorn from the lion's paw. If you ever test that out, let me know how it goes. But we know that providing a quick and permanent solution is a way to win trust.

Seth Godin calls that changing your customers. Alan Weiss calls it improving your customer's condition. Either way, you've had a beneficial impact on them. Some customers may just pay the bill and say thanks. Others will see this as the beginning of a beautiful friendship. It's that second category we're interested in here.

Sparking innovation across your community

When you bring a new product to market—or a proven product to a new market—you are presenting that market with new options. A new approach to solving old problems or a whole new way of operating that obviates those old problems.

You have to prove that the product works, of course, to your early adopters as well as to yourself. Once you've proven your case, something magical happens. You've begun to spark innovation outside of your business.

This has been the biggest driver of the technology industry. In the cases where new technologies have worked, they've transformed entire industries. Made them technology industries. Banking has been a tech industry since the '60s. Travel since the '90s. You know the rest of the list, and it's growing year by year.

But these transformations do not come for free. More technologies miss expectations than exceed them. True successes usually arise out of courage, adaptability, and a close partnership between technologists and their customers.

Innovation within your business is ambitious, but it doesn't count till you share it. Innovation with your customers is success.

Whose penny for whose thoughts?

Somebody—usually you, if you're the vendor—has to lead with a credible answer to an expensive problem or lucrative opportunity for the customer. And the customer must want the answer enough that they're prepared to fund the work and trust your abilities in order to invest in you.

The proposition has to be attractive to both parties. You can make your first customer partner very happy when you deliver on their need, but that's just a one-off. You can learn from your early customers, but you'll have to add a layer of thinking to capture the broader market need. Sometimes that means following your customers, sometimes it will mean leading them, or declining their requests. Do this well and you'll stay friends.

Recruiting innovation partners is a cyclical process:

1. Have an idea.
2. Find someone who will partner on the early work.
3. Prove the concept (or disprove quickly and move on).
4. Find others with a similar need.
5. Repeat.

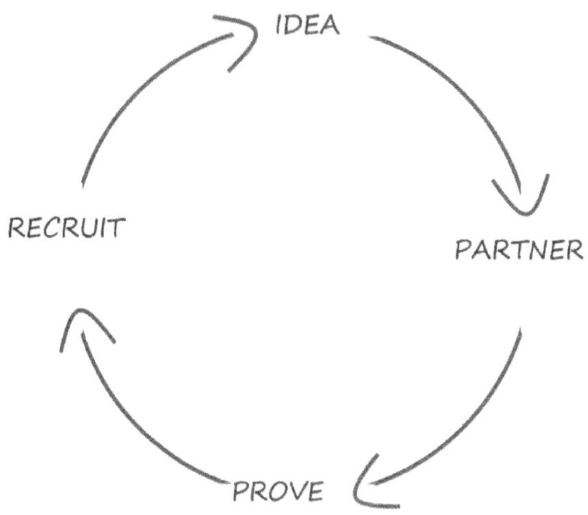

Building innovation partnerships

When you are funding your business from revenue—bootstrapping—your customers are your angel investors and venture capitalists. Their gain is a better business or a happier life. Your commitment is that every investment they make will be spent in the delivery of a product that fits their needs *and* creates a more mature offering capable of sustaining you as their partner. Every good deal you sign will do two things:

1. Create enough value to cover your costs and make a reasonable profit.
2. Improve the net value in your product offering that appeals to other customers.

If your customer wants a solution created entirely to their specifications, they should hire a custom product developer and be prepared to bear the costs of support and enhancement for as long as they need that solution. If you accept such a deal, you're in the customization business, not the product business. All well and good as long as you don't confuse the two.

If, on the other hand, you're creating something to sell to other customers later, and they want to share the ongoing costs of maintenance and improvement with those others, you both need to strike a compromise.

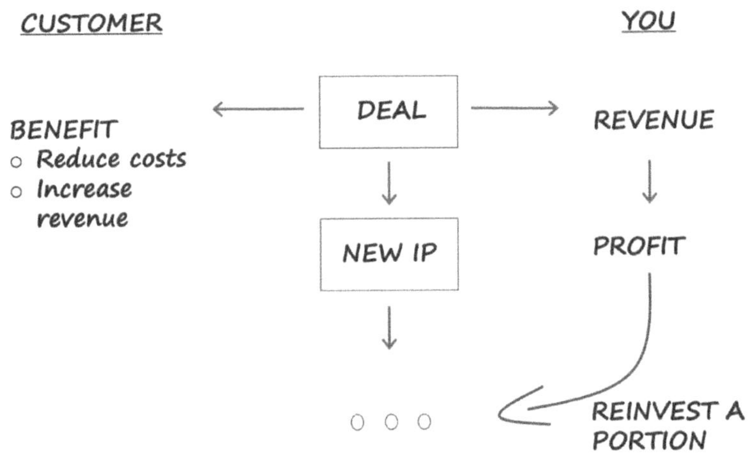

The IP outcomes of a deal

Changing together

The next chapter covers the topic of change. You've heard, of course, of change management, which prepares, equips, and generally helps employees deal with changes that have been decided upon by those higher up in the organization. Change leadership applies more in the market environment where you can't "tell" your customers to change. They are at liberty to decline, so you'll need to do everything you can to convince them to head in your direction and to make it as easy as possible for them in the going.

Ultimately, your partnership will reflect what each of you has at stake. Do you need them more than they need you?

If change management is tough, change leadership is Darwinian. Only the strong innovations survive.

Engage with enquiry and influence

You'll need to do everything you can to convince them to head in your direction and to make it as easy as possible for them in the going.

As for that "easy in the going" thing, customer partnership is all about learning, and learning is all about being agile. As preface to Chapter Six, let's assume that:

- If you can plan, do. That's Waterfall.
- If you know the problem but little about the solution, figure out what needs to be learned next and learn it quickly—with an agile board.

If you have all the answers and know for sure that your customers will agree with you, you won't need to partner with them. But market uncertainty is generally the biggest risk to progress—bigger than technical risk and resource risk.

You're most likely to succeed if you engage with a learning—agile—mindset. We touched on at that in Chapter Three and will revisit in Chapters Six and Nine.

THE CUSTOMER AND YOUR BRAND

To this point, we've established a few areas of collaboration with your customers:

- Creating the right customer experience for you and your customers.
- Partnering on innovation—customers funding your product development with their interests at heart.
- Your most loyal customers referring you to their friends.

The question for you to answer now is how these customer partnerships will move the needle for your business. In the short term, the answer may be "not much." After all, these things take time.

It can take years, for instance, for a mediocre experience to erode a customer's loyalty, particularly if finding a better alternative will require them to commit time, research, and switching costs. If your experience is "good enough," they won't care to move, and you'll end up with a bunch of mildly dissatisfied customers. Yippee!

And innovation rarely takes hold overnight. Apple launched their iPad tablet in 2010. By 2016, the tablet category had penetrated 50 percent of US households. Smartphones and social media saw a similarly precipitous climb.

Six years from launch to domination. You'd likely notice if a similar innovation started to take root and rise in your field. But would you notice in time to respond effectively? In Chapter Nine, we'll talk about staying close enough to the leading edge to strike. For now, let's not get complacent about fending off the competition.

Nokia and RIM made that mistake. They held massive market advantage and lost it over a period of, say, ten years. And they reacted fairly quickly.

If there's any chance that your business could die by overlooking customer experience or ignoring the innovation signals, would you choose to take that risk?

The alternative is to build customer intimacy into your brand—and mean it. Technology is not the only way to do this, but few companies have built such intimacy into their brand this millennium without the help of technology. Better understanding, more efficient delivery, faster product changes, more responsive customer care.

Your customer's comfort zone

We all have our comfort zones, and we look to friends, colleagues, coaches, and partners to help us grow. Part of your role as a partner of choice will be to give customers confidence that you can take them further than they could go without your help, further than with a competitor or on their own.

If you are known—recognized—for your thinking, customers will prick up their ears. If you are a great thinker in your field but are not recognized as such, it's clear where your marketing dollars should be spent this year and next.

If being seen as a thought leader opens doors, having credibility opens checkbooks.

If your customer believes they need help to get someplace important and they see you as a candidate to get them there, your job is to extend their comfort zone. Ultimately, your job may be to make your role redundant in their business, but good customers have a habit of finding new opportunities for trusted partners to help.

Employee experience

"You can't have happy customers without happy employees" feels like a trope, but Gallup provides evidence that sales benefit.[12] We've all been in the customer's seat listening to a call center agent apologize that "our system is slow today," or worse, "our system's down." How frustrating it is to be the service-oriented person on the other side of that call. "I just want to help, but my pencil broke."

If you ask your colleagues to be customer heroes every day, don't squander that initiative by giving them crappy tools. Disappointment will spread like a virus from colleague to colleague and on to your customers.

> *If technology is your product, keep it front and center.*
>
> *For the 95 percent of businesses that do not sell technology, make it invisible.*
>
> *It's what the tech can do for your customers that's front and center.*

12 "State of the American Workplace Report (2016)," Gallup, accessed June 30, 2019, *https://news.gallup.com/reports/199961/7.aspx*.

Give your employees great tools from the front line to the back office, and they'll operate an efficient process with insightful support that will delight everyone.

Invisible technology

"What's tech got to do with it (do with it)?" you ask.

You'll find out in the next few chapters but it's important to emphasize one thing at this point....

So what if they can do it...?

Before we move on, let's make time for a spot of inspiration.

Have you ever looked at someone in awe at what they've achieved? And then asked yourself, "What if I could do that?" What if I could sing like Freddie Mercury? What if I could write like Stephen King? What if I could free solo El Cap like Alex Honnold?

If you have, the next test will be easy. And if you haven't, try it anyways.

Take the If They Can Do It... Test to prepare for the *so can we* part.

Done? Good.

In the remaining chapters, we'll go deeper into the components of mastering technology in your business. As you read on, it's my hope that new *what-if-I-coulds* come to mind. If that happens, be sure to return to these notes and record them for later. You'll be using your list in the final chapters.

CHANGING WITH YOUR CUSTOMER—IN A NUTSHELL

You've just spent a chapter with your customer, walking alongside them to understand their perspective. This understanding will inform your actions for the rest of this book and for your technology mastery journey that will follow.

We all assume that we know what we do for our customer—and inherently we probably do—but it's important to constantly validate our assumptions. The world changes, and our customers change with it. If we don't keep asking them, we're apt to fall behind.

And if, in asking, we find the need to step up our act, technology is there to help. By placing ourselves in the customer's process, we get out-

If They Can Do It… Test

Think of some companies whose achievements you have noticed. Maybe they've excelled in serving you as a customer. Perhaps someone who's brought products to market that have revolutionized your market—or any other market. Or maybe they simply killed it on NYSE.

Now think about how technology helped them do what they did. Write the list out and park it for later. If you wake up in the night with a new idea, note it down before you fall back to sleep.

I'm trying to plant a bug in your subconscious that'll help you live this stuff every day and ask yourself "what if we could do that?" Chapter Ten has a bunch of suggestions, but here are some simple examples to get you started. What if you could…

- Fulfill orders like Amazon?
- Understand data like Google?
- Design like Apple?
- Entertain like Disney?…

When those companies pioneered their special sauces, it was hard to do. But these capabilities are now within your reach.

side the confines of our own day-to-day and leap into theirs. What better place to be than in your customer's pocket?

Remember that customer experience is not an event, a department, or a philosophy. It's simply a commitment to viewing your business from the perspective of the customers who fund it and acting appropriately to improve what you see.

In this context, technology helps you design and monitor the experience, create insight at scale with your customers, and do what you do for them more efficiently and effectively.

Knowing how the customer regards you—whether they need you, are ambivalent to you, or don't remember your name—informs you how much they care. Mapping their journey from *need identified* to *need satisfied (or not)* renders their experience visual. If you can see it, you can decide where to improve it. How to make the best first impression and maintain a strong and lasting impression.

In the best cases—with your best customers—you'll form the long-term partnerships that are vital to your success with experience, product direction, and all that follows. These partners afford the ability for you and your customers to change each other.

❐❐

Booksite extras at www.trustingtechnologybook.com/chapter4 include a template for your Customer Journey and the workbook for all tests.

CHAPTER FIVE

BUILDING CONFIDENCE

Achieving Change with Expertise, Clarity, and Confidence

In which we take a different spin on the most written about business topic. Let's face it—change should never come as a surprise. In order to successfully pivot when you need to, build a team that is confident and sees change as an opportunity to thrive.

I'm hoping by now that you're beginning to see why I'm so jazzed about the potential for technology. And what would make me really happy would be to hear that I've sparked new ideas about the potential for your business. If your goal is to pursue the biggest outcomes with all haste, there's one big hurdle we need to talk about.

Change. And nothing rings "change" like technology.

Change may be the most written about business topic. That's indicative of the havoc it wreaks—the challenges, limitations, and stress it exacts on us all. Yet we live with change every day of our lives. Plans change, things we count on happening don't happen. The unforeseen has a habit of cropping up.

Just when you get used to it, somebody changes something.

Is that somebody you?

If so, it pays to master the art and science of setting your team up to be change-savvy. In this chapter, we'll explore components of successful change and the expertise you'll need to develop or acquire for success. And although technology mastery can't happen without this, you'll find only scant mention of tech in this chapter.

SHARPEN YOUR AXE

> *By failing to prepare, you are preparing to fail.*
>
> *—Benjamin Franklin*

When the water's cold, I like to dive straight in. It's quite warm once you get used to it.

You can take the same approach with your next change initiative. But if your team doesn't have confidence that they can pull it off, that it's the right thing for the business or that it's the best thing for themselves, they're apt to get stuck in mid-dive. That's a hard, *Matrix*-like trick to pull off in the real world but a very natural act when you're facing an unknown transition. After all, don't you hit the brakes when you drive into the fog?

How can you keep your team from getting stuck while diving into new changes? The answer lies in preparation. More precisely, the trick is to enact *just the right amount of preparation*. To figure that out, let's begin by looking at why change is so challenging.

Don't mess with my world

When was the last time your day went exactly as planned? When you sat down at your desk and had no surprise emails or phone calls that merited your urgent attention? Or when you jumped into the car and encountered zero traffic on your way to a meeting that went exactly as you'd expected?

If you've had such a perfect day in the last month, you're lucky. Fact is, we all face the unknown every day. We adapt and survive. When we turn setbacks into opportunities, we thrive.

Why, then, is change considered so hard?

The brain burns around 25 percent of our daily calorie consumption.[13]

13 Ferris Jabr, "Does Thinking Really Hard Burn More Calories?" *Scientific American*, July 18, 2012, *https://www.scientificamerican.com/article/thinking-hard-calories/*.

- A familiar routine means we have fewer new challenges to deal with. Chaos means more thinking, more energy, perhaps a higher calorie intake.
- We feel better when we know what we're doing. New stuff puts us in a place of uncertainty.
- We take comfort in predictability. It's nice to know we'll be able to keep up the mortgage payments.

When we decide to make a change in our lives, it's because we believe it's the best path for us to take. We buy in before we act.

But when some Joe comes along and tells us things have to change, we take some convincing before we'll leave the familiar behind. *Is the status quo so bad?* we ask. And if we appreciate that change is better for the business, we may still see it as a threat for ourselves. However loyal, hardworking, and committed your team is, it's likely they'll still resist the idea of change.

As a leader, you simply need to acknowledge that resistance. Who is feeling it, why it's there, whether it has merit (it often does), and how to reflect that insight in your plans. Ignore it, and it may undermine your goals. Glass half full—that resistance may provide valuable nuggets that could make the difference between success and failure.

The tension between *operate* and *upgrade*

Any team—any business—can only do so much at once. There's a tension between operations (getting work done that pays the rent) and upgrades (getting better at doing that work).

This tension may be the biggest single barrier to upgrading your business, and it's one you'll have to address if you're to achieve technology mastery.

Many businesses are staffed to operate efficiently—to do the day-to-day transactions and processing that brings home the bacon, pays salaries and rent, and funds any upgrades you're able to make to your business.

An organization needs to be resourced for upgrades. Obvious? Yes. Often overlooked? Abso-flippin-lutely. To take on change without giving your best people the time to do the work is setting everyone up for a big disappointment.

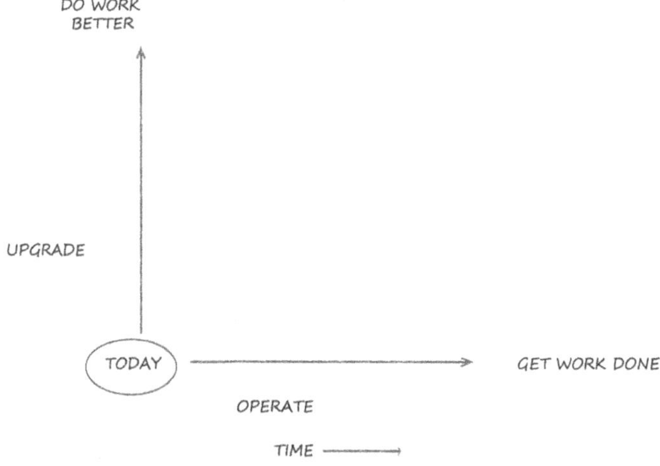

The tension between Operate and Upgrade

There's no secret sauce, silver bullet, or magic potion to solve this one. It's a question of commitment. What operate/upgrade balance do you need to achieve your goals?

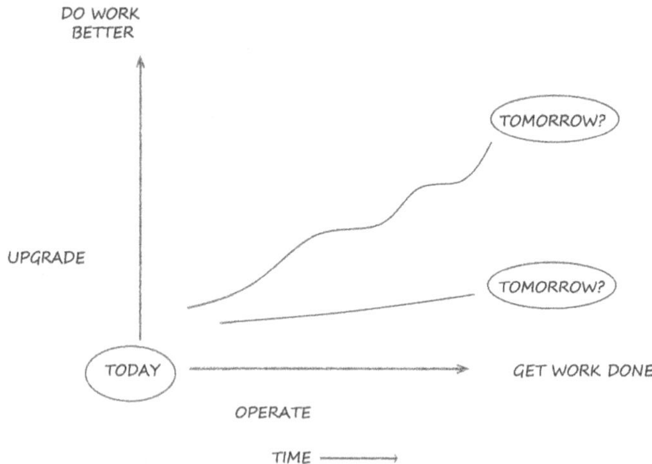

Find the best operate/upgrade balance

Doing things better means doing things different

When we innovate, we set out to do things better. To improve the way the thing we're innovating gets done. That applies whether we are loading the dishwasher more efficiently, taking a shortcut on our trip to work, or writing software to help our customers secure product delivery in one-tenth of the time it used to take.

> *Tech is a four-letter word: "something that doesn't quite work yet."*

Some goals—like 10x improvement—are only achievable with a whole new approach. If that approach takes work off our plate, we're apt to be happy unless and until it breaks. And new things have a habit of breaking.

We humans are at the top of the food chain because we evolve rapidly by finding better ways to do things.

We must experiment our way to "better"; there's often no other way. In other words, we have to earn a state of "better" through change. The less uncomfortable we can make that change, the faster we'll improve.

> **An unintended consequence**
>
> You don't always need technology to do things better. But when you do use technology, you yield some level of control. Without that control, you can't take your time to adapt. If something goes wrong, you're often reliant on someone else to fix the issue—and that someone may be busy helping fix another issue.
>
> So you wait. You pause your work, and that makes you a little testy. If you're working with a customer, they may get testy too. I hear some people have an instinct for patience, but eventually your survival instinct will kick in and you'll find a workaround.

Changing complexity can mean doing things worse

Lots—dare I say most—innovation has happened in the palm of our hands so far this century. The smartphone has given us pocket computing and over a billion apps. Or is it ten million? I forget, but who cares.

This is change on a massive, industry-disrupting scale. But most of these apps are solving simple problems. Sending messages in every digital medium yet invented. Millions of bouncing disgruntled birds across the screen.

Business is diverse and complex. That complexity makes it very easy for intended innovation to have unintended consequences.

Without some way of handling breakdowns quickly, the change falters.

The silver lining payback—we *like* change

You could fill a library with books on change management. I have. My favorite is Bill Bridges's 1992 book entitled *Managing Transition.*[14] I cite Bridges's work because it excels in focusing on the journey.

The silver lining is that everyone likes change-for-the-better. Eventually.

It's the journey that can be painful. Knowing this, knowing that "it's not just me," can help.

Bridges describes the change journey as a *transition* in three steps. Many other change gurus talk about eight, nine, or ten steps, but Bridges's three provide the most pliable starting point. They are:

1. Endings
2. Neutral zone
3. New beginnings

You can't begin a transition without letting go of the status quo to begin an ending (an ending, meaning the end of the way things used to be done). You can't arrive at your destination without embracing new beginnings. The neutral zone is in between—where you do the hard work of figuring out how you'll get to those new beginnings. In some cases, figuring out exactly what they will look like.

Emotionally, this is tough. While other change experts such as John Kotter[15] and Jeff Hiatt[16] do a good job of breaking down the activities into actionable chunks, they're kinda engineering-y. Bridges focuses on the emotion.

Change, or transition, is an emotional topic. It's important to keep that front and center in any thinking.

---

14 William Bridges and Susan Bridges, *Managing Transitions, 25th anniversary edition: Making the Most of Change* (Boston: Da Capo Lifelong Books, 2017).

15 John P. Kotter, *Leading Change* (Boston: Harvard Business Review Press, 2012).

16 Jeffrey Hiatt and Timothy Creasey, *Change Management: The People Side of Change* (Fort Collins: ProSci Learning Center Publications, 2012).

In the spirit of building on the shoulders of these giants, I offer five turning points that I've found to impact the course of my five hundred or so change initiatives that were enabled and perhaps inspired by (but not *driven* by) technology.

More on that shortly, but first: where's the fun in all this?

If life is a journey, you might as well enjoy it

Life is a journey, enriched by growth. But we get stuck in our ways.

In the business context, this is the dilemma that you address as change management. You know that change is constant whether you like it or not, and you adapt in little ways every day. Yet so many businesses frame change as an event, something that happens every few years. Piling up the pain. Storing up reasons to adapt the machinery of the business—the advent of the smartphone, the increasing cost of doing business "the old way," the aging of once-reliable business systems. The straitjacket of status quo only grows tighter.

When this mound of reasons reaches a critical point, you take a deep breath and resolve to invest whatever it takes to rip off the Band-Aid and make the change over the next year. Then when you're in mid-change, some unanticipated event causes you to reset. So the change takes two years and some compromise. Job done, you take another deep breath, celebrate your relief that that is over, and hope you don't need to face a change like that again. For the rest of your career.

What if you made one small shift in mindset? Consider not that you will need to make a big change sometime soon, but that you're already changing. Resolve that your team should get better at understanding how to do what you already know, call out what you don't, and intentionally learn what you need to know to take the next step and the one after that.

Then pivot to taking small steps. Beginning today. And don't expect this to end. Adjust your mindsets, your budgets, your business plans, maybe even your vision.

Could you sign up for a career like that?

TURN THE TANKER WITHOUT SINKING THE TUGBOATS

Atul Gawande achieved fame as the guy that restored just enough OCD to the medical industry. In his 2009 book, *The Checklist Manifesto*, Gawande demonstrated how attending to a simple checklist could save lives. By urging surgeons to "please wash your hands" he may well have saved many.

His retrospective on a large medical systems implementation—transparently entitled "Why doctors hate their computers"[17]—is a classic. In this *New Yorker* article, Gawande tells the story of a major system implementation across a dozen hospitals in New England. He could have been describing many major systems-enabled change initiatives in finance, insurance, or just about any industry you care to mention.

The stakes don't get any higher than in healthcare, of course, and this project was budgeted at $1.6 billion (yes, that's a "b" not an "m"). The folks involved all knew what they were doing and all were experts in their field, whether medical or information systems, digital health or administration.

The idea was to make it easier for healthcare providers to digitally access and interpret patient information so that the hospital could run more efficiently. Yet something subtle was missed that could have undermined the whole endeavor. I urge you to read the whole piece, but here's a summary for our purposes:

The technology provider—Epic—is one of the leading medical systems providers. They've been in the business for forty years and know their stuff. The implementation team offered a detailed consultation to representatives from every stakeholder group—patients, doctors, nurses, administrators, support staff. Many showed up, though some were too busy saving lives to voice their opinions. Requirements were gathered, and the system went ahead.

Skunkworks work

Have I mentioned how I love skunkworks? They so often uncover the best solution, unencumbered by bureaucracy.

New ideas, small risks, and launch when it works. That's the essence of effective experimentation.

Legitimatize skunkworks in your business.

17 Atul Gawande, "Why Doctors Hate Their Computers," *New Yorker*, November 5, 2018, *https://www.newyorker.com/magazine/2018/11/12/why-doctors-hate-their-computers*.

It wasn't until after go-live that significant flaws became evident. For instance, data that the doctors had previously been able to interpret in two minutes had become almost useless to them, the details of each patient's history being lost in a jumble of notes.

Towards the end of the story, Gawande hints at a happy ending. One of the leading surgeons took it upon himself to partner with a member of the technical team in a skunkworks project that tailored his piece of the system to meet his needs—without screwing it up for anyone else.

While the leader in this case *was* a brain surgeon, you don't have to be one to instill successful change.

This story is resplendent with lessons, including many we will return to later. For now, consider these aspects of the hospital *transition*:

- The ability to maintain notes helped the support staff but made the data much harder for the doctors to interpret. This is an example of unintended second-order consequences.
- Despite a rigorous design, development, and test process, many problems surfaced after launch. Go-live is never the end—simply the end of the beginning.
- Gawande does not mention any prototyping or small sample testing before the system was released to thousands of users. Starting small and isolating issues could have minimized the adverse impacts on hospital procedures. (Smells like a skunkworks...again.)

Before we go on, I'd like you to think back to any systems initiatives you've experienced where "people hated their computers." Pause to reflect that computers are smart enough to do exactly what we tell them but not smart enough to make mistakes. Now reach for pen and paper and take the Kick the Computer Test now.

Will you do anything differently next time? Like what?

Let's look at a few change fundamentals that, given due consideration, will protect against setbacks and learning lessons the hard way.

Momentum

It takes about twenty minutes for a fully loaded oil tanker to stop. In an emergency, some can perform a "crash stop" in fourteen minutes, but

Kick the Computer Test

When did issues surface?

How long did it take to diagnose and fix the critical issues?

What was the impact to the business—project cost, sales, customer experience, and more?

Could the adverse impacts have been avoided?

I don't like the sound of that. Those things weigh up to half a million tons.

Oil tankers have a turning circle of two miles—it's a bad thing if yours is pointing in the wrong direction. They are the biggest man-made example of the power of momentum.

Except for changing your business.

Consider that every change in your business is a change to the daily routine of several—often many—individuals. Each member of your team and each customer will adapt at their own pace. If the change is significant, they'll travel along a personal change curve that looks something like this:

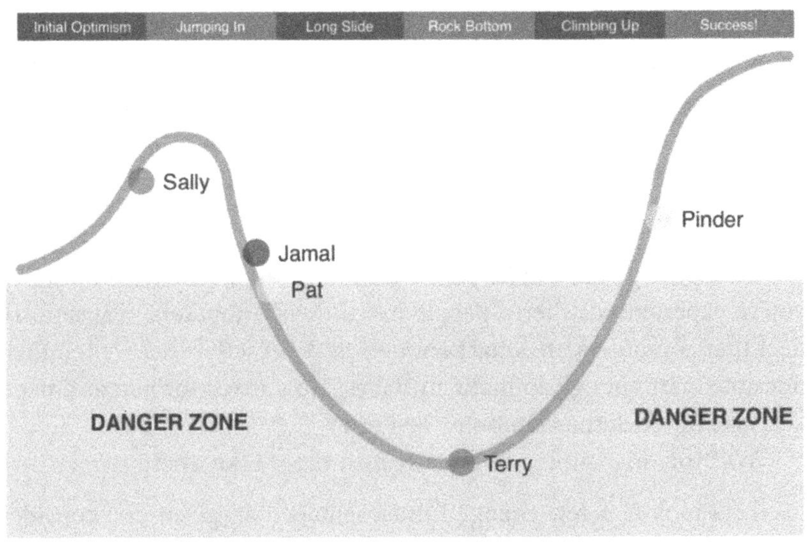

The you~curve personal change journey[18]

18 "The you-curve Online Tool," Courtesy of you~curve, accessed June 30, 2019, *http://you-curve.com/step-two-the-you-curve-online-tool.*

If each of us is uncomfortable with changing our little piece of the world, how much more complicated is it for *all* of us to adapt in sync? We all have to see the value of the change, coordinate all our dependents and dependencies, and take the journey together.

It takes many leaders to make progress but only one naysayer to scupper the work. As a leader, you need to pace your team with realistic goals. Take the Pace Your Team Test to explore small, meaningful steps you could lead with.

Pace Your Team Test

List a few members of your team. Three or four is fine.

For each team member, describe their change resistance as low, medium, or high.

What measures could you employ to bring the team along at the best pace? Examples:

- "Sell" the change concept more thoroughly to the team.
- Hold 1:1 conversations to explore "what's in it" for each member of your team.
- Share outcome ownership between low and high resistors.

Embrace second-order consequences

Second-order consequences are rarely obvious ahead of time. They tend to arise as a side effect of the intentional changes. When Epic provided the editing flexibility that the majority of users requested, no one recognized how that would slow down the doctor—the most critical cog in the machine—until the system went live. As this consequence emerged, doctors were inconvenienced and were able to see fewer patients, which rather defeated the whole purpose.

Second-order consequences are not always bad—after all, penicillin was discovered by accident. In Chapter Six, I offer a process to tease out the secondary benefits of a project—side benefits that you can take advantage of.

Epic or episodic?

I wrote earlier about the pile of pain that accumulates before you begin that once-a-decade upgrade. If you run your car until oil is leaking everywhere, a hole yawns beneath the passenger seat, and two of your tires go flat, you're likely to be stranded one day. If your business is running on failing systems, you run the same risk. You get by, until you don't.

You're placing your bets on epic change. Your next systems upgrade will be massive and urgent—and that's not a recipe for success.

At the other end of the scale, if you refresh your systems—or their components—more frequently, you're changing faster and more likely keeping up with the needs of your customers and colleagues. You're making serial—or episodic—change. Each change is small, your team has adopted that "already changing" mindset, and the world is a happier place. No longer playing catch-up, you can leapfrog the competition and be a standout supplier to your customers.

Pace Your Work Test

Think of a change initiative you've completed and list each phase of the work. If you only have one phase, that's OK.

Next, list the bigger tasks delivered in each phase.

Now consider how you could have broken those phases up into smaller ones.

How could this affect your next initiative?

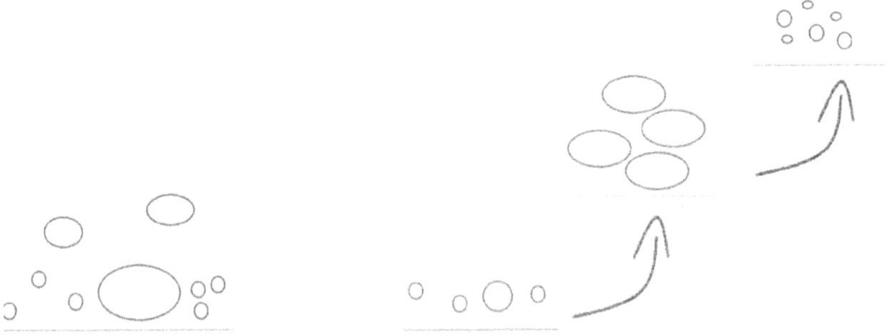

Epic or episodic? Piles of pain

Where would you rather be? Take the Pace Your Work Test to find out.

CONFIDENCE IS ALL

Being comfortable with uncertainty does not come naturally to most of us. If you're one of the few, take note that the majority of your colleagues will probably need some convincing.

> *All you need in this life is ignorance and confidence, and then success is sure.*
>
> *—Mark Twain*

Most take comfort in predictability, yet in the business world we're expected to guess the future—what will our customers value in five years? What might our competitors do to leapfrog the market? Where are the economic, political, and technological trends headed? We don't have any choice but to deal in uncertainty. Success follows when we get it right.

Fortunately, we can be confident in some predictions. For the rest, we have to keep doors open to opportunity, get good at hedging, and do what we can to increase our odds.

We gain confidence through achievement, and the very best way to adapt your business to change is to build a team with confidence. Confidence that they will make the best choices with the information available to them—confidence that they can pivot when a better path is revealed.

Building confident teams

Teambuilding has become associated with social events, framed as an opportunity to hang with your colleagues outside of work. For instance, bowling night or tough mudding. Sometimes such events create genuine camaraderie, but more often they feel forced.

> **Vote of Confidence Test**
>
> What gives you confidence?
>
> What gives your boss/board confidence?
>
> What gives the members of your team confidence?

But take on a shared challenge together and win—*that's*

team building. There is no better way to build camaraderie than overcoming a difficult challenge together. It's the reason why war veterans get together decades after the battle and why sports teams play together for longer than their bodies would like.

We're going to look at the lifecycle of a winning team. But before that, I'd like you to set the stage by taking the Vote of Confidence Test. Grab that pen and paper again…

Your innovation squad

I don't hold with talk of "dream teams." I've seen too many embryonic teams roll their eyes at the notion they could sign Michael Jordan or Wayne Gretzky. Much better to build a team with humility and confidence. A team with self-esteem.

Maybe another sporting analogy will help us think about this stuff. Any good (or great) sports team has clear attributes:

- **Balance**: every soccer team has eleven specialists. They all know how to kick a ball with at least (mostly) one foot. But stopping, creating plays, and finishing are specialties that dictate each player's role in defense, midfield, and attack. If you put the top eleven all-time goal scorers on the same team, they'd lose every game.
- **Experience and youth**: young players run faster; experienced players know where to run. Every great squad has the right blend.
- **Coaching**: the best coaches are rarely great players themselves, but they know how to get the best out of the team they have. They do that by guiding them on the path to confidence.
- **Visibility**: when we watch a match, we see the constituent parts, the specialist roles, and where teams are weak and strong. Visibility makes it easier to improve.

The process of soccer is, essentially, to stop the other team from scoring, move the ball within range of the goal, and score more times than your opponents. The better the team works, the more games they win, and the more confident they become.

Confidence drives achievement drives confidence —but which comes first?

Consider, then, the process of change. We find a need to focus on, design a solution that addresses the priority concerns, build it, prove that it works, and launch. That's how we put the ball in the net.

Simple stuff, right? But here's the thing. It's all too easy to focus on the inputs and outputs—the needs and the launch—and forget the part in the middle—the design, the learning, and proving that it works. Yet that's where the quality is determined. Can you get this right the first time, or do you have to reset the project? Will your roadmap deliver additional value, or will you be playing catch-up to make good on the failings of your first attempt?

Returning to our soccer analogy: think of the team that keeps possession of the ball—reducing the other team's chances of scoring—but never gets close enough to put the ball in the net. Best outcome is a snore draw. Oftentimes, one late slip can cost the game.

Building a balanced squad

While every business has unique needs, the core roles in a change team are consistent:

- Business sponsor (on the hook for outcomes)
- Project leader (day-to-day decision arbitrage)
- Project wrangler (project management, coordination, hustle)

- Business designer (business specialists, arbiters of readiness)
- Builder (technical roles—think architects, developers)
- Quality facilitator (~~anal~~ detail-oriented test designer)
- Sanity checker (systems thinker, usability advocate)
- Knowledge facilitator (capture minimal effective documentation)
- Someone who's been there, done that

Each role requires special attributes. Odds are you will already have people in roles that seem like the best fit. Here's a litmus test—questions to ask of each of them. If you're taking on one of these roles, answer the questions of yourself.

Business sponsor: does your candidate have the most to gain from the success of this work? Will they get timely decisions right most of the time? As a bonus, do they have the coaching skills to bring the team along with great questioning?

Project leader: is this person execution-oriented? Can you empower them to make most decisions that the team cannot? Do they have the capacity to give this work the time they need to? Can they coach decision-making across the team and be accountable for the results?

Project wrangler: Is this person an organizer? Can they coordinate teams? Will they set clear expectations and hustle with empathy? Will they make and maintain friendships and avoid alienating the team? As a bonus, do they have experience as project manager?

Business designer: Are these people the best business specialists you have? Can they articulate a vision for improving their areas? Are they systems thinkers that will understand the whole and make appropriate compromises? Are they a good judge of when the work is ready to go live? Let's be clear—this is a multi-faceted role, and it's rare that you'll find someone who doesn't need the support of the other experts. This person is the core of your team—the "customer" and the "director"; Atul Gawande's brain surgeon, if you will. *This role distinguishes a business project from a technology project.* Surround your business designer with the requisite skills.

Builder: Do these folks have the technical chops to build (code, configure) the technology? Do you have an architect who owns the technical vision?

Quality facilitator: Is this person ~~anal~~ detail-oriented? Can they create test plans that meet the designer's needs? Can they facilitate efficient quality testing? Have you empowered them to postpone a deliverable if quality is in question?

Sanity checker: Is this person a usability advocate that understands the full context of the project? In Gawande's story, this person would have headed off the doctors' data issues.

Knowledge facilitator: Can this person engender a spirit of knowledge-capture across the team? Will they advocate minimal effective documentation? Can they be accountable for enhancing information sharing across your organization? (The most valuable outcome of change is often improved self-awareness of your business—how it works and how it can work better.)

Advisor(s): Do you have enough been-there-done-that in the team above? If not, consider adding one or more advisors to the mix. Their role is to preempt pratfalls and transfer expertise to the team. The question, of course, is how much is *enough*? If in doubt, check credentials and add more early on. You can always phase out the advisory role as the team grows in experience.

> *Visit the Trusting Technology booksite to build your Squad Skills heat map.*

Balancing experience

Every strong team has the right blend of experience and learning. That is to say, if you're charging your team with achieving something beyond any of their collective experiences, that's a great pep talk but destined for disappointment. You need the right level of "been there, done that" on your team.

Let's dispel a myth here—*no* initiative is totally original. Unless you're planning to land humans on Mars, somebody somewhere has done something like this before. The harder it is to find those people, the more you need them if you're to manage your risk. If you're bringing a novel new product to market, find someone who's brought a novel new product to market before—anywhere. If you're creating something with high technical risk (meaning you've no idea if the project is even possible) find someone who's worked in basic research before.

Ideally, your experienced associates will be great teachers—excited to share of their expertise and see your team develop.

If you cannot find this experience within your organization, you have three options:

1. Seek partners to de-risk your current assignment and coach your team to become self-sufficient in these areas.
2. Hire the skills fulltime—if you're going to need the core competence.
3. Roll the dice and load up on trial and error.

For what it's worth, I have never seen option three lead to universal happiness.

Partnerships define your business

If no one on your team knows the answer to some part of the puzzle, recognize it and find someone who does.

That someone may know exactly how to solve an ongoing problem. Or they may have a way to help you figure it out faster and cheaper. The gig economy is here to stay, and that makes it more likely that you'll be able to find the right help whenever, and for however long or short, you need it.

With every generation, business becomes more complex. As a result, specialists abound. Experts in specific technologies, in change management, in coaching.

Seek help and try them out. Once you're confident in the work, you have a partnership.

In the same way, your business is defined by the partnerships you form. If some other organization can fulfill your need faster and cheaper than you can, you should at least

> *"Surround yourself with people who will stretch you and with whom you aspire to be a peer"*
>
> *—Alan Weiss*

speak with them. If you'll have that need for a long time, you'll want to get good at addressing it—with their help.

Partnering is a specialty in itself; collaborating across teams requires a skill. You know well enough that silos exist within your own business. Collaborating with partners is about breaking down the silos at the boundary of your business by:

- Being candid about each party's objectives. If you're the customer, you're paying. If you're the partner, when conflicted, you have to favor your business. So the customer doesn't quite come first.
- Taking the best advice. You pay partners for their best advice. If they don't tell you what you want to hear, suck it up. Or hire a parrot that will always say yes.
- Act like you're in it together. Because you are.

Language matters. Supplier suggests a subservient relationship. Partner, on the other hand, implies a relationship of motivated peers who respect each other's interests. If I'm your supplier, it's because I need to be. If I'm your partner, it's because I want to be. Which sounds like the healthier relationship?

A coaching culture

Take the example of a change management company. Like all growing consulting businesses, they face the challenge of cycling new blood through the ranks. Consultants move on, especially the best ones—fact of life. To build a great consulting organization, you have to hire well, ramp new folks up as quickly and effectively as you can, and maintain the highest quality for the client. Our change management company's creative approach to the challenge is to assign a coach to every new hire. Someone who will not only show them where the washrooms are but also guide their on-boarding and act as counsel for any client challenge.

It appears that everyone and their dog is a coach today. Shingles have been hung and advice dispensed. Results are mixed and the reputation of coaching has taken a hit.

Fact is, coaching is a great way to strengthen the skills of teams and individuals. A skilled coach imparts expertise through *asking*, not telling.

The art of coaching is underestimated. And under-appreciated.

You have all kinds of experts in your organization. Odds are, they learned most of what they know through the school of hard knocks over a long period of time.

But I'll put five dollars on your having only one real expert in some of the critical areas of your business. One gal that knows that part of the code. One guy that remembers why that thing works the way it does. If that rings true, you're running a one-bus business.

Obviously, we all hope these folks stay healthy and don't accept a better offer from some other company. But even then, having single-expert bottlenecks in your business won't cut it down the line when your competition speeds up.

Sure, experts sometimes hoard the information. Much more likely, they've under-shared because they were never granted the time to share their knowledge.

Teams are dynamic. Everything changes. Projects come and go. Teams form, make their marks, and disband.

You may start by building one great team, but it's not enough to end there. A successful change initiative will create a buzz. The team members will be looked up to like champions. Others will want to sign up for the next challenge.

Your pioneer teams can go forth and multiply. Each can carry their early lessons into other initiatives and other teams. It pays to invest in their coaching skills—it's the fastest way to turn a championship team into a squad.

How much better would your business tick if your experts and pioneers were also great coaches? Propagating their expertise to anyone who will listen. Transitioning others in to fill their shoes. Taking on bigger and better challenges.

What could this coaching model do for your business?

Transitioning expertise

Here's my favorite model for transitioning your expertise:

1. I do it—you watch.
2. You do it—I watch.
3. You do it—call me if you need help.

You'll call me at first, but that won't last forever.

THE FIVE TURNING POINTS OF CHANGE THAT YOU HAVEN'T READ ABOUT

So how to avoid the challenges of change?

There's a lot of good reading in the bibliography. To add to that, I promised earlier to share my five turning points. Here they are...

1. Integration—strategy and technology
2. Deep, concise goals—value workshop
3. Out of the blocks—launch program
4. Decision making—keeping your finger on the pulse
5. Closure—realizing benefits

Integration of strategy and technology

This is a book about building trust in technology as your platform for a better business.

But at no point do I suggest that technology is essential. First and foremost, I want you to be inspired by the work that others have done with the best technology for their context. It's my fervent hope that such inspiration will generate ideas that you could apply in your business. And then to help you gain the confidence to pursue these ideas until you either reject them (quickly) or hit the success button.

What technology can best influence your strategic success?

This all comes down to answering one simple question:

What have others done that could broaden my strategic horizons? If this has merit, what would I need to achieve in order to mirror their success in my context?

You could approach this question by saying, "Here's my strategy—what do I need to do to execute?" But consider:

- MITS shipped Altair, the first PC in 1975. Jobs, IBM, and a host of others created a new industry.

- Archie pioneered web search in 1990. Page and Brin nailed it in '98.
- Sixdegrees launched a social network in 1997. Mark Zuckerberg was inspired.

This prompts an even better question:

If it's worked elsewhere, someone else has done it. If they've done it, why can't you? Whether it be Silicon Valley or any of a thousand other business breakthroughs, you know that somebody, somewhere has proven that something works that could change your business.

What if you could do the same thing?

This melding of strategy and technology provides a confident starting point, based on the proof possible of others' work.

Deep, concise goals—value workshop

This change that you're planning will be the work of everyone on your change team. You're going to be asking them to work above and beyond—stretch thinking, longer workdays, on call for emergencies. You can demand compliance, but you need commitment. Pump them up and you can rule the world. Engage with reluctance and you're handicapped from the start.

People like exciting work, but many don't get to try it out. Change should generate excitement over the future, not fear.

All of this means one thing—you need to engage what I call 360° Motivations.

That means sharing leadership goals and enlisting wins for every stakeholder. How is the new beginning going to look for everyone? How will that improve things? Will their day-to-day job be easier? Better still, will they be able to focus more time on creative work, thinking about how to better serve your customer and putting their ideas into action? Or perhaps roles will be different—change brings an opportunity to develop new skills. Can you make this deliberate?

The value workshop principle is simple:

1. Invite representatives of every stakeholder—a dozen is a good number. Invite every stakeholder if you can.
2. Leadership supplies the overarching goal.

3. Everyone generates additional value that can be attached to this goal. Individuals or breakout groups work best.
4. The group quickly reviews the value ideas. If you can't achieve them all, vote down to a shortlist.

Well facilitated, that can all be done in an hour. If you can assemble without buying a plane ticket, that's always best. If not, the process works almost as well remotely.

Precision and conciseness are vital. Sometimes this gets in the way of the ideation process above. It's worth taking a second pass at crafting the wording.

The work that remains depends on what you need to make yourself comfortable. Return on investment, cost/benefit, and so on. You can run proofs of concept, viability tests, and the like later.

Capture the final value list on one slide, twenty-four-point font and put it everywhere—desktops, screen savers, mouse pads, posters. Go crazy—because the team will refer to this list when making every decision between here and the finishing line.

Out of the blocks—launch program

The pace of work is about action over time. If you were to chart this, it's apt to look like this:

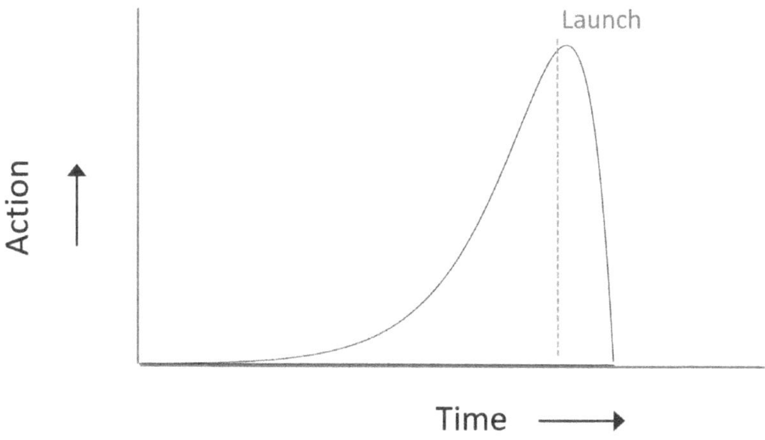

The Everest Approach—a risky climb to major change

When any change initiative is launched, the immediate challenge is to get up to speed alongside the work that your contributors are already doing. You're turning that oil tanker when you modify the status quo by supplanting existing—often long-standing—habits. It's very doable but needs special attention. Absent this deliberate shift, the change work will take time to build momentum—the long slow climb that occupies the left half of the Everest illustration.

Visit the booksite to benchmark your Action Over Time.

A well-crafted launch program begins by addressing the required shift in habits by having the team answer questions like:

- What changes do I need to make?
- What's preventing me from focusing on the new priorities?
- Which of the old priorities can we discard? What can we stop doing now?
- What's the most efficient way for us to work together?

Once the time has been freed up, the work of change can begin.

- What decisions can we make now?
- How can we break the work down to both divide up between us and to deliver frequent, complete chunks?
- What's the overall plan and how will you maintain it?[19]
- What outcomes do we need over the next few weeks?
- Who's doing what?
- How can each of us help other team members?

Visit the booksite for help in turning Epic change to Episodic.

19 *A plan is a theory that identifies the bigger tasks, calls out risks and mitigation, and identifies what you already know and what you need to learn. This allows progressive discovery that tests the theory in action. Find a setback, an assumption that turned out to be wrong? Update the theory and press on.*

Here's my Foothills Model—how I prefer to see the Action Over Time chart:

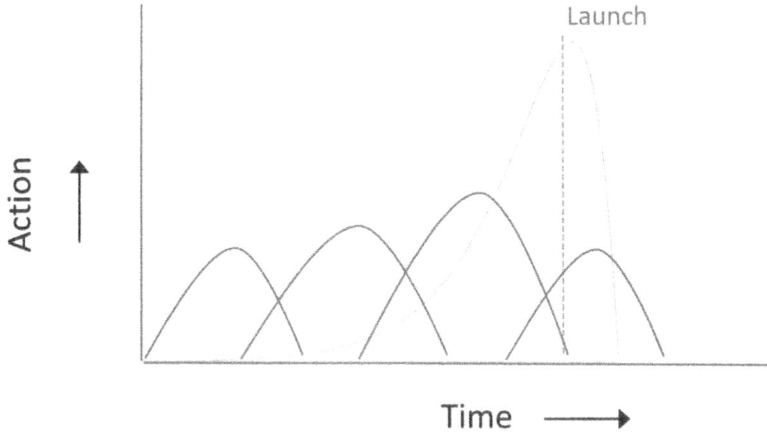

The Foothills Approach to Minimalist Change

The key change here is to break up big, complex initiatives into series of smaller contributions. Sequenced by risk (address the most important unknowns first), dependencies and priority outcomes, these "foothills" spread the risk, make each project smaller and therefore easier to begin and complete, and usually deliver usable chunks throughout the course of the work. In so doing, you avoid the "big go-live" and its concomitant risks.

A note about serial-changers: Organizations that have mastered change can pivot on a dime when new information infers the need. They do so by moving rapidly through small adjustments. An organization that has mastered this no longer sees change as an event, but more as potential everyday action. Agility becomes visceral. Fundamentally, such organizations no longer think of change.

Decision-making—finger on the pulse

Did you spot something? Decision-making is the fourth of my five turning points, and you're only now starting the work. If you're like *dude, when do we get going*, you're forgiven. But understand that the goal here is to point your rocket at the right planet—or rather to where that planet will be when you get there—before engaging the boosters. Aligning with, perhaps expanding, business strategy, uncovering all the value you need, and setting a series of frequent small goals will have you launching in the right direction.

Once the work begins, it comes down to doing the right things well enough. The execution is generally not that hard—assuming you have a qualified team—but the "picking the right things" merits special attention. This is all about making good decisions (avoiding bad and sweating over great) as soon as those decisions are needed. You'll do this well if you:

- Monitor the important outcomes to track your position relative to the goal.
- Recognize the few big decisions that are worth thinking through.
- Are willing to settle for .600 hit rate on the others in return for fast continuation of work.
- Empower the right peo-ple to make decisions.
- Spend optimum time on decision-making and team communication.

I'll expand on the secret sauce regarding that last point in Chapter Six (the Decision/Action loop), but for now, recognize that there's a fine line between efficiency and bureaucracy.

You may have blended the new work into everyone's schedule, but that doesn't mean everyone's day job can be paused. The business still has to be run and (unless you have the scale to pull off the miracle of dedicating your best people exclusively to the change—see Change Assignments sidebar) that means everyone has to be efficient with the time they spend.

On change assignments

This is the textbook approach but is a luxury that can only be resourced by larger organizations. You want your best systems thinkers on the change team, but you likely also need them to contribute to the daily transactions that pay your rent.

Since I'm hoping to put you on the path to becoming a Versatile Organization, you'll need to master this duality.

Dedicated change teams are not the best model—as you'd find out when the change is integrated into the business.

The key is Simple Steering—keeping everyone's finger on the pulse without a ton of meetings.

> *Visit the booksite for more on Simple Steering.*

Stop when you're done—benefits realized

If you're surprised that we began the work with the fourth turning point, I'm gonna blow your mind when I say that we've reached the end of the work with the fifth. But this one's the most important, the reason for it all, and your guiding star.

While it's exciting to begin the work of change, it can be a relief to end. (The excelling organizations never see an end, but they could probably celebrate success more often.) The question is, of course, when does it end?

Here's my simple definition:

When the target outcomes have been achieved.

To which you could add:

And you're ready for the next important outcomes.

Realizing benefits means that the "go-live" or launch is the end of the beginning. If you've done your job well, it'll be the beginning of the end. Either way, your plan will have a way to measure progress once the work has moved from the lab (workshop, dev environment, drawing board, take your pick) to the real world. This begins after your work has passed the preparatory tests and ends when your work has arrived in the customer's hands and is being used to do what you set out for them to do.

The point is, you don't launch the rocket and assume it will land on Mars. Mission Control's most important work begins after achieving exit velocity.

There are many ways to track success:

- Number of critical reported bugs
- Adoption of the tools
- Completion of tasks using the tools
- Requests for more

Path to Success Test

Spend a few minutes refreshing your memory on your chosen project. Then answer the following.

How did the work further progress towards your strategy?

What value was expected at the outset? How did you define success?

Plot your action over time. How do you feel about this?

How did the timeliness of decisions impact the action-over-time curve?

Did you achieve the success criteria? Did any secondary—bonus—value emerge?

What will you change when you begin your next project?

The key is to have crystal-clear measures at the outset.

Recall a recent project of significance to your organization that has now completed. Complete the Path to Success Test with this in mind.

A LEARNING TEAM IS A CONFIDENT TEAM (I)

This chapter has been all about change. More specifically, about building change confidence through achievement across your business. Before we move on, let me re-emphasize one thing:

A shared achievement is the best team-building exercise.

When you pull a new team together, think about some small, valuable challenges you can set early on. Achievable but not easy. Fix a painful problem together. Or plan a launch week where everyone gets to be creative together. Everyone gets to build a plan they can call their own.

We'll dig deeper into building teams in Chapter Nine (**p. 242**). For now, just make a start by naming your squad. Think of a change you would like to make this year. Who needs to be on that team?

Done? Great. With this team in mind, we can move on to the cadence of the work.

Visit the booksite to track the Path to Success for your next project.

BUILDING CONFIDENCE—IN A NUTSHELL

This chapter sets out to help you identify the right amount of preparation to move your organization to the next level of change. A quick review:

- Adopt a learning mindset that embraces experimentation.
- Recognize endings, new beginnings, and deal with the challenges in between, but realize that you're already changing.
- Understand your team's pace of change and accelerate just ahead.
- Identify second-order consequences as early as possible.
- Embrace small steps.
- Decide which change philosophy is best for your needs—epic or episodic?
- Build your change squad around a balance of experience, partnership, and confidence.
- Consider what coaching and transition skills could do for your squad.
- Attend to the five turning points—integration, value, launch, decisions, and benefits.

Name Your Squad

Name names:
Business sponsor:
Project leader:
Project wrangler:
Business designer:
Builder(s):
Quality facilitator:
Sanity checkers:
Knowledge facilitator:

Now put names against the soft roles:
Who are your Coaches?
Who's done this before?
Who are your Partners?
What Gaps are you still concerned about?

Agility is all about *confidence* with change—a spirit of learning creates confidence.

And now—to work!

❏❏

Booksite extras at www.trustingtechnologybook.com/chapter5 include:

Build your Squad Skills heat map
Benchmark your action over time
Help in turning Epic change to Episodic
Tools for the efficient Simple Steering approach
Track the path to success for your next project
The workbook for all the exercises

CHAPTER SIX

GETTING IT RIGHT BY DOING THE QUICKSTEP

You Won't Know What You're Doing till You're Halfway There

(aka the art and science of informed guesswork)

Seems like the tablet computer is everywhere these days.

Tablets take your order at the takeout counter, play your favorite TV series in bed, and display your findings at your team meeting. Heck, you may even be reading on one right now. In a relatively short amount of time, tablets have become a pervasive device in our professional and personal lives.

The successful generation of devices dates back to the iPad launch of 2010, quickly followed by a competitive range of Android tablets. But there were previous generations of tablet. Wacom pioneered the professional market in the '90s, but do you recall Microsoft's attempts to build a tablet platform? The year was 2002 and the software giant held sway over 90 percent of the PC hardware industry through their ownership of the Windows™ standard operating system. If Microsoft said, "boo," the hardware vendors jumped.

So, when Gates and gang decided it was time for a tablet revolution, the industry scrambled to be there on launch day. I was with Alias at the time, and we spotted an opportunity. Alias had long provided the best high-end sketching software to the automotive design industry.

Your car probably started as a sketch created on a Wacom tablet with Alias software.

Alias was big in the automotive, industrial design space. Also in the movie effects and gaming industry, but that's another story. You probably own a hundred products that were styled with Alias software. Anyone who drove a car, watched a movie, or played a computer game probably benefited from our work.

But no one outside the design industry had ever heard of us. Microsoft's tablet launch provided an opportunity to change that.

Bill Gates announced to the PC industry that he would be launching Windows Tablet PC Edition at a major New York City event to be held in November 2002. To do so, he needed hardware...and innovative software that would take advantage of the platform's pen-before-keyboard ethos.

That was our opportunity. If we could produce a tablet PC sketching application that was ready for Bill to demo that day, Alias could be featured on the main stage. Since it was Bill Gates in front of millions of viewers, it was critical that the software didn't crash. There would be huge challenges in turning out a robust product in just a few short months, but our motivation was that Alias could become a household name, just like the products that we equipped the designers to create.

So we went for it, and SketchBook was born. We had some idea of how to go about this when we began. We had the advanced digital sketching capabilities, sure—for a sophisticated user on a very different platform. In order to appeal to novice and skilled sketchers alike, the user experience would need to be completely redesigned, and moreover, the software would need to be modified to run on the Windows Tablet PC platform.

But we knew less than we would have to learn. I can't tell you how impressed I was as I saw the software evolve over those intense few months. Every week or two another version would pop out. A pool of enthusiastic techno-sketchers was enlisted to test and provide feedback on their experience. The Alias research team included some of the most talented User Interface thinkers in the world, and SketchBook was the ideal place for their innovative ideas to flower.

A product development of this magnitude simply couldn't have been realized in the old-fashioned way—design, build, test, and launch would have taken too long. Instead, the agile approach allowed the team to build on what they knew and learn what they didn't—through user feedback, research, and close collaboration with Microsoft's Tablet PC operating system team. (In the spirit of great partnerships, Microsoft learned a few things from Alias in the process.) To refer back to this chapter's title, we had to do the quickstep.

It takes courage to admit to what you don't know. After all, we're all hired as experts. But when you set big goals, you're setting out on a unique journey—no one has ever done what you are about to do in your exact context. Your big journey truly starts with a single step, and that step is to recognize what your business needs to know and planning to learn as you go. In this chapter we'll discuss how you can proceed with caution but still move quickly.

SketchBook was launched on November 7, 2002, by Bill Gates in NYC as the premier sketching app on a platform that was designed for pen and pencil. Fifty million USA Today readers saw the Alias name the next day. It was a turning point for our business.

Looking back, the key to success here was that realization—that we knew less than we would we need to learn. Because of this, we adopted the agile development process, the approach that best allowed us to recognize—and resolve—our ignorance on our way to creating the product.

Microsoft's tablet program ultimately did not succeed and went into hiatus until the Surface was launched ten years later, a couple of years after the iPad had re-established the market.

SketchBook's fortunes followed the hardware path, and when the tablet platform was reborn, it continued to prosper. The software—still known as SketchBook Pro many years later—is used by over forty million people.

And I'm one of them.

ADMIT IT—YOU'RE GUESSING!

> *When it comes to ambitious projects, you won't know what you're doing till you're halfway there.*

Boom! I said it. If you don't like the sound of that (or even if you do), please humor me for this chapter.

We all like to think we know what we're doing. And when we do have doubts, we often hide them behind a veneer of confidence rather than share.

Technology has a reputation for missing expectations, for running way over budget, for perennial tardiness. We need to fix this. The practices laid out in this chapter have largely been developed in the context of technology-driven work, but they can be applied when facing down any complex endeavor. Whether you're using tech or not, uncertainty is a challenge.

Fact is, you probably don't know how to solve your next big challenge at the outset. But you probably know how to figure it out. Over time.

Embracing uncertainty is the first step towards enlightenment. (I think I read that somewhere.) Embracing uncertainty enables us to set out to learn what we need to. If we commit to a guess and press on until we're "proven wrong," it'll take longer, cost more, and we'll all lose confidence in the outcome.

The fundamental innovation behind "agile" is simple—admit you don't know the answer, and design your work to learn what you need next. That's it—simple but not easy.

Like any miracle panacea, agile is best viewed as a shift in thinking, not the entire answer.

Admitting we don't know all the answers runs counter to conventional business wisdom:

Risk feels lower if there's "a plan."

A plan signals that someone has thought this through before seeking funding and leaping into the void. It's conventional wisdom for a reason—particularly for more established businesses with more to lose. Yet clearly there's value in the startup model as well, which relies more heavily on improvising 24/7 to find a product/market (customer) fit.

Being average isn't an option when you're burning cash. But it's easier to be average when you have a revenue runway.

I'm not going to say that "the world moves faster" and "there's less certainty than ever." I think the world has always moved a little faster than our ability to adjust—that's the exciting part.

You will find the right balance between upfront planning (thinking) and on-the-job adjustment. The following section will help you focus and keep your teams on task regardless of your pace.

SEEING IS BELIEVING

We all like to see things laid out. It exposes uncertainty, renders clarity, generates insight and action, and inspires confidence. We'll talk about how technology can help you do this in your business in the next chapter. Today's topic, though, is about bringing clarity to execution at four levels:

1. Objectives—why are you doing this, and how will you know you're done?
2. Plans—what is your current theory for success? What could go wrong, and what will you do about it?
3. Progress—how's the work progressing; how are you validating or adjusting your plan at each step?
4. Design—what will the solution look like?

Let's unpack those one at a time.

What's the point?

We choose to go to the moon this decade...because that goal will serve to organize and measure the best of our energies and skills.

—JFK, September 12, 1962

A simple declarative statement of outcomes is powerful. It provides a meaning to the work, something that every contributor can get behind. Kennedy sure did that—it was less than seven years later that Neil Armstrong took the giant leap.

Coming back down to earth: are you thinking of taking on a complex endeavor? Then you need to articulate three good reasons to undertake it. Why three? Many projects are easy to justify for one reason, two could be a coincidence, but three really focuses you on your best opportunities.

Take the Three Reasons Test now and see for yourself.

Three Reasons Test

Looking at a past or present initiative, why was that work selected over the alternative opportunities? Can you recall one, two, or three reasons?

Now think ahead to some new investments you're considering. List two or three, then come up with three reasons to do each.

Is your decision clearer now?

We'll come back to this later, but I wanted to plant the seed with you now.

When Kennedy made his shoot-for-the-moon speech, it was pretty clear what he meant. But when we get a little deeper into the weeds, clarity becomes harder and, for that reason, even more important.

Play that back to me

Clarity is the best investment you will make. Miscommunication is a killer. Fortunately, that's a match made in heaven.

True story: a friend of mine was asked to book a flight to Oakland for an urgent meeting. He dutifully called the travel agent, bought his ticket, and made the flight. To Auckland. That's an extra fourteen hours in the air. You see, my friend had a heavy accent and when he said "Oakland," the agent heard "Auckland." He missed the meeting.

You've also probably witnessed a variation of this story: One time a vendor was giving my client a first view on a major deliverable. The vendor was anxious but proud of the work they had put into it. As we walked through the demo, I noticed my client's expression transform from excited anticipation, to confusion, to actively frowning.

Not the ideal reaction. "You look pained," I whispered to her.

"Yeah," she answered, gesturing to the demo. "This is not what I asked for."

We see the consequences of miscommunication way too often—lots of wasted time and work. It's painful to observe and costly to fix.

It's also easily avoidable.

Life's potential for ambiguity seems unlimited. You speak—I hear. But did you convey your intent clearly enough? Did I comprehend fully and have an opportunity to challenge the approach and enrich the outcome?

The best way I know to close the communication gap is to make a simple request:

Play that back to me.

In business, we are often asked to solve complex challenges. Unfortunately, teams can dive into the details too early. And any time before the goals have been clearly shared and played back is too early. Sometimes the goals are lost in the detail; sometimes they are never fully developed and communicated (meaning sent *and* received).

At the same time, we have to be clear on what's intractable (goals that the outcome must achieve, the "why") and what's malleable (the "how"). I advocate:

1. A short description of what we are trying to achieve; a simple, measurable outcome that anyone on the team can recite. (This is a *not* a list of features.)
2. A list of steps that we think will *achieve* the goals, a plan to test the approach as we go, and a readiness to adjust as we learn.

This goal should inform *every* decision that anyone makes in the course of the work—what decision should I make to best serve the goal? If they can recite the goal, they can apply it; if there's any confusion or misunderstanding, the best decisions will be overlooked.

While your goals should be declarative, they should be light on prescriptive. Boiling goals down to the essential outcomes leaves room for creativity in the team's solution. You want this.

Good Goals	Bad Goals
Reduce average service call by 25% while increasing customer sat by 10%	Spend less time on the phone by following the attached script. Check the customer's Net Promoter score before hanging up.
Enable users to complete 20% more jobs using our software without increasing their active time in the system	Increase product use by 20% amongst existing users. Add the three new functions we discussed last quarter.
Increase revenue by 35% over the next year without reducing margins	Just do it

Good and bad goals—you can spot the difference

Clarity Test

Looking at past initiative, how simple were the goals at the outset? How clearly were they defined from the start?

Did your team fully embrace the goals? Could they recite them, and did they refer to the goals when making every decision throughout the initiative?

Or did they get lost in the fog of war as the work progressed?

Now apply these same questions to a present or upcoming initiative. What would you change?

In tech, "play that back to me" translates to a common understanding that all parties agree on. That may mean a contract, or a detailed specification, or (often best) an evolving prototype that can be touched, felt, and sculpted to the best outcome. The more complex the specification, the less likely that the team will absorb it, recite it, and base every decision they make on whether or not they are moving towards the goal. Anything else is a waste of time.

Spending time on clarifying the objective will save 10x the time downstream.

Measure this for yourself with the Clarity Test.

There are many techniques for describing outcomes in a simple but comprehensive manner. I recommend that you create an Agile Vision Statement with your team. It's about what you write down but also about what you leave out.

What's so good about this technique? Well it answers the questions "who's it for?", "why might they need it?", what *it* is and how it differs from the alternatives. All on one page. What's not to like about that?

For: *«target customer»*
Who: *«needs»*
The: *«product name»*
Is a: *«product category»*
That: *«product benefit. Reason to buy»*
Unlike: *«competitors»*
Our product: *«differentiation or value proposition»*

The Agile Vision Template

Can't you just picture developing this vision statement with your team, sharing it with all the contributors you recruit, hearing them recite it and asking "how does this contribute to the goal" with every decision they make?

Returning to our Sketchbook story, here is an agile vision that Alias developed at the outset. First came the product definition…

For: graphics professionals, primarily, and visual communicators, secondarily,
Who: need to explore and present ideas and designs using high-quality sketches anywhere,
The: Alias SketchBook Pro Application
Is a: simple, elegant, and innovative software product of uncompromising quality
That: transforms a Tablet PC or other pen-based PC into a digital sketchbook.

Then a number of competitive statements…

Unlike: physical pen and paper,
Our product: allows users to instantly switch brushes, undo and redo, manipulate layers, compare and present digital sketches and annotated images.

Unlike: paint solutions targeted as production art tools,
Our product: is an instant access, lightweight application that provides the essential tools to make sketching, annotating, and presenting visual concepts as fast and efficiently as possible, preserving creative flow.

Unlike: PowerPoint and linear presentation applications,
Our product: enables users to create and deliver dynamic, non-linear presentations, seamlessly alternating between image viewing, comparison, annotating, and sketching to promote visual discussion and decision-making.

Unlike: ink-based applications
Our product: delivers high-quality and responsive artist tools that simplify working with digital images.

Then we used this vision as a basis for business and engineering goals and design principles. The business goals set out the strategic parameters, and the engineering goals and design principles set the standard for the implementation.

Business Goals

Enter Broader Markets: Establish Alias in larger graphics and business markets.

Brand Expansion: Hundreds of thousands of users touching Alias products.

Innovation: Changing the way people work with images.

IP: Produce opportunities for protectable intellectual property.

New Partner Relationships: Working successfully with a new set of hardware and software industry leaders.

Integrated Product Line: Create a SketchBook product line based on pen input that works seamlessly with the entire Alias family of products.

Integrated Brand Experience: Develop well-defined, connected, and satisfying experiences at all customer touch points: marketing, web, retail, partner, application, and support.

Engineering Goals

Technical Excellence: Full commitment to highest quality.

Optimize: Fastest possible speed and smallest code size.

Stable: Zero tolerance for real defects.

Reusable: Code can be used in the Alias product line.

Focus: Do only the essential.

Design Principles

Promote Flow: An interface that doesn't interfere with the user's artistic experience.

Stylus Friendly: Taking full advantage of, as well as minimizing problems with, the stylus.

Innovative: A user interface that others will want to copy but can't because of patent protection.

Maximum Work Area: Interface elements with no window clutter.

Performance: Starts quickly and performs responsively.

Self-Revealing: Approachable. Users can figure out the functionality by exploration.

Engaging: A pleasure to use.

Elegant Simplicity: Features are used by most users most of the time. Features are not added just because they can be.

High Aesthetic Quality: Cohesive, consistent, pleasing visuals. Part of the Alias family of new products.

Last but not least, a roadmap strategy defined what comes next and made explicit the things that Version 1 would *not* address....

Version 2 Strategy

Sketch: Add the core functionality needed for graphic professionals to create conceptual artwork: custom brushes, custom colors, layer and selection tools, hotkeys, and UI enhancements.

Book: Add the essential functionality to support single user sketch organization and presentation: thumbnail viewing, seamless toggle between sketch and book views, intelligent image comparison, and maximum screen real estate.

Present: Support fluid linear and non-linear presentations of one or more sketches to promote visual discussion.

Focus: Reduce the emphasis on business users and focus on artists and visual communicators.

Granted, it took some work to pull together this definition, but the discipline of conciseness makes for a pointed outcome that's easily understood by your audience. OK—at some point we passed everyone's capacity for recitable, but this still fits on a page. A page that we pinned to office walls and dropped on our computers' desktops.

Could this technique help you clearly and concisely define your next major initiative?

Yes? Great.

No? Then refer to the booksite for more examples and techniques for clarity.

At the end of the day, it doesn't matter what technique you use as long as you hear your team play the right goal back to you.

The best laid schemes o' mice an' men

...Gang aft a-gley.
—Rabbie Burns

Roughly translated, I believe Burns would agree with my point—plans go astray. Your plan—any plan—is just a theory. An expectation of the way things should go down. Hopefully, it's based on some solid thinking by folks who have done this kind of thing before. But I guarantee that no plan will happen exactly as predicted at the outset.

Allow me to add another truism:

Optimistic planning is disappointment, delayed.

Ouch. Here I am coming out against optimism—and you thought I was a glass half full guy, right? Well I'm still the same guy that said you should build your plans around opportunities, not problems.

But many of us have a natural tendency to optimism when it comes to the work we can get done, and that's damaging. I'm here to steer you clear of damage. Let me expand.

Setting the right expectations is the first and most important step to success.

Being overly optimistic is a sure way to sabotage the best investments, accurate timelines, and delivery of the intended outcome. And since estimation is the bedrock of planning and expectation setting, it's a strength worth investing in.

I once helped two different clients through a couple of project sessions. One was a retrospective that I had been asked to attend as an observer, and the other a project launch that I led. The projects were remarkably similar, but comparing their outcomes is a useful exercise.

In the case of the retrospective, the completed project had exceeded timeline estimates by 50 percent. Compromises had been made to wrap up at that point, and the shortcuts were continuing to drag on the business.

Disappointment filled the room. After listening to the roundtable discussion of outcomes, I asked the team to describe their project launch process. Turns out that the sponsors had spent four hours preparing the business case and timeline estimates and reckoned on a six-month timeline.

The allotted six months became nine months and, understandably, the pressure had mounted during the overrun. Everything the team had accomplished had a black cloud over it.

As for the new project launch session: we brought eight stakeholders and contributors together for over two days. During this time, we crystallized the project goals and made twenty-seven key decisions. We tested use cases, shortlisted essential outcomes, mitigated risks, and developed a plan for benefits realization. The group had confidence in the plan they had built.

A year on, we, too, conducted a retrospective. The team delivered on the timeline, despite a couple of curveballs in their marketplace, and the benefits now being realized are 15 percent better than expected.

Here are some takeaways that I took away from these two experiences:

1. Good estimation drives great expectation-setting, which gives the team room to succeed.
2. Successful planning requires an environment that promotes candor and preparation.
3. Experience counts most at the outset of any project; posing the right questions, examining the work to be done, challenging assumptions, and mitigating risk.
4. Breaking the work into smaller chunks is the best way to chip away at uncertainty.
5. Be clear where the risks lie and develop mitigation strategies to counter them.
6. Enumerate assumptions and adjust during the project if things change.
7. Things change.
8. If you are repeating work that's similar to projects you've done before, you have a benchmark to build on and can apply lessons learned. You can then focus on what's different this time around and adjust your previous plans to accommodate the new.
9. It's harder to estimate work that is different from anything the organization has done before. You need to talk to someone who's been there and done that. If they have the ability to quickly adapt

their experience to your context, get them on the team, even if only in an advisory capacity.

10. A "good" estimate pegs cost, effort, and timeline within plus or minus 15 percent. You should plan for the upper bound and deliver within that budget.
11. Always conduct a retrospective, whether the outcome is good or bad.

In short, businesses run better without unpleasant surprises, great expectations are laudable, and we all like happy endings.

Expose fantasy planning

How do you ensure that you're dealing with reality? When building your plan, make sure you answer three questions:

1. What is your current theory for success?
2. What are your unknowns?
3. How will you address them?

Many "plans" unfortunately stop at the first question. This is how it's going to go down, unless something unforeseen comes up. And we'll jump off that bridge when we come to it.

Well guess what? Something unforeseen will happen if you don't spend the time to foresee.

Let's begin by describing your current theory for success. Knowns are predictions that we are comfortable making. You have evidence and experience that suggests you don't need to sweat about these outcomes. When evaluating knowns, consider:

- What do you know to be true?
- Which parts of the work are you confident in?

Recall from Chapter Five that job number one is to get the right experience on your team?[20] Who has done this kind of thing before? How do the circumstances differ? You know enough to connect the dependent tasks and estimate the effort. Step one of your plan could look this Waterfall chart:

20 "Balancing Experience," *Trusting Technology, p. 115*

What you know how to do, and the missing links

> **A word on formatting**
>
> In this section's figures, the shaded boxes represent Knowns, the unshaded denote Unknowns that need to become Knowns and the shaded without border are Learning activities in progress, designed to answer these questions.
>
> Unknowns
> Learning
> Knowns

The next step is to plan for uncertainty—how to address those missing links. Remember that uncertainty is inherent in any original work that a team takes on. How can everyone know exactly what it will take if they have never done the work before? There are several strategies for reducing this uncertainty, but *not* planning is not one of them.

You'll be able to address some missing links by seeking guidance from someone who's done this before. Find that someone and get them on the team.

OK, that deals with what you know. Everything else is either a known unknown or, somewhat trickier, an unknown unknown. Let's begin to address these by asking more questions:

- Which of your "knowns" have risk, and what exactly are those risks?
- If you did this before, what's different this time? Where should we proceed with caution?
- What do we need to learn?

You can't avoid uncertainty en route, but you can identify it. Making your knowns and unknowns visible keeps you honest and focused on learning what you need to learn to make the best decisions you can today.

Try this. Pick an important initiative and consider its components—let's call them building bricks. Take a pad of Post-its and write the name of each brick on its own sticky. Now find a big wall in your office and spray paint two vertical black lines in the middle. (You can use removable tape if you're less committed.) On the right of the two lines, stick the Post-its for bricks that you understand well—things you have already built or are convinced will be easy. Put all the other Post-it bricks to the left of the two lines.

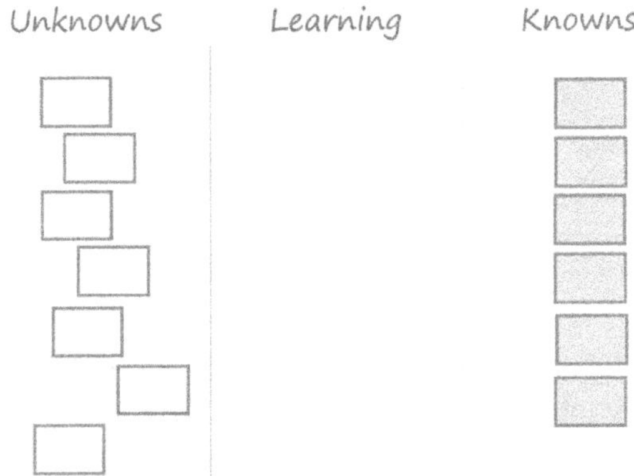

Call out your knowns and unknowns and bare your soul

Your mission between now and the end of the job is very simple—move every unknown Post-it on the extreme left to the extreme right or throw them in the recycle bin. You'll do that by picking the one or two unknown bricks that are most pressing and move them between the two lines—your "active learning space." Then you'll figure out what you need to figure out in order to move them into the known zone on the right.

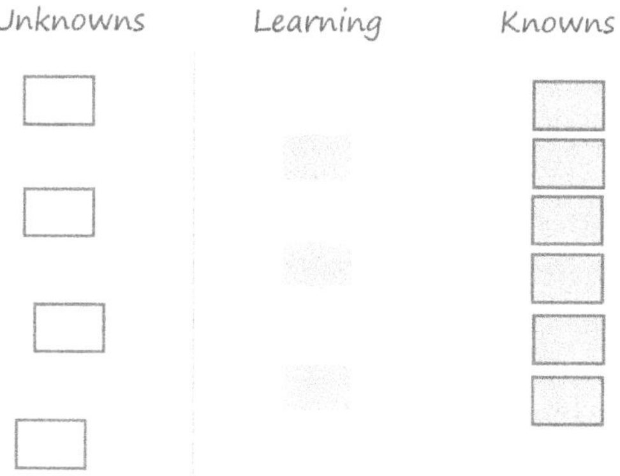

Keep your learning progress visible at all times

How does that process sound to you?

a) creative or

b) vandalism?

If you answered b, would you believe me if I told you that's the way that the world's most creative companies have operated for the last twenty years? IDEO, Google, and the rest of the gang have been solving problems with stickies for a generation. Have you read about agile, scrums, and the like? Well for all the fancy talk, this is how it's done. With stickies. Really.

Making these challenges visible helps individuals see context and helps teams see where to swarm.

Business tends to favor linear processes; they feel more orderly, and it's hard to get lost if you can only move forwards. But if you approach innovative work as a linear process, you tend to get stuck in bottlenecks, miss connections, and lose the plot. Instead, if you understand our dependencies and focus only on the next small step, you'll make better progress.

Waterfall or Agile?

Brothers and Sisters, we now reach a point of religious debate—in tech circles at least—do we run this work as Waterfall (a preplanned sequence of steps) or Agile (a defined and evolving learning path)?

My answer may surprise you, but first some history.

There was once a time when it took years—like five or ten—to build computer systems. One reason was that the hardware was built just ahead of the software, but the main reason was that software development practices were modeled on the construction industry. First you needed an architect's sketch, then a building permit, a detailed blueprint, and then a lengthy build phase. Some form of testing (to make sure the building is safe or the software works) followed by repairs to resolve important items on the deficiency list.

Seemed to make sense. Enter Fred P. Brooks.

Frederick P. Brooks led the major (five-year) development project for the IBM System/360 hardware and operating system. When he left the company, IBM founder Thomas Watson asked him why software projects were tougher than hardware. He later shared this hard-earned wisdom in *The Mythical Man-Month.*[21] There aren't many classic software development books, but this is one. Brooks expounded an approach that coupled small teams with cross-disciplinary skills. Some twenty-five years later, the Agile movement was formed just in time for the new millennium, and it's clear that the founders had read Brooks.

What had occurred over the intervening decades to bring this about? Well, software development had matured as a practice. It had expanded beyond its beginnings in the military, science, and banking industries (though admittedly, Citigroup still had more developers than Microsoft) and gone mainstream in business.

In the years following the Agile Manifesto,[22] the world changed again. The smartphone ushered in a new wave of consumer tech, hardware became cheap and rentable—which meant you could start a software business with no capital outlay. And the consumer market drove demand for a gazillion apps—a few of which were actually useful. The open-source movement made software components readily available.

All of this meant that it became much, much easier to build software. The old construction paradigm no longer applied. And the Agile model offered developers an easy way to avoid the associated bureaucracy.

---

21 Frederick P. Brooks, *The Mythical Man-Month: Essays on Software Engineering* (Boston: Addison-Wesley Professional, 1975).

22 Mike Beedle, Arie van Bennekum, Alistair Cockburn, Ward Cunningham, Martin Fowler, Jim Highsmith, Andrew Hunt, Ron Jeffries, Jon Kern, Brian Marick, Robert C. Martin, Ken Schwaber, Jeff Sutherland, and Dave Thomas, "Manifesto for Agile Software Development," AgileManifesto.org, accessed June 30, 2019, *https://agilemanifesto.org/*.

The pendulum needed to swing. And swing it did. Too far. Suddenly, you couldn't be cool unless you were an Agile addict. Remember those Apple commercials where the hip young Apple dude was chatting with the geeky, older Microsoft guy? Well in this case, Agile is the hip dude and Waterfall's the, well, old-fashioned guy.

Things got really exciting. Just. Build. Software. Then reality bit.

Teams tasked with building software weren't producing when expected. If you ran a startup, unexpected delays meant you needed more cash to burn. If you ran a profitable business, your profits got hit. Good results came too late.

And Agile seemed particularly difficult to apply in the world of business systems. Over the decades, the Waterfall approach had been built around *big* implementations. Systems vendors took some time to adapt to the demand for faster implementations. Many have yet to make the shift.

So where are we now? The industry has learned (in the best tradition of Agile) that neither extreme—Agile or Waterfall—is best, and that the most effective approach depends on the context.

Context, here, is a factor of the business you're in, your customers' demands, your culture, your team's comfort with each approach, and the specific needs of the project you're undertaking.

If that sounds too complex, pick your position on the scale below to figure out where your next project should fit on the "Waterfall-Agile" scale:

1. You know exactly what you need and can write down every detail at the kickoff meeting.
2. You have a culture that is attuned to Waterfall.
3. You favor predictability and will pay a premium to get it.
4. You're repeating work that you have done before and have confidence that your playbook will work again this time.
5. You have a very short list of critical goals and don't care how those goals are achieved.
6. You have a team that's really good at Agile.
7. You're solving a problem for customers and the best solution isn't known yet.

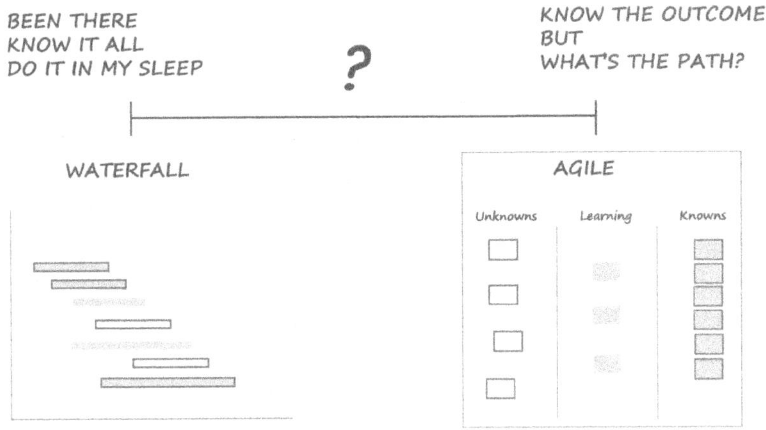

Balance knowledge with discovery on the Waterfall-Agile scale

If you find yourself relating more to statements one, two, and/or three, the more you should lean on Waterfall—if you find yourself nodding more at statements five, six, and/or seven, the more likely you are to win with Agile. You may notice that the degree of uncertainty increases with the numerals. That's no coincidence.

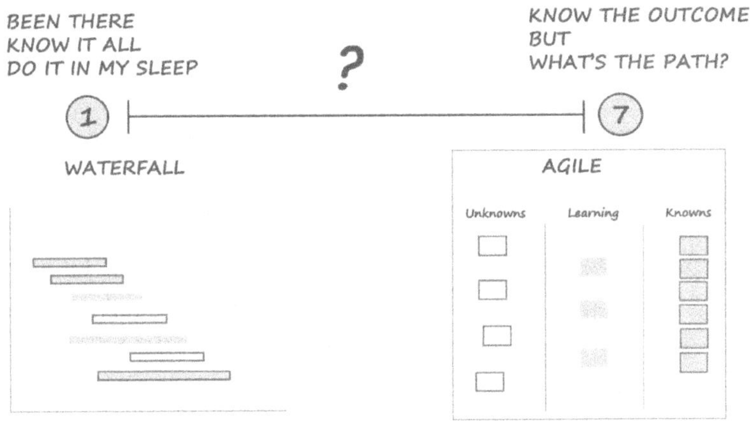

Are you a 1, a 7, or somewhere between?

Are you wondering what my answer is to the Waterfall/Agile debate? Simple—*plan what you know and leave space to learn what you don't.*

- If you can plan, do. That's Waterfall.

- If you know the problem but little about the solution, figure out what needs to be learned next and learn it quickly—with an Agile board.

When you combine your plans, they'll look something like this … let's call it WAgile.

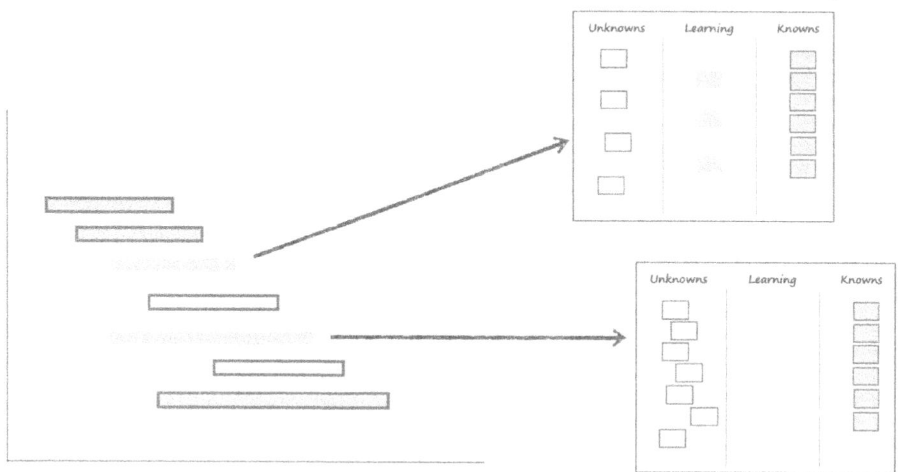

Merge what you know (Gantt) with what you must learn (boards)

Every map needs a compass

If the plan (theory) provides a map, visible progress tracking serves as your compass.

It shows your current coordinates, where you're on track, and where a course correction is required. Your success will be determined by the pace at which you recognize the need for course corrections—where planning assumptions have not panned out—and how quickly you decide and act to get on the new track.

In its simplest form (and we like simple around here, don't we?), your compass lists the big chunks of your work and highlights three things:

1. A statement of health:
    - Thumbs up—we're good. Let's not spend much time on this today.
    - Questionable—slipping. Here's a plan to get back to green. OK with that?

- On fire—at risk of impacting the whole project. All hands on deck.

2. Brief on what's been done since our last milestone.
3. Brief on what you'll do next in response to what you know today.

Your milestones could be daily stand-ups, bi-weekly steering meetings, or quarterly board meetings. This format works for all. And it all fits on your front page.

Health Done Next

Simple Steering dashboards are best

Seeing and believing is all about exposing the key elements of the work—the goal, the path to reaching it, the evolving design, current coordinates, and next steps—to every contributor, every stakeholder, at all times. There are lots of tools available to help you do this, from whiteboards, to software, to napkins. That part is easy.

> *Visit the booksite for more Simple Steering tools.*

All you need to do is commit to the practice. Then your next step is to do the absolute minimum necessary to achieve that crystal-clear goal.

MINIMALIST CHANGE

Basecamp, a project management software, is a paragon of the software industry. Not because their only outside investor is Jeff Bezos, and not because they've written the most brilliant code ever. Basecamp stands out because they provide ten million customers with a solution to a complex problem. (They're also entertainingly opinionated guys—I've included a few references that I recommend you check out.)[23]

They're germane to this topic because of the way they work. They've built their business around six-week calendars, thinking time, and effective (read: "few") meetings.

A philosophy of minimalist change is one where you do the least possible amount of work to meet the goal—without compromising quality and design thinking. You turn out a solid solution to an incremental problem, then rethink your next steps. To illustrate this further, let's return to the way that work can be approached.

> *"Silicon Valley has become especially good at turning software, the highest margin product ever, into many of the worst performing businesses imaginable. With few exceptions, the amount of money being lost by the leaders of the new school is absolutely staggering."*
>
> *—Jason Fried, Founder and CEO Basecamp (formerly 37signals)*

I'll take five whys with my three reasons please

Remember my mantra—find three reasons to do anything and you'll have your shortlist? Recall the story that opened this chapter. Our three reasons for creating SketchBook Pro could have been:

1. Launch a product in a new market.
2. Do it now to take advantage of the massive publicity.
3. Cement our partnership with Microsoft.

We didn't think deeply about an ROI—these three reasons were enough. SketchBook Pro now has forty million users.

Once you've decided what to do, you'll be facing lots of different ways to do it. There's another mantra, courtesy of a little 1940s Japanese

23 Basecamp (*https://basecamp.com/*) books include *Rework*, *Remote*, and *Getting Real*. You can find their entertaining blog at *https://m.signalvnoise.com*.

start-up called Toyota—keep asking why. They say that if you ask "why?" five times, you'll not only sound like an inquisitive five-year-old, you'll also find the real reason for doing something.

If you respond to the observed symptoms, you may end up mitigating those symptoms at the cost of finding—and fixing—the root cause. Five-*whys* offers a powerful technique for root cause analysis—ensuring that we spend time solving the right problems.

Continuing with our theme of simplicity, five-*whys* is straightforward:

Why *are we drowning in faxes?*
Because *we require customers to apply by fax.*

Why *do we ask them to do that?*
Because *our staff needs to key the data into our system.*

Why *is that a problem?*
Because *we don't have enough staff to handle the peak load.*

Why *do they need to do that?*
Because *there's no other way to enter the data.*

Why *not?*
Because *we haven't given our customers a way to apply online.*

Practice this right now, if you will. Pick a nagging problem for your business, substitute that core symptom in the My Five Test, and keep going until you find the root cause.

"Five" is, of course, a guide, not a rule. Stop before three and you'll miss the point. If you go past eight, you need to reset.

Five-*whys* is a five-minute habit that saves hours, weeks, or months in fixing symptoms. Where else will you get the kind of return on your time?

Rip it up and start again

Your design is how you see the work—the artifacts that will evolve into your desired outcome. It's hard to know what the solution will look like until you've seen a first draft. Enter the prototype.

My Five Test

Why <observed symptom>?

Because ____________________

Why ____________________

Because ____________________

Why ____________________

Because ____________________

Why ____________________

Because ____________________

Why ____________________

Because ____________________

We learn by reading, asking, and listening, but most of all by doing. If I have a great idea, I can describe it to you and you may get it, but if I show it to you, you'll know what I mean, and we'll both make better decisions as a result.

Prototypes rock because they're visceral, almost real. We trade expedience for incompleteness—napkin sketches, cardboard models, html mock-ups, or throwaway code. The goal is maximum reality under extreme time constraints.

Don't be one of those who see throwaway work as a waste. Done right, the only thing that's being thrown away is ignorance. Set a direction, mock it up, and decide it's good or not. And think of all the time you'll save by avoiding the wrong direction. If it helps, allocate 10 percent of the project budget to prototyping—work that's done simply to facilitate better decisions. If you're breaking truly new ground, make that 25 percent.

	Napkin	Mock ups	Pilot	Final product
Innovate	50m	2d	10d	20d
Create	10m	4d	50d	250d
Sunk cost	60m	6d	60d	270d

Innovate at speed before you build your product

Take a look at these numbers, representative of the process of innovating and creating output that represents your ideas. When you innovate, you find an answer by trial and error. At which stage of this process would you prefer to make errors?

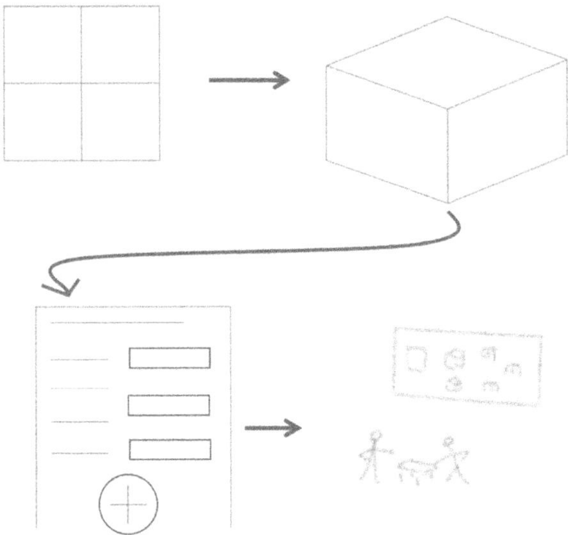

Evolve your prototypes with many tools

Action/time—watch out!

You'll recall the contrasting charts of Action Over Time from Chapter Five. The first is a caution on the big bang approach…

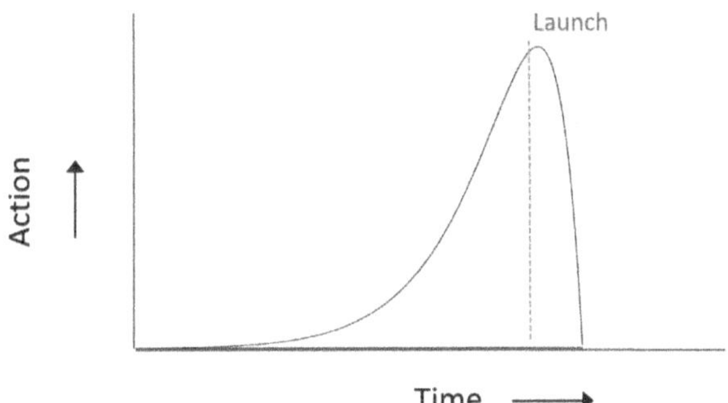

The Everest Approach—a risky climb to major change

…and my Foothills Model shows an alternative.

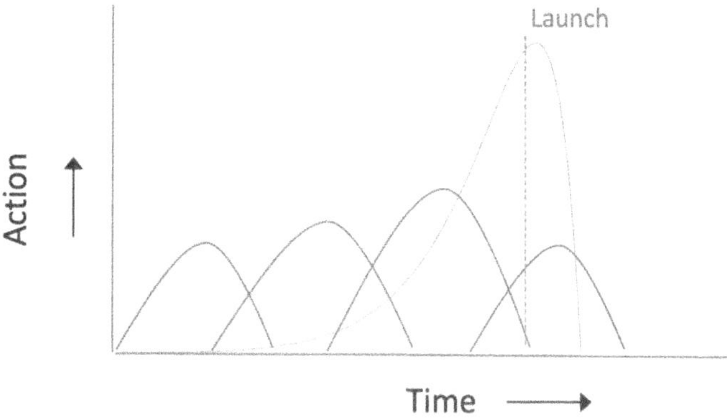

The Foothills Approach to Minimalist Change

Here are three reasons to prefer the foothills approach:

1. You see frequent results—fully functional slices of the work.
2. You learn as you go and make course corrections more readily.
3. No big crescendo of risk at the big launch—margin for error.

Which is the best way to reach your outcome—a big bang project or series of small wins (minimalist change)?

THE ART OF ESTIMATION

Major construction projects are, on average, delivered one year behind schedule and 30 percent over budget.[24] On many large industrial projects, high levels of complexity create productivity bottlenecks that can slow work to a crawl.

The stats for technology are less clear, but probably no better. The primary cause could be slow delivery but, more likely, optimistic or naïve planning that results in weak estimation—poor expectation-setting at the very time you need great expectations.

24 Tom Brinded, Raja Sahulhameed, and Andy Thain, "Accelerating late-stage construction: Mastering the sprint finish," McKinsey & Company, February 2019, *https://www.mckinsey.com/industries/capital-projects-and-infrastructure/our-insights/accelerating-late-stage-construction-mastering-the-sprint-finish.*

Since every plan is a forecast, things will never actually go down exactly that way. But this is not a reason to skimp on the preparations.

> *"Plans are useless, but planning is indispensable."*
>
> *—Dwight D. Eisenhower*

The triangle of levers

Whenever planning an endeavor, you have three levers to pull:

1. Scope—the amount of work you need to do to finish the job.
2. Time—the number of days between your start and end dates.
3. Resources—the effort that your team can put in and other budget items.

If you increase scope, you'll need more time or more resources or both. If you decrease scope, the reverse applies—simple stuff you probably know, but worth reiterating before we delve into the art of estimation.

The challenge of the crystal ball

"It's hard enough to figure out complex change without having to put your neck on the line and commit to some date or other. And I can't give a budget number until we're a few months into the work."

Odds are you've probably heard some version of this lament—or felt it—a dozen times. I have. And it's valid. Every plan is a theory, and last time I looked, none of us had a crystal ball. If you're beginning challenging work that's new—to the world or just to this team—there's no way you'll have all the information about how it's likely to go down. And if you have to put your reputation on the line and guarantee a date, you'll want to hedge until you have enough information to go on.

Fact is, you'll never have enough. Just when you think you're there, some surprise could pop up and take you in a new and lengthier direction.

Is it any wonder that you'd rather just get on with the work and see what happens? Or give a wildly pessimistic number—and risk a poor ROI killing the project before the kickoff meeting? Or, what the hell, pull a number out of the air, present with confidence, and white-knuckle the ride to inevitable failure?

Do any of those options sound good to you?

I thought not. So let's try something else.

Why predict at all?

Whether you champion a new initiative or are excited to be handed a challenging assignment, it's all too easy to start with the remit and work our way through to the end of the assignment. But then you run the risk of missing the main point. Why are you doing this? What is the context? What is the chain of initiatives that precedes your work, and what downstream work is dependent on your delivery?

Let's not miss the whole point of why we're here.

Everything you do is part of a chain—your contribution to the world. That applies to work, family, community, and the universe in general. The last three of those are beyond the scope of this book, but the first one isn't.

If you've been asked—or are asking someone else—to improve your supply chain efficiency, provide customers with better channels of communication, or improve the performance of your product by 75 percent, it's because someone needs that to happen. Those people are now your stakeholders. They're dependent on your success and just need to know when you expect to deliver. That way, they can build the results into their sales plans, delivery plans, or whatever plans.

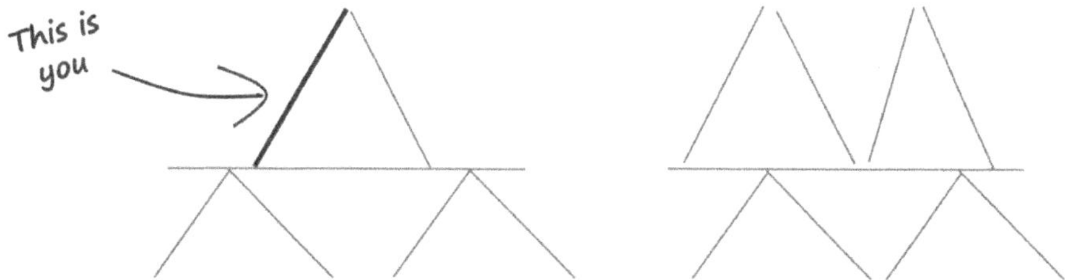

Your work is part of a puzzle

They trust you to deliver, give them a *reasonable* delivery date, and keep them posted if things change. They're excited have you to contribute to their success. And that's an honor.

No pressure, but people need an idea of when you'll be done

The best way for you to build that trust is to share your estimation challenge. Not in a whiny way, but in an objective, "here's our theory, here's what could go wrong, and here's how you can help" kind of way.

Here's our theory
Here's what could go wrong
Here's how you can help

Engage your dependents with responses to each of these statements.

In the same way, you'll be dependent on upstream activities being delivered. You need answers to the same questions from the folks who are delivering to you. If you don't have those answers, ask them the same questions *while* you're building your plans.

In a perfect world, we'd have one long happy chain of activities with timely communication of change impact between teams. And if a butterfly flutters its wings upstream, everyone will know the likely impact right away.

OK, so that's crazy talk, but if you can improve your estimation and dependent communication by just 20 percent, I guarantee remarkable improvements for your business.

(Feel free to apply these principles to family, community, and the universe in general, by the way, but just know that my guarantee doesn't apply everywhere.)

If it was easy, everyone would have a crystal ball

Absent a crystal ball, your best bet for 20 percent better estimation is to relax, eschew perfection, think it through, and share your logic—concisely—with your stakeholders.

As is always the case (well, at least 90 percent of the time) clarity and communication resolve a ton of problems.

If, like me, you're a recovering perfectionist, you'll have spent years aiming for great accuracy, but have now realized that's a fool's game. The 80/20 rule applies in spades here. Do some good foundational thinking to answer the estimation questions above for yourself, accept some answers that are just ranges, and set realistic expectations with your stakeholders.

Pessimistic	⇔	**Realistic**	⇔	Optimistic
Missed opportunity		*Confidence*		*Delayed disappointment*

Dire consequences of fantasy planning

THE FIVE FALLACIES OF PROJECT "MANAGEMENT"

I've been around over five hundred projects, and I've joined many of them part of the way in. It's rare that I'm asked to help with a project that hasn't come off the rails. When this happens, the one person on the team—aside perhaps from the sponsor—who most often looks like a deer in the headlights is the project manager. The title can bestow the weight of the world on one's shoulders yet can often feel like shuffling the deck chairs on the Titanic.

Project management is a vital role. It takes steel, organization, empathy, and a proclivity for clarification to do the job well. Notwithstanding, it's often the case that this person is not set up for success.

Let me present five fallacies about the role of project manager, along with a tip as to how you can strive to empower your PMs:

Project managers are "managers"

Managers in the conventional sense have the authority to command that things be done. We use the term "leaders" for those that inspire work to be done. While it's possible for a project manager to be a leader through force of personality and influence, they are very rarely managers. When you consider that most project team members are often doing double duty from their "day job," it's easy for the PM to be placed in a position of responsibility without authority.

Empowerment tip: *support your PM's negotiations with the team members' line managers.*

You can learn project management from a book

Amazon has over thirty thousand books on project management. I'm sure many of them do a good job of the logistics—timelines, risk management, efficient meeting habits, *et al.* But I've yet to see one that is a substitute for experiencing a few difficult projects. PMP certifications, like any certifications, do not an expert make.

Empowerment tip: *when you interview PM candidates, ask them to describe their three toughest project situations, what they did, and how things turned out. The tougher the challenge they overcame, the higher they should be on your list.*

Anyone can do it

So often, a project manager is picked because they're already on the team as an expert and they have the greatest passion. Or because they "can make the time." Smaller projects rarely need a fulltime PM, especially when efficient communications have been established. But be sure that you have someone who *can* establish and maintain a streamlined project approach—such as the efficient Simple Steering techniques—and communications that allow people to stay abreast without distracting time from the work itself. (You can find some useful tools for this at the booksite.)

Empowerment tip: *support the PM in establishing an efficient project machine. Do not treat this part of their role as an afterthought.*

The project manager is responsible for getting the project team to do their work

I'm a fan of PMs that make good wranglers—people who can stir things up, motivate the team to keep moving forward, go the extra mile. But this is not the same as chasing team members down for simple status updates (tried Slack?), or for tardy meeting attendance. You want your PMs to be wranglers not shepherds.

Empowerment tip: *hold the team responsible for results—good or indifferent—not the PM.*

The project team has all the time they need

Let's go back to that double-duty thing. Can you honestly say that the project team has been cut some slack on their other responsibilities in order to contribute what's required to get the project work done? If so, congratulations. If not....

Empowerment tip: *help every member of the team avoid overestimating their abilities. A slower, realistic commitment beats an unachievable commitment every time. Hands down.*

Setting your project managers up for success

Most of all, if you are the sponsor, the best way to help your PMs succeed is to be present early on—and as often as necessary after that—to ensure full engagement of the team. Do a good job at the start, and you'll be surprised how much easier (as in better results with less work) it gets.

When I see PMs that are really kicking it, their role is akin to a Project Navigator. (I'm not a fan of jazzy job titles like Chief Unconventional Officer, but navigator just, well, fits.) Here's the job description:

- Help the team design the work—coordinate creation of the WAgile plan and ensure maintenance going forward.
- Run the regular update cadence (daily scrums, bi-weekly steering, take your pick) to engage each member of the squad listed at the end of Chapter Five at the right time and for the right questions.

- Help the team navigate the work—what did we just complete, where are we, what do we need to do next, and what could go wrong?
- Be the avenue of escalation for any new decisions that need to be made, and make sure the Decision/Action loop doesn't ever—*ever*—slow the work down.
- Direct focus onto what matters and quell distraction with what doesn't.
- Anticipate and avoid barriers to progress.

That's it. If they have time left over (which they often will), they can spread their goodness around multiple projects. Or the polymaths can take off their Project Navigator hats and don another to contribute even more to the core project.

Have I convinced you to hand out those new "Project Navigator" business cards?

A LEARNING TEAM IS A CONFIDENT TEAM (II)

You know how I feel about confidence and change. What do you consider to be the attributes of a confident team? A team that's nearing the completion of a major project should be feeling good about themselves. That's because they've faced up to the challenge and are on the brink of wrestling it to the ground.

At the heart of any happy team is a spirit of camaraderie and of mutual trust built on results delivered together. Of sharing experiences. Of helping each other to grow.

A team that learns these things together has extra gas in the tank. Any member's challenge is the whole team's challenge. All opportunities are shared. Individuals learn at different paces—a learning team moves at the pace of the fastest third but leaves no one behind.

Rapid learning is vital. It means sufficient, efficient communication. "Here's what I learned yesterday—tell me if you want the details."

We all thirst for knowledge, and that thirst begins with embracing ignorance. A vital outcome of any project launch is that the whole team is on the same page regarding the outcome, and each member is clear on the roles they will fulfill.

Equally important is that everyone knows where to go for help in specific areas—and where the team simply doesn't know that answer yet. The next step is to determine who's best to figure that out. Can they consult someone from outside the team who's been there, done that? Is experimentation merited? How important is it to get the answer; should we focus somewhere else in the near term?

Empowerment Test

If something's not working, who on your team can authorize a change in direction?

What level of decision does the leader need to approve? Has this ever delayed the work?

How imperfect can the answer be; how good is good enough? How much latitude do we have to experiment? It's ok—usually good—for experiments to fail. Does everyone get that?

Here are some simple techniques to cultivate greater Project Knowledge, all designed to be completed in fifteen-minute learning bursts.

- Keep records—scribe all meeting decisions, outcomes, and actions.
- Document as you go—have everyone spend fifteen minutes on their daily journal, first thing or last thing in the day. Share headlines and detail. This can be written, spoken, or videoed.
- Conduct fast retrospectives after any major achievement. Don't save these till the end—you want to apply lessons learned ASAP.
- Go all out to have at least one customer participate. Their pragmatic self-interest is worth a dozen theories.

Is your team empowered? Take the Empowerment Test to find out.

WHAT'S TECH GOT TO DO WITH IT (DO WITH IT)?

I mentioned it once or twice, but I think I got away with it.
—Basil Fawlty

Although this is a book about *Trusting Technology*—using it with ambition and confidence—it's mostly about complementing the machine and community of your business. The principles outlined here apply whether you're using high tech, low tech, or even no tech.

That means you need to consider the question of whether technology can speed the achievement of your outcomes. While I hope you'll find a reason, one question should be asked at the outset:

To tech or not to tech?

Here are some ways tech can help:

- Speed of platform.
- Rapid experimentation to match customer need with solution.
- Scaling an already effective solution.
- Stand on the shoulders of others' success.

This last one is important. There's nothing new under the sun—basic research innovation is rare and risky. The odds are heavy that someone somewhere has already done what you're trying to do. Technology provides numerous ways you can leverage their perspiration and inspiration to save your own.

GETTING IT RIGHT BY DOING THE QUICKSTEP—IN A NUTSHELL

Taking effective and efficient action on business upgrades calls for the right mindset. Here's one path:

1. Admit that your plan is a guess.
2. Plan what you know:
    - Leverage your team's experience.
    - Expand your team to fill the gaps.
3. Learn what you don't:
    - Test ideas and prototypes with customers.

- Adopt a spirit of exploration and experimentation (try out new ideas, methods, or activities; create a theory and prove or disprove it—quickly).

4. Make everything visible:
    - Objectives—why you're doing this.
    - Plans—your current theory for success.
    - Progress—validation of correction at each step.
5. Give yourself room to succeed:
    - Estimation.
    - Banish fantasy planning.
    - Make minimalist change.
    - Don't ask your project manager to do it all.
6. Replenish your confidence with every win and every lesson learned.

If you are ready to apply the ideas that we've covered in Part II, you're about ready to move from competence to technology mastery. If you're confident enough to make that leap, read on!

❒❒

Booksite extras at www.trustingtechnologybook.com/chapter6 *include* Agile vision examples, more techniques for clarity, more Simple Steering templates and the workbook for all tests.

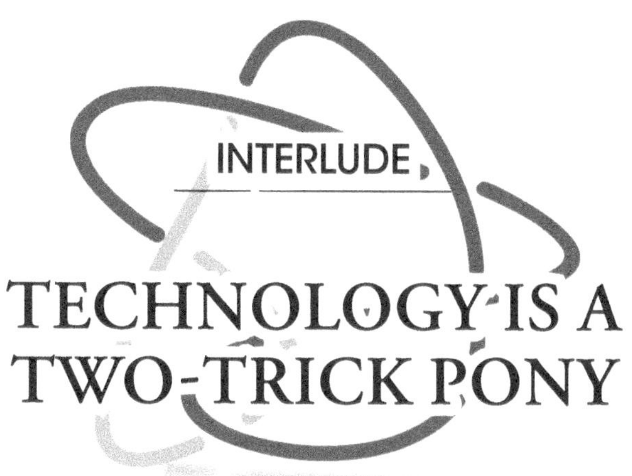

INTERLUDE

TECHNOLOGY IS A TWO-TRICK PONY

Technology does two things well:

1. It helps us generate insight and choose actions.

2. It enables fast, economical action.

That's it.

In Part III, we'll explore both in detail.

Chapter Seven looks at the generation of insight through the gathering, sense-making, and distribution of information to the right people at the right time—so they can make decisions that prompt their next actions.

Chapter Eight covers technology's role in enabling action—faster, more economically, and at massive scale with near-zero marginal cost. If you can describe the way a job is done, it can be coded. When a job is coded, it becomes enshrined in a software asset, capturing the intellectual property you deliver to customers.

Chapter Nine pulls together the constituent parts of technology—the what, why, and how—to help you build your path to technology mastery.

In Chapter Ten, we close with some example achievements to inspire your work—shoulders on which you can build.

PART III

MASTERING TECHNOLOGY

LAYING YOUR FOUNDATION FOR CONFIDENCE

Finding the Digits that Inspire Insight Across Your Community

In which you will discover new ways to inform decisions across your community—gather the information already available to you, learn how to make sense of it, and reveal your potential to provide new and valuable insights across your business community.

Before we act, we think.

At least, that's the theory. We make thousands of decisions every day, each one preceded by at least a smidgeon of thought.

Some decisions, most in fact, come easily with instinct and experience. "This has always worked for me" usually wins the day. And thank goodness—the brain already burns 25 percent of the body's calories. Imagine how much we'd have to eat if every decision was painstaking.

But instinct and experience come with their own dangers. Experts have a blind spot for new ideas precisely because they know the ways that have always worked in the past. You know that—you're an expert. Insight requires vigilance for new information that changes our thinking.

Information feeds insight—ideas that could lead us to take valuable action. But what information, when, and to whom?

We sure don't lack for information in the twenty-first century. Way too much for anyone to process, so much so that many of us have turned off those news alerts that once seemed useful. Unfriended ex-friends with TMI-itis.

Call it a crisis of curation. They say information is free, but facts cost money and relevance is worth paying for. The value, the skill, has moved from sourcing information to curating it. Separating the wheat from the chaff.

If you take one thing from this book, it's that your path to tech success begins with the understanding, channeling, and mastery of information to drive exponentially more insight across your business's community—customers and colleagues alike. In this chapter, you'll identify the information that currently exists in your business and the information that *could* exist. With this in hand, you'll paint a picture of how that information can be delivered to whoever needs it, whenever they need it—to make the best-informed decisions, fast. As a bonus, we'll spend some time on information security and highlight what you really need to know in order to critically think about your data protection.

BETWEEN THE BLAND AND THE BOUNTIFUL

Commerce thrives on information. Always has. Who needs your product, when will they need it next, and how much is it worth to them? You can never fully answer these questions, but you can answer them well enough to grow your business this year, and the next, and the next.

Maybe your questions go beyond the dollars and cents. What long-term impact will you have on your business community and on the world at large?

In a world so chockablock with raw data, the answer is out there somewhere. The question is whether you can find the answers that will generate your most important insights and do so with reasonable investment of time and resources.

It's all about inputs and outputs. You gather data for inputs and generate information for outputs. If the information is on the mark, insights will ensue. Technology has become the medium by which you can gather, curate, and distribute information a thousand times faster. For that reason, the information challenge has shifted from sourcing a scarce resource to curating a plentiful supply.

Business technology has mastered the gathering part. Your business systems log events—such as transactions, website visits, and emails exchanged—that you choose to record. Internet resources accumulate countless videos, photos, and messages exchanged. Data is the raw material of insight, but how do you process it to extract useful information?

Yet, if you teleported a 1960s COBOL programmer to the twenty-first century, business reporting would look pretty familiar to them:

- Lists of numbers (data) about things that happened last week, month, or quarter.
- Reports prepared for management—the higher ups—often labeled "top secret."
- Some analysis of those numbers to predict (speculate) what will happen next.

Sure, the spreadsheet somewhat democratized the ability to create reports and conduct some analysis, and many are now equipped to pretty-up the numbers into a report or presentation. Not to underestimate the revolution that VisiCalc, Excel, and friends brought to business, the fundamentals remain the same:

1. Log transactions in a business system.
2. Store the information in a database.
3. Extract the information in formulaic ways.
4. Review the same reports every day, week, quarter, or year to see what happened.

Let's reimagine that for a minute. Ask yourself what value this process presents:

- What analysis is possible? What expertise does the reader need to have?
- What work is required to make this useful? How much is manual and how much automated?
- What information is *not* being factored into decisions?

- And how broadly is that value being utilized—how many of your colleagues benefit?

And now ask the fundamental questions:

- How many of your colleagues are *not* being fed insights?
- How long are the decision/action/feedback loops?
- How does this help your customers?

Let's recall the Big-O model. Information is exchanged within your organization, between colleagues and customers, and between customers and prospects every day. If you're going to be serious about the business of generating insights, surely, you'd want to enrich all of these exchanges?

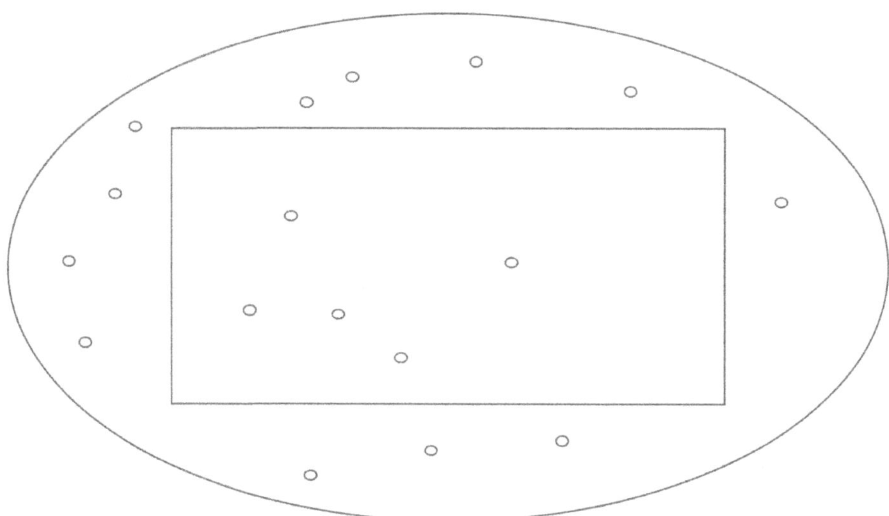

Consider the insights that could spark across your business community

There's no question that technology has sped up the making of good decisions over the last fifty years, but most businesses still aren't fully exploiting the potential of recent innovations.

The first step of mastering insight is to be clear on what you know and what you need to know.

ANSWERING THE RIGHT QUESTIONS

Information processing is here to serve, to help answer your questions. But you have to ask the right questions.

You make decisions with the information at your disposal. Logic accounts for about 25 percent of our decision process. The rest is emotion. Emotionally fueled influences include risk aversion and bias as well as personal connections and trust.

The amygdala is the part of our brain most concerned with emotion. Interestingly, research has shown that people who have suffered damage to the amygdala cannot make decisions[25]. This is pretty strong evidence of the role of emotions in decision-making.

Think about how your own emotions influence your choices. Comfort with what you know, trust in who you know, risk of error, courage to make decisions that push against the grain. How can insight influence your emotions and help you to make better decisions?

Every single one of your colleagues has to make everyday decisions that they are not comfortable with. Odds are, they're overlooking other decisions because they just don't know. Consider your org chart and the decisions each level is concerned with for a minute:

- **Executive**: what to do next quarter, next year, and three years out; how to handle any immediate and public demands.
- **Divisional**: how to hit targets, make the plan, hit the revenue and expenses; respond to departmental issues.
- **Project**: adjust the course of deals in flow and handle business upgrades based on lessons learned and shifting priorities.
- **Front line**: handle each customer moment as if it was the first and last chance to impress; solicit colleague help and advice wherever required.
- **Firefighters**: (whoever is assigned) see the smoke early and muster immediate support to do whatever it takes to prevent or douse the fire.

25 Jennifer S. Lerner, Ye Li, Piercarlo Valdesolo, and Karim Kassam, "Emotion and Decision Making," *Annual Review of Psychology*, June 16, 2014, *https://scholar.harvard.edu/files/jenniferlerner/files/annual_review_manuscript_june_16_final.final_.pdf*.

Need to Know Test

Using the "What do folks need to know?" table as a starting point, list a similar sample of the decision-maker "types" in your organization—name examples if that helps.

For each, list the information they receive to help with their decisions.

Then fill out the information that may also be available.

This isn't an exhaustive list, but it's a reasonable cross-section of the decisions that are made in your business every day. As the research indicates, most of those decisions will be made with a fair degree of emotion, but let's consider how to help with better information.

Consider, if you will, the kind of information that could be valuable for each of these decisions. Take the Need to Know Test on behalf of your colleagues.

Once you've created your own version, I suggest you go sit with the colleagues you've listed and get their input. Ask them about some major decisions they've made and what they wish they'd known then that they know now.

Decisions	Information Today	Additional Information
Executive What to do next quarter What to do next year What to do three years out How to handle any immediate and public demands		
Divisional Manager What to change to hit revenue targets What to change to hit expense targets How to react to departmental issues		
Project Leader: What to adjust to complete the project How to react to lessons learned and shifting priorities		
Front line—Sales, Support, Call Centre: How to handle today's customer moments Who to ask for help and advice		
Fire-fighting: (whoever is assigned) See the smoke early Muster immediate support to prevent or douse the fire		

What do folks need to know?

Reasonable doubts

We've talked about confidence before. When the stakes of a decision are high, it's healthy to challenge the information you use to place your bets. Doubts like these may arise in the decision-maker's mind:

- How do I know my information is correct? What degree of precision do I need?
- Is this up to date, or has something material changed since the information was provided?
- What are the gaps in my knowledge?
- Is this *my* decision to act on, or do I need someone else's blessing?

Information needs to be trusted, and trust is hard-won and easily lost. Ultimately, confidence in accuracy and timeliness is the goal of your data quality practices, which we'll talk about shortly.

That last doubt is a question of empowerment. Technology can implement approval processes, but the bottom line is that you need to provide everyone with clear parameters on the responsibilities you entrust them with, and who can help when there's doubt. A RACI-type chart—a matrix of all the activities or decision-making authorities undertaken in an organization set against all the people or roles—can play a part in streamlining your decision/action/feedback loop. Check the booksite for a RACI template.

The expert's dilemma

Experts develop an instinct for their area of specialty. This instinct is honed through experience and practicing the same thing over and over in a variety of contexts. It used to take years, even decades, to become a recognized expert. The glut of expertise—real or imagined—that the internet now provides has hastened this process. You can become an expert with some intensive research and application. (More dangerously, you can *think* you're an expert with the research and skip the application. Would *you* hire a twenty-year-old life coach?)

Then again, let's not forget that expert's blind spot for the new. Maybe you could learn something from that young life coach after all?

While access to information helps us become an expert, it can also challenge our instincts, presenting evidence-to-the-contrary that challenges our beliefs. The mark of a true expert is one that adjusts opinions with new information. That ability, I would venture, is wisdom.

Surprise me!

I'm something of a *muso* and have curated my own library—tens of thousands of tracks that mean I keep having to buy a bigger iPhone. I've become an "expert" in my own musical taste, bolstered by the positive feedback I receive whenever I DJ a gathering of friends.

Some time ago, however, I noticed that I'd stopped hearing new music. Most radio stations just play the old stuff. I found a few podcasts that introduced me to some appealing new stuff, but they faded away. And I don't find that the "similar people also listened to" services do anything for me that my friends couldn't. (What is a similar person, anyway?) Now I rely on happenstance—TV show tunes and clothing store and coffee shop background music.

> **Happenstance Test**
>
> How many new ideas do you receive every day? Where do they come from? What influence does happenstance have on your actions?
>
> Now consider how you could help your colleagues to broaden their horizons? What idea sources could you place in their path, for instance?

It's important to recognize the role of happenstance in our learning. The injection of a healthy diet of new ideas is how we learn about new things. Take the Happenstance Test to see how this is working for you—and how it might work better.

Your crystal pyramid—enriching your historical record

Business is about prediction.

OK, this book will not tell you how to predict the future. If it did, I'd be charging a lot more for it. But I can offer the next best thing to a crystal ball—my crystal pyramid.

Let's look at an example of how you could enrich your historical record to gain a glimpse of the future that might make you more comfortable about your predictions.

Imagine you were in the building supplies business; one of the biggest players, in fact. You sell billions of dollars of supplies every year, so you obviously know your business pretty well. But you're still encountering unnerving swings in demand that cannot be attributed to the usual seasonal trends.

How can you create deeper insight?

Plumbing contractors account for a good chunk of your company's customer base. When you seek to better understand the macro trends underlying your business, it makes sense to not only mine your transactions records but also study the factors that impact your customers' business. And it turns out that household renovations drive more demand for plumbing supplies than new builds. This distinction is important since the markets for renovation and new builds peak and trough at different times.

Having joined the dots with your research, you are now able to predict your business six to twelve months out with a high degree of accuracy—by using renovation forecasts as a leading indicator.

Take the Where Are You Headed? Test now to list out the leading indicators for your business.

What does this have to do with the information that you feed your business? Let's walk through that example again. If you've been in business for more than a year and have kept accurate records, your starting point will be the history of transactions recorded in your accounting system—the numbers that tell you what happened this year.

Where Are You Headed? Test

Split your buyers into a few segments. Don't go crazy in detail—two to five segments are fine at this stage.

Now list out the underlying trends that affect the market for each of those—the factors that dictate how *their* businesses will perform over the coming six to twelve months.

What information can you find to help forecast the impact of those factors? What do those trends mean for your forecast?

And how can you prepare now to exploit the opportunities and mitigate the slowdowns?

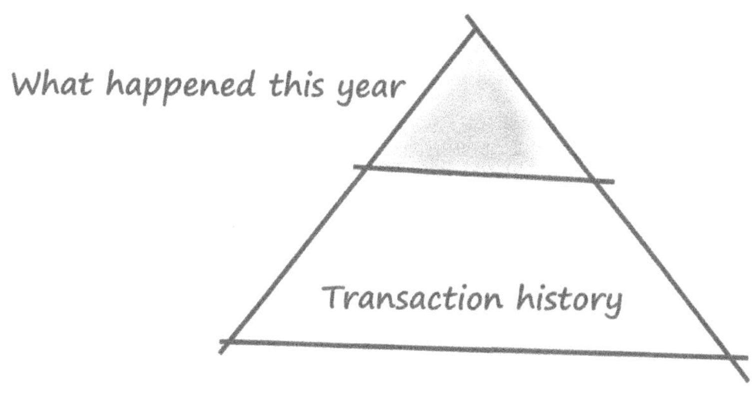

Information tells you what happened—typically your transaction history

As an aside, transaction records tend to be pretty accurate for one simple reason—your customer will let you know if you ship the wrong product or over-bill them (though they may overlook an accidental discount). The data is being "exercised" frequently (exercised meaning that the data is checked and errors are fixed *at source* on a regular basis) and stays in good shape. We'll see later on that this is not the case for all data. For now, let's assume your transaction records provide a sound basis for further research.

It's important to know what happened, but this data is a bit dry. How can we pump some excitement into it by helping us predict the future with some degree of confidence?

You measure the things that are easy to measure because, well, because they're easy to measure. Sales offer a cut-and-dried basis for bonuses, website visits tell you how many people dropped by, and transaction histories are simple ledgers.

In contrast, lines of code or bugs fixed per week are poor ways to measure programmer productivity. A better measure is the pace that complete and tested functions are delivered to the customer. Good metrics focus on the outcomes, regardless of the measurement hurdles, whether you're tracking HR, service, or any other part of your business.

If you drill deeper, beyond the easy measures, you can make the numbers sing, provided you're prepared to accept some uncertainty. Rounding numbers isn't good for your accounting practices, but it's as good as it gets for forecasting.

When you looked deeper, you found the influencing factors that explained why what happened happened. When transactions were up, it so happened that the renovations market was in full swing. When renos hit a valley, transactions dropped. Presto!

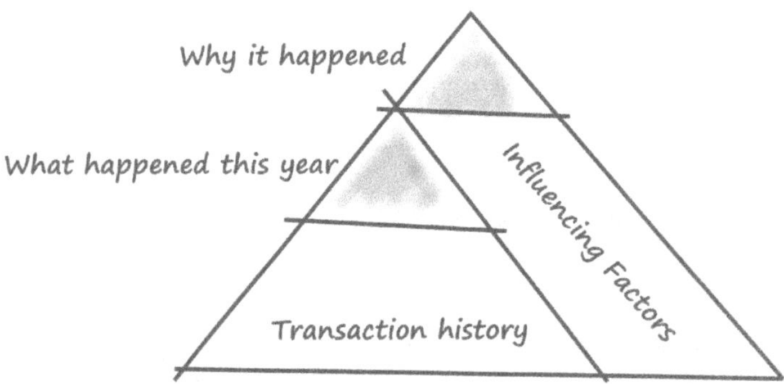

Interpretation allows you to understand why it happened

OK, fine—history is interesting inasmuch as it helps us isolate cause and effect. In our example, you used this information to isolate leading indicators in the construction market and factored these indicators into *your* forecast. And while a more accurate forecast allows you to set shareholder expectations, there's a much bigger benefit. A more accurate forecast allows you to react with advance warning and deploy programs that can mitigate a downturn and exploit an upturn. Now you can hit a higher forecast!

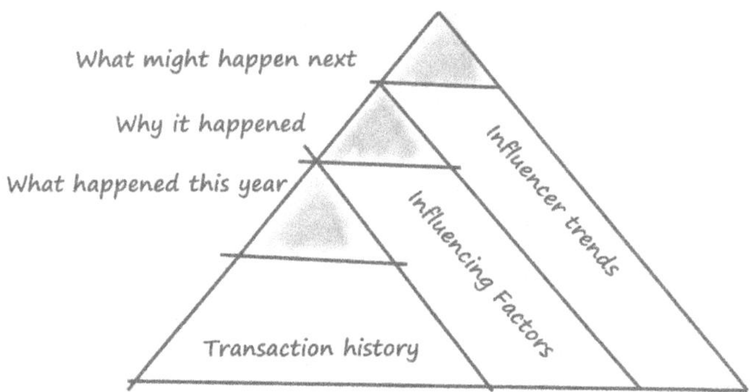

Anticipation allows you to understand how to prepare

Let's be clear, the information required to do this may not all lie within your database today and may not even be in your line of sight. But it's likely out there somewhere. Your first step is to kick off a research project to design your version of Project Anticipation. When you've run ad hoc research enough times to generate predictable improvements, you can decide whether or not to invest in pumping the information through your systems to your colleagues at scale.

What's an insight worth?

Insight generation isn't free. You'll need to invest in research at a minimum. If results merit scaling, that adds some cost. So how do you know what an insight's going to be worth before you invest in the research?

Here's a simple exercise—ask yourself what you would do if you knew the answer to a question you're considering. Jot down three or four possible answers, then decide for each what action you would take if each answer were to prove true. If your answers are equivalent, meaning you would take essentially the same action regardless of the answer to your question, then that question is moot. If, on the other hand, the answers would lead you down quite different paths, it's worth finding that answer. If three of the four are similar, maybe you just need to rule out (or confirm) that fourth alternative and proceed accordingly.

Answer	Action
1	A
2	B
3	C
4	D

4 actions—is the answer 1, 2, 3, or 4?

Answer	Action
1	A
2	B
3	B
4	B

2 actions—is the answer 1 or > 1?

Answer	Action
1	A
2	A
3	A
4	A

1 action—who cares what the answer is?

Consider your potential actions to find the real question you need to answer

This thought process offers a way to assess whether you should put the time and effort into learning something.

Note that it does not apply to happenstance or random research—these techniques aim to broaden your perspective. That end in itself is worth some of your time.

Every datum tells a story—if you let it

The outcome of all information work—generating insights—is so often lost at the last mile. You know what questions you need to answer, you've found the information to provide that answer, and the information arrives.

But it's incomprehensible. Someone dumped stuff in a table that takes four sheets of legal to print. The report has so many numbers, you can't see the forest for trees. Then there's the ten-for-the-price-of-one dashboard that tries to answer every question but answers none.

Information needs to be presented with clarity if it is to generate insight. Otherwise, you just need the Tylenol. Information is subject to the rules of usability—no distracting clutter, redundancy, or clipart. Don't make the reader do the math. In general, prefer graphics ahead of numbers, and use just enough text to avoid ambiguity.

For more reading on this, start with Avinash Kaushik.[26]

Invest some of your organization's time in understanding how to present information. Your insight depends on it.

SOURCING THE FACTS

Having posed a few new questions, let's look at how you might go about sourcing the answers.

There's gold in them thar hills

Don't stop at the obvious when sourcing your information. You're not limited to what you know.

What information lies within your business? When you consider your business systems—accounting, order management, procurement, sales tracking, website data, HR, payroll—there's a lot of data in your

26 Avinash Kaushik, "Occam's Razor," Kaushik.net, accessed June 30, 2019, *https://www.kaushik.net/avinash/*.

databases. In the tech world, we call this "structured data" as it is stored in a format that's designed for computers to extract and analyze.

But don't stop there. Your unstructured data includes email archives and the gazillion documents stored on somebody's disk, somewhere. If you've created documentation for colleagues and customers—user manuals, operating procedures, training videos—that's all data too. Some of it will be searchable, all of it is informative and capable of inspiring insight.

And don't forget paper. Look around your office. What's in that filing cabinet? If it's share-worthy, you have the technology to digitize that paper.

Then there's microfiche…OK, I'll stop.

But wait—isn't the internet plastered with documents, images, video, audio, and other data? Hell yeah. Undoubtedly, you and your colleagues are already using lots of this, but are you:

- Using YouTube as a medium of exchange with your customers and suppliers?
- Tapping into the wealth of public domain data on government websites?
- Buying valuable information about your business community from third parties?
- Conducting sentiment analysis on any social mentions for your business?
- Creating automated personalized email conversations with your prospects?

If you've answered yes to all these questions—congratulations. If no or maybe—opportunity alert!

(You might ask why that last bullet is a *source* of information for your business. Think of automated personalized email conversations with your prospects as an online version of a dinner party conversation with every one of your customers. What questions would you ask, and how would you respond to their answers? Email me with your thoughts.)

A word on when to buy information from a third party. Wikipedia, Google and the like have conditioned us all to think we can find the answer to anything in two minutes with a browser and an internet connection. For *free*.

Truth is you can find *an* answer, but nobody is vouching that it's the right answer or even a correct answer. These tools make cursory research dead easy, and that's fine for many enquiries. Here are some situations where it's worthwhile to seek out a vouched-for, trustworthy, expert source of data and paying if that's what it takes:

- When the stakes of a decision are high. Weigh the cost of information against the cost of error.
- When the data source is very large and you only need a bit of it. Postal address validation, for example, draws on millions of addresses to confirm that your system has it right.
- Where the data changes often and you need to be *bang* up-to-date. Bloomberg sells real-time trading data to a market where yesterday's news is useless.

Rule of thumb: move bits before you move atoms.

Think about the ways your business moves information. If you're moving *any* information with atoms—take paper, for instance—what opportunities do you have to move digitally instead? Or before you ship? Take a look at the reasons for your product returns—could you reduce the associated time and cost by confirming information before you ship it? You could share the design for approval, confirm the product spec and bill of materials—all digitally.

Glance back at your notes for the Where Are You Headed? Test. Do any other useful sources of information come to mind after reading the last few paragraphs? If so, add 'em to your list.

In$ights in sight

While you're at it, turn the tables for a moment and consider what information your business accumulates, cleanses, and maintains that could have value for an existing customer. What about an entire new market? If you can curate useful information, what's that worth to your customers? Could you sell this information and become the Bloomberg of your market?

Data cleanliness *is* data godliness

OK, OK, Graham, lots of data out there. I get it. But isn't most of it garbage? How do I know what to use and how much to trust?

How can you trust your sources?

Newsflash—questionable information isn't confined to the internet. Have you conducted a data quality exercise on your business systems lately? If not, sorry to say, there will be errors. Whether those inaccuracies are material or just rounding errors, data quality activity is a vital part of any information-driven decision processes you adopt.

In Essence: Data Quality measures

Data atrophies without exercise—just like your body. Again, exercise means that the data is checked and errors are fixed on a regular basis.

There are several ways to take your data to the gym:

- Validate on entry—don't allow bad data through the door.
- Verify accuracy often—this happens naturally with most financial data because you, your customers, or suppliers will notice when the money is wrong. But other data errors may not be noted as a matter of routine—mailing addresses, email changes, service records.
- Define valid and reasonable ranges for data, and build alerts into your systems to report exceptions.
- Automated techniques include pattern recognition for anomalies and trends, checksums, triangulation of multiple sources.

By these means, you can ensure that the insights you generate are based on the best data you can make available.

Now, aside perhaps from your CFO, I'm the last person to suggest that you take the accuracy of information for granted. Verifying the credibility of your sources is not just a job for the *Wall Street Journal*. If you can find equivalent data in multiple places, it's a great idea to triangulate three sources, or double-check two. If they line up, odds are the data is accurate. If they don't, well, someone is fibbing.

Decision precision—you can estimate almost anything, but should you?

> *It is the mark of an educated mind to rest satisfied with the degree of precision which the nature of the subject admits and not to seek exactness where only an approximation is possible.*
>
> *—Aristotle (384–322 BC)*

He knew a thing or two, that Aristotle. Different decisions call for different levels of precision. Living out this principle can have a profound effect on how fast you move.

When you're homing in on a direction, you can make initial decisions with reasonable data. If you grow cranberries and you're choosing between the cranberry juice or cranberry sauce market, you only need enough accuracy to pick the biggest opportunity. But you're likely to need more precision when narrowing down whether to ship cranberry jelly or chunks. Precision is not always worth the time and cost.

> *Rule of thumb: most decisions should be made when you have 80 percent of the information you would like to have.*

Have you ever stopped to think how often the Pareto principle applies? Why does it only take me about ten minutes to pick up 80 percent of the things on my grocery list, and another fifty minutes for the final fifth? (You too? Uncanny, isn't it?)

Just as 80 percent of something can often be completed in 20 percent of the time, acting when you're 80 percent ready is a good maxim for information gathering. The last 20 percent of accuracy isn't likely to impact your direction, and by the time you get there, the decision may be moot.

In *How to Measure Anything: Finding the Value of Intangibles in Business*, Douglas Hubbard[27] offers the best background I know on the

27 Douglas W. Hubbard, *How to Measure Anything: Finding the Value of Intangibles in Business*, (Hoboken: John Wiley & Sons, 2014).

application of probability to business. Anyone who makes business decisions every day should be interested—or at least conversant with—sampling techniques.

If that's you, Hubbard's book is about as light a read as you're ever going to find on statistics. As a taster, here's his reminder about another mind-blower—the rule of five:

1. Write down thirty or more numbers at random.
2. Take a sample of five numbers from your list.
3. Sort your five in order and look at the lowest and the highest.
4. Count how many of the thirty-plus original numbers lie between the low and high.

The rule of five states that 93 percent of the thirty originals will almost always lie within this range. If you want to prove or disprove this, go ahead and run the exercise as many times as you like. I'll still be here when you get back.

So what? Well it just goes to show that you can narrow down a range of values with a very small sample size. Estimation is a tool!

OK, enough of the statistical stuff. If you want more on that, go read Hubbard.

Rule of thumb: **Graham's Progressive Precision Principle** *states that the accuracy of your data should increase as you home in on a decision.*

Rule of thumb: ask your CFO for help if you're researching important numbers that begin with $.

INFORMATION PLUMBING

Hopefully, I've whetted your appetite on the untapped potential for information in your business. Between answering new questions, providing insights to your colleagues and customers, and that small sample size thing, you're probably exploding with ideas.

But where to you begin to test this out in your business?

Let's find out.

Information's circle of life

Information is only useful when it flows.

Store it up, by all means, just know that it's a waste of disk space unless it's shared, read, consumed, considered, and eventually generates insight.

The first step in information plumbing is to recognize the way your information passes through this life cycle:

1. Find information.
2. Capture it somewhere useful—in a database, from paper to digital, audio/video recording—and keep the confidential stuff safe and sound.
3. Prepare it for use—cleanse it, confirm its "quality."
4. Maintain it—keep the data accurate and current.
5. Share it—deliver the information to customers and colleagues at the place and time of their need.
6. Destroy it—when it's no longer needed. Only hoard it if you have reason to.

Poor data is cheap—good data is an investment.

This life cycle dictates everything you do with your information. How you source and store it, how much you trust it, who sees it and when, and how much you should invest to make this happen.

Place	Type	Details	Format
Sales	Prospect	Name, email, interest	Data
	Customer	Name, address, email, orders	Data
...			
Accounting	Customer	Name, billing address, email, phone number	Data
...			
Website	Marketing broadcast	Collateral, About Us, ...	Web
	Video	About Us, Training	Video
...			
File storage	Contracts	Text and images	Document
	Resumes	Text and images	Document
	...		

What do you know?

Take control of your data

Any business over a day old has a body of information. While most businesses can find the information they need every day, many overlook much of their data.

Cataloging what you have, where it is, and where it travels is the first step in taking control of your data. Knowing what you know also exposes what you don't know—the gaps in your information that you could usefully fill.

Take the What I Know Test to make a start on your catalog.

When you're done, you'll have something like this:

Your list is not intended to be exhaustive, but it should be enough to provide a cross-section of the information that you should include. In short, everything you can think of—information in all its forms, shapes, and sizes. Data in databases, spreadsheets, Word and PDF documents, video, text, and audio.

For fun, share your list with colleagues and ask them to add or correct as they see fit. Remember that you're talking about *types* of data, not individual records or exhaustive

What I Know Test

Reach for pen and paper, or screen and keyboard, and make a list of the major systems your business uses today. The places where your accounting, sales, production, support, and other data is stored. Write these down the left of your page and leave a few lines between. This test may take more than one page so leave plenty of room. If you get to the bottom, pause the list and complete this page before continuing.

Next to each system, write the types of data in a second column. For example, your sales system will provide customers, prospects/leads, and orders. So write that and finish the page.

Now go back to the customer and list what your systems "know" about them—name, address, email, and so on—all on one line. Then do the same for prospects and so forth.

When you've finished the sheet, turn the page and continue with your list of places. Systems, disks, filing cabinets, whatever.

Within ten minutes, you'll have an OK catalog. Good enough for now.

lists of documents. No one person needs to spend more than ten minutes on this. At the end of the day, you'll have a solid list of what your company "knows."

Time and need

Now, an interesting thing often happens when you pass this list around—colleagues will see information they've forgotten (or even never knew) you had. Either way, they'll start to think what they could do with this newfound treasure trove.

People need information at different times depending on the work they're doing.

- **Front line** folks in your sales, support, and call center teams are talking to your customer all day long, day in and day out. In order to give the best advice they can, they'll want information that's relevant for this customer, and they'll want it in their faces, for every call or meeting, in the moment, on demand, just in time.
- **Planners**, like your management team, sales leaders, project managers and the like, will want to know how things have gone compared with the plan.
- **Planners**, same groups, would *really* like to know what might happen next. Leading indicators—remember your pseudo-crystal ball.
- **Problem-solvers**, like everyone, want to know when something is about to go wrong and what they can do to prevent it. Predictive trends, diagnostic reports. In their face.
- **Accountants**, every once on a while, need the information to be exact. Month-end accounting processes are built around the need for precision. This doesn't mean that folks can get sloppy, but the time it takes to prepare financial reports is a useful indicator of your data quality.

Most information needs are predictable—folks can tell you the circumstances when they need particular insights. In our information-engorged world, it pays to hit people at the right time. We are conditioned to treat topical stuff as urgent.

There are, of course, the unpredictable enquiries:

> *Rule of thumb: the faster you close each month's books, the better your data quality.*
>
> *And the simpler your business.*

- One-offs, when someone's thought process pings a "what if" and curiosity jumps in. If that person is in the Exec Suite, these idle curiosities can receive more urgency than they merit. But hey! Having well designed Key Performance Indicators is the best way I know to head these things off at the pass.
- Happenstance. Random injections of news and insight will enrich everyone's thought processes. While that may account for less than 1 percent of the twitter-sphere, curated insight can provide value. "Boss, you better see this…."

Follow up with your colleagues to find out what they don't know but would like to. As a bonus question, ask them when they would like to know it.

Spreading the word

At the risk of beating the information-as-water analogy to death, seeking information in a data lake can be something of a fishing trip. While it's easy (and therefore inexpensive) for me to ask accounting to "just run some numbers by the end of the day," it may be time-consuming (and therefore distracting from some other priority) for someone to just do that.

Keep a log of these requests and look for patterns. If the same question gets asked month in, month out, it's a candidate for building a canned answer. And once an answer is canned, you can ask me to run my own damn numbers. Teach me to fish. Then check in a few months later to see whether I actually took the time to answer my own curiosity.

When you know who needs to know what and when, you can share those insights efficiently—in their inbox every morning or with a pop-up alert on their screen. The news industry has perfected the art of interrupting us whenever there's a headline. You can do the same with important business information—if you know who needs what and when.

Information architecture

We're on the brink of a deep precipice of detail here, but there's one more topic we need to touch on to give you a rounded view of information plumbing.

That customer address in your sales system will also be in your accounting system, assuming they pay you at any point. Allow duplication and you're headed for errors and confusion. Stamp out duplicates—you only need one version of the truth in your business.

Your information architecture redraws the What You Know table in a way that has *only* one version of your customer data, and likewise for each of your other data types. If different systems actually need their own copies (a universal flaw of system business design, I'm afraid), then your architecture says which version is the truth. Your system of record for customer information is…what?

Your information architecture also connects the parts that will refer to each other. It could look like this:

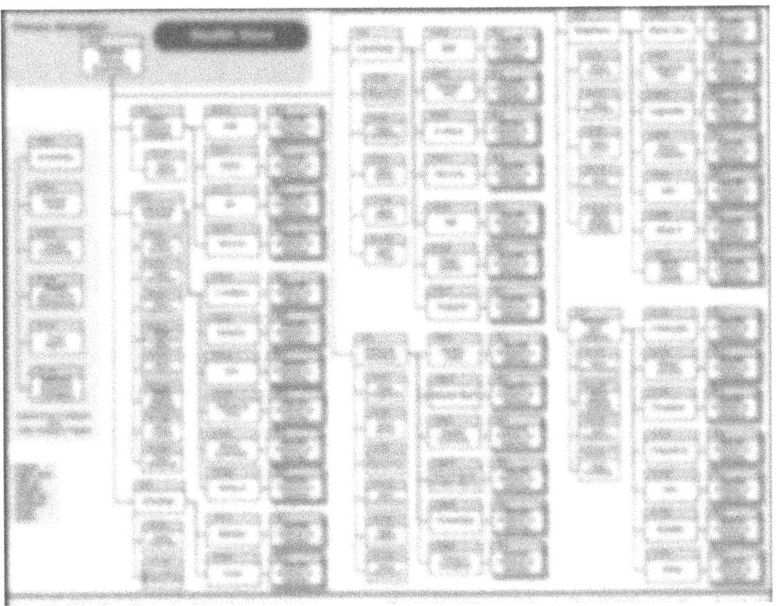

Information architectures tend to be complex, but invaluable

All a business leader needs to know about security

Your business community thrives on good information. Some need to know everything; everybody needs to know something. **Technology has reduced the cost of information distribution to near $0.**

Some of your confidential information may have value on the black market. **You need to understand the data you have and what it's worth.**

There's a burgeoning—illegal—industry in monetizable data and disruption. Bad actors employ talented hackers to find and steal information or install tools to blackmail businesses. **Regard these folks as very smart businesspeople.**

The hacker industry invests in tools to test the protective measures in place at any business that's connected to the internet. Where those measures prove easy to penetrate, they will delve deeper to search for booty. **If your outer security shell is weak, you will attract attention.**

The larger the quantity of monetizable data you have, the more attractive you are to the hacker industry and **the greater your defenses need to be.**

Most security breaches are a result of employee naivety, error, or mischief. **Employee training is foundational and provides the biggest bang for your buck.**

Customer data in your keeping does not belong to you. The owners have entrusted their data to your keeping. When you request and gather customer data, you are accepting responsibility and liability. **This must be reflected in the protective measures you take.**

Information security is a tech-enabled phenomenon, for good and bad. But security is first and foremost about good policy and procedure. Technology measures are only there to implement these rules. Security is not simply an IT responsibility. **Security is a CEO responsibility.**

The process of implementing security policy is straightforward:

1. Catalog the data you have and wish to have.
2. Create policies that allocate a level of sensitivity to each data type. Three or four levels will do for 99 percent of businesses.
3. Deploy technology to build protective layers, beginning with your outer shell. Whether your data is on-premises or in the cloud, take equal measures and monitor performance of those protections.
4. Create policies that define how your business, employees, and customers must treat data and how you will handle exceptions.
5. If you owe your customers or regulators some evidence of how seriously you take security, submit to a third-party audit to receive verification that you're doing the right thing. *Never* share your security strategy with a third party without an NDA.

That's it. A one-page model for your security strategy.

I'll stop there for now, but take a look at the booksite if you would like to go deeper on this topic.

OWNERSHIP, CUSTODY, AND SAFEKEEPING

All a business leader needs to know about security

It's a shame that the tech industry has such a knack for confusing the vast majority of the population that don't care for techie folderol. Serial confusion is alienating, and readers tend to switch off when deluged with detail.

In that vein, we're about to cover the tech topic voted most likely to confuse by CEO polls everywhere. Among all business technology topics, none is more poorly presented than security.

The essence of security is simple. All the information that a business leader needs to know to start down the path of understanding can fit on one digestible page. And here it is…

The devil, as always, is in the details, but a simple explanation like this will help you move you further along the security journey.

And a journey it is. Security is a changing landscape. You evolve your protections until they meet the standard you've set for yourself. You maintain their daily operations to detect and respond to the breach events that will occur. When the hacker industry develops new threats, you respond.

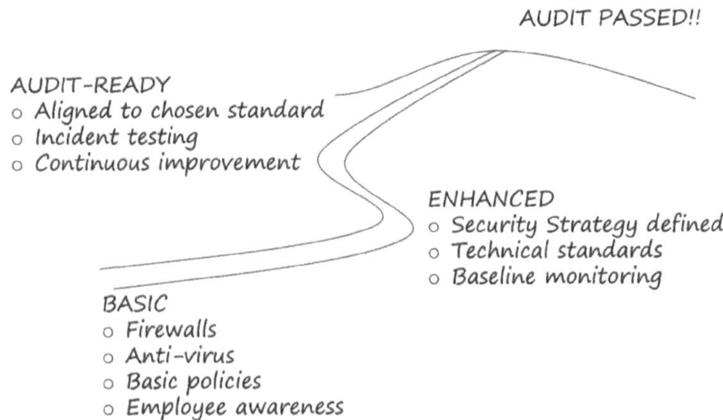

The security journey

> *Myth-buster: Security is not a project. It's an evolving part of your daily operation.*

This is not the place to delve deep into your security plan, but let's reflect a little before we move on. You completed—or at least made a start—on step one (your data catalog) when you did the What I Know Test. As a second step, consider the consequences of each type of data falling into the wrong hands and assign one of the following categories to each type on your list:

- **Top Secret**: Could shut down the business, perhaps result in litigation.
- **Confidential**: Would damage the business, perhaps cause public embarrassment.
- **Private**: Would cause minor inconvenience.
- **Public**: You want this in front of every customer and prospect!

Security is not a blanket. It's more of an onion. When you're done, you'll have a list that will allow you to place each type of data somewhere in your Security Onion.

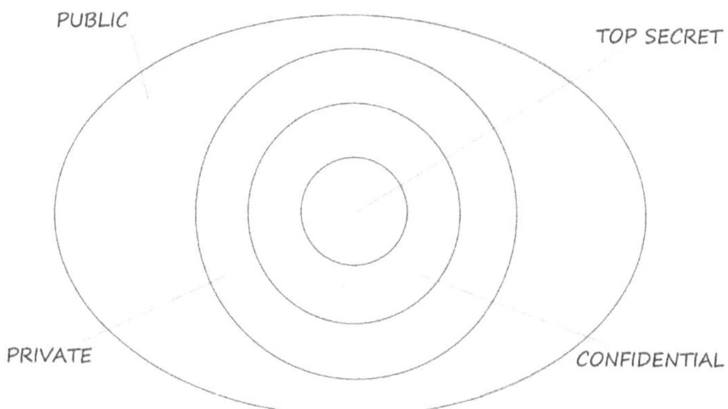

Your Security Onion—several layers of protection

Think of any James Bond, Jason Bourne, or Pink Panther mission where our mischievous hero determines to steal the biggest diamond in the world. They scale the wall, drug the Rottweilers, disable the alarms, break the window, dodge the laser beams, and somehow shatter the unbreakable glass box that contains the prize. Of course, our hero has read the script and knows all those measures are there before they do the job. But anyone hacking your defenses will have to discover your protections as they go.

Rule of thumb: Information is only useful when it flows.

Your onion sketch will help to define the security measures to be taken for each layer. You will present any intruder with increasingly greater challenges as they encroach from the outer edge to the inner core. And at the center is your top-secret version of the Koh-I-Noor diamond.

Bear in mind that the outer—basic—layer is to repel a hacker's initial probing. Everything inside there is to deal with the guys that make it through, and monitoring is your burglar alarm.

Where do you draw the line on sharing?

Now that we've removed the mystique surrounding information security, it's worth spending a few minutes to redraw your line around sharing. When security is a black box, there's a natural tendency to err on the safe side by under-sharing. Having digested the outline in the last section, this is a good time to reconsider your comfort levels, recalling what we said earlier:

Keep your top-secret information under lock and key—sharing exclusively on a need-to-know basis—but don't compromise the value of the insights hidden elsewhere by under-sharing.

Take the Sharing Test now and often to double-check your proclivity for privacy.

Sharing Test

Does every trusted colleague that needs your top-secret or confidential information have the access they need today?

What information do you keep company-confidential that you could share with customers, protected by the necessary controls?

Beware the curse of toxic data

When the internet blockbusters—Google, Facebook, and the like—were establishing themselves, most consumers expected to pay for software. These titans created business models by granting free access to their software. With no financial barriers to entry, adoption simply took off—never before had one company acquired billions of users. The quid pro quo was that they would keep the data they capture from you in return. At the time, consumers were prepared to make this trade-off. Business flourished and the companies stockpiled googols of dollars.

Fast forward a decade or so, and it appears that the data these guys have gathered has been used in ways that consumers don't appreciate. Targeting ads—OK, if occasionally annoying; involving you in propaganda schemes—worrisome. And then those nefarious activities that no one can put their finger on—not keen on that at all.

Consumers have been trusting with their data since the mid-oughties. These businesses were established on the assumption that they can use our data in return for free software.

But now there's a backlash. European GDPR legislation is a milestone—consumers want ownership of their data back

What this means for the average business is that security—keeping other people's private data private—is a responsibility with increasing gravity. If you collect this kind of data, you better protect it well, and you'll have to provide a means for the owners to see what you know about them and enable them to delete their information whenever they choose. Security systems have not been built to handle this level of transparency. The industry will adapt, but until that time, the processes for legal compliance will be a dog's breakfast.

Rule of thumb: Only collect data that is useful. Never collect data on a whim.

One other salutary lesson—customer data is an asset if you use it well and responsibly, but unused and unnecessary data can become a toxic asset for your business.

YOUR INFORMATION HIGHWAY REVISITED

When Al Gore spoke of the information highway, it was the "man on the moon" speech of its time. The highway proffered the promise of instant access to anything digital. And so it happened. The telco industry invested massive amounts in infrastructure—for which we, the consumer, are still paying—in order to create way more bit-moving capacity than we knew what to do with. But nature abhors a vacuum, and we soon figured out how to use it.

Broadband.

Netflix alone uses around 20 percent of the internet's capacity worldwide. Think about that—the information highway is used to deliver whatever you and I choose to watch. Like all highways, the information highway filled up. It's now wired and wireless, and the pipe continues to grow.

Your business has its own information highway. We've come a long way in this chapter, but let's wrap with a look at how you can fuel your business and your community with insight.

Returning to our Big-O model, imagine new information sparking anywhere in the oval-shaped community area. Imagine further that you could direct this information to the right places to create insight for your colleagues (for instance, predictive signs that a customer is about to need help) and your customers (help is at hand).

If that sounds too Arthur C. Clarke or Philip K. Dick for you, I have two questions for you:

1) How could a service like that help your customers?

2) Why do science fiction writers use their middle initial so much?

Just know that this is happening today. We'll find out where and because of whom when you've had time to consider your answers.

We all exist in an insight chain, sharing our expertise for someone else to build on. The vast majority of these insights do not originate with us. But we can absorb them, add something, and pass them on. How is your business placed in the insight chain?

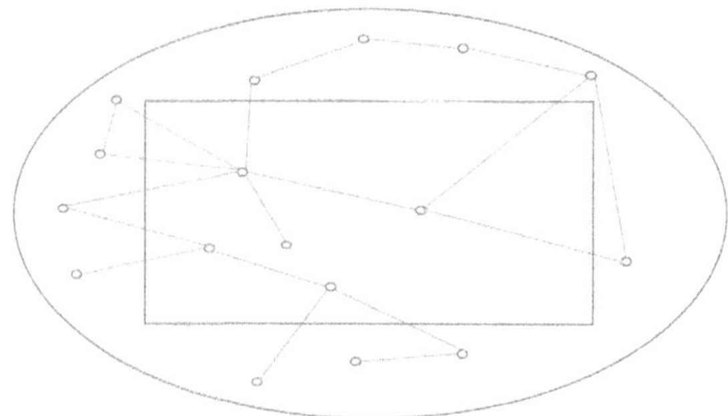

Your business community's insight chain feeds off exchanges of information

Talk about insight!

For a fun wrap-up to this chapter, take the Need to Know More Test.

Keep these notes in a handy place. I'll be asking you to bring them out again later.

Need to Know More Test

Go back to your notes for the Need to Know Test. In light of all you've read since you took that test, add any insights to the final column.

For extra brownie points, add rows for the customer and figure out what they know. Is that all they need to know?

What's your biggest insight from this test?

Insight feeds action

I've thrown a lot at you in this chapter on the art and science of business information. We'll return to the topic towards the end of the book, but first, we'll take the next chapter to consider how technology can help you turn insight into action.

INSPIRING INSIGHT—IN A NUTSHELL

Your business thrives on great information and starves without it. Technology excels at capturing, storing, and transporting data. You just need to fill the gaps by asking the right questions, tapping the right sources, and delivering the information to feed the right people with the right insights at the right time.

I've offered one path to this insight bonanza:

1. Think beyond bland reporting of trailing indicators by asking:
    - What work is required to make information more useful?
    - What information is *not* being factored into decisions?
    - How many of your colleagues have the best information you can provide?
    - How does this help your customers? And how could you help them more?
2. Answering the right questions:

- Drill deeper with your colleagues—what are their questions and how can you inform better answers?
- Experts get comfortable—how can you help them stimulate new insights?
- How can a crystal pyramid enrich your data?

3. Sourcing the facts:

    - Don't stop at the obvious.
    - Don't just measure the easy-to-measure.
    - Enrich your insights with data from third parties.
    - Be open for opportunities to monetize your own data.
    - Data is not free. Invest in cleansing your information.

4. Information plumbing:

    - Respect your information's life cycle.
    - Know what you know and take control of your data.
    - Focus on time and need to feed insight across your community.
    - Identify your one source of the truth.

5. Ownership, custody, and safekeeping:

    - Everything a leader needs to know about security fits on the page provided.
    - Solid security can give you the confidence to share more.
    - Recognize your custodial responsibilities.

6. Your information highway revisited:

    - Your business community has an insight chain.
    - Re-imagine your role in this chain.

7. Insight feeds action—coming up next!

As a bonus, here are my rules of thumb for insight generation:

- Move bits before you move atoms.
- Most decisions should be made when you have 80 percent of the information.
- Graham's Progressive Precision Principle states that the accuracy of your data should increase as you home in on a decision.
- Ask your CFO for help if you're researching important numbers that begin with $.
- The faster you close each month's books, the better your data quality and the simpler your business.
- Information is only useful when it flows.
- Only collect data that you know is useful. Never collect data on a whim.

Booksite extras at www.trustingtechnologybook.com/chapter7 *include RACI samples, more on information architecture, and* the workbook for all tests.

CHAPTER EIGHT

BOTTLING INNOVATION

It's Just an Idea Until It's Shared

In which you will consider ways to deliver innovation every day.

Seth Godin says it's just an idea until it's shared. No matter how much genius you apply, it doesn't count until someone has read it, reviewed it, or used it.

There are many ways to innovate: high tech, low tech, and no tech. No matter how you approach this, rapid deployment, feedback, adoption, or retirement makes for an innovative community. Technology affords the quickest means of distribution and feedback.

And when you do share an idea that works for your customer, you have the opportunity to create something of value for your community and an asset that could show on your balance sheet. This is how we distinguish an investment from an expense.

THE YIN AND YANG OF TECHNOLOGY

In the last chapter, we talked about the role of technology in generating insights—by plumbing information between the right people at the right time. In this chapter, we will address the other role of technology—supporting the actions required for your business to deliver value.

The Yin and Yang of Technology

The implementation of business technology—products and systems—has long been a boon/bane cycle. The excitement generated by the promise of new technology often dissipates as the complexity of the problem and magnitude of the work dawns on the team. By the time the work goes live, the overwhelming feeling can be one of relief—*thank goodness that's over.* And that can leave little appetite for the further work required for continuous improvement.

In Chapters Five and Six, we dealt with the emotional and collaborative aspects of change. In this chapter, you'll lay a foundation for the best outcomes from another perspective—to build business assets on technology, tools that can connect your business community to your machine for delivering value.

Let's begin by examining the difference between an asset (what the technology does) and a solution (how it does it), then expand your definition of system, answer the $64-billion-dollar question of how to build the operating system of your business, and posit the goal of delivering innovation as frequently as your customers need it. That and no more.

TURNING IDEAS INTO ASSETS

Ever wish you could bottle the things that make your business unique?

Your business stands out because of what you know, what you do, and how you do it. The last chapter talked about what you know—and need to know. Here, we move on to consider what your business and customer community do with that knowledge, and to bottle the way you do it.

Rule of thumb: If you can describe the way you do a job, someone can code it.

When Paul Newman's dinner guests gave his salad dressing the thumbs up, it was a natural next step to make a lot more of it and bottle it for sale. As software has allowed us to capture ever more complex activities, businesses have been able to bottle their own special sauces. Figure out how things should be done, abstract those processes to a general case, and write code to describe that abstraction. Voila number one—process in a bottle.

In Essence—Building software

Creating software is a black box to the 95 percent of the population that haven't honed their technology skills. (I didn't make that number up—just ask the US Bureau of Labor Statistics how many people are employed in tech. And how many aren't.) This mystique has, unfortunately, driven some tech salaries to unjustifiable levels.

I promise this book will not attempt to turn you into a software developer beyond the very basics. And here they are:

You create software by:

1. Targeting a specific problem or opportunity.
2. Understanding what is needed to solve that problem or opportunity well.
3. Describing the information and automation required.
4. Capturing those rules, sequences, logic, and formulae in code.
5. Ingesting data and pushing it out in a new form.
6. Taking the time to make the user's experience as pleasant as possible.

Actually, that last one is a bonus. Most software has been created without due consideration of the user's feelings. Ignore at your peril.

There are, of course, many layers of complexity beneath these creations, but the essence is really that simple.

The software that results can be used a million times with minimal incremental cost. It can be sold or licensed to others for use or remain proprietary. And if you find a better way to do the job, you simply change the code and ship an upgrade. Voila number two—continuous improvement.

If your business has a secret sauce that only a few people understand, you can only deliver at the pace those folks can manage. You're also at risk of losing that uniqueness the minute they walk out the door. But if you capture that recipe in software, you have an asset that you can protect—maybe patent—improve, and sell at scale. Perhaps an asset that can appear on your balance sheet.

Kill-a-cliché—Digital Transformation

Origins: Likely around 2005, when tech marketing was looking for a new term to generate demand for new technology.

What it *could* mean: Depends where you start, but your business can be transformed any number of ways.

Try this instead: moving to digital information and automation *only* when it better serves your business's community.

The vast majority of businesses have adopted accounting software and other operations systems, but the time is right for broader thinking. The potential for software to run your business is so broad, however, that it's all too easy to miss the best investments—to invent ways of doing things that should simply be outsourced to partners and to miss the best investments that will create value unique to your business. We'll look at how to find these investments shortly, but first let's consider what an asset really is.

Creating assets

My Dad was an accountant, and he would have defined an asset as:

A resource owned or controlled by an individual, corporation, or government with the expectation that it will generate future cash flows.

Kill-a-cliché—Innovation

Wow, Graham—did you say that innovation is a cliché?

You betcha—try finding ten people who agree on a definition. If you'll humor me, I will use this book to advocate this definition:

Innovation = Insight + Action

That *is the yin and yang of technology.*

Your IP Test

Make a list of the things that your business has created that are unique. If your list is under ten, add things that are rare.

If your list droops over your desk, check the ten best and park the rest.

Don't overlook the possibility that you provide unique combinations of value (the iPod, for instance, was an original combination of proven technologies).

(Btw, we're friends here—no patents required.)

The traditional—shall we say pre-digital—definition of assets contemplates financial and physical properties with residual value—building, plant, inventory, cash, and receivables. Innovations may be included in the form of patents—intellectual property that has been protected by law.

The digital revolution offers new ways to create assets with the means to "generate future cash flows." Enshrining your business's important work practices in software, for instance, or the intuitive (but largely unproven) value of megatons of data.

Whether or not this stuff does end up on your balance sheet, the notion of a company being the sum of its protectable parts holds true. For all the truth behind the idea that your business *is* its people, employment law insists that you cannot restrict their ability to move on when they find a better opportunity. Sooner or later, every one of your colleagues will leave the company.

By investing in your business operating system, you get to create something bigger. If you focus on the things that draw loyal customers, you'll create the best kind of value—that which the market doesn't already have.

I'm going to pause here while you take the Your IP Test and jot down things that your business has created that are unique or rare.

What's it worth?

Patents were invented to protect the commercial implementation of new ideas. (*New* ideas, not necessarily *original* ideas, though, as it's worth noting that the patent goes to the first to file, and that's not always the originator. Just ask Alexander Graham Bell or John Logie Baird.) But patents are a blunt instrument for comparing innovation. There's no notion of relative value—is the printing press more valuable than the mousetrap? Will history regard the car or the smartphone as the greater innovation?

If you look at the table below, Samsung has filed more than double the number of patents that Microsoft has, and six times the number of its greatest rival—Apple. But does Samsung deliver six times the value of Apple? The market caps of these businesses would suggest not.

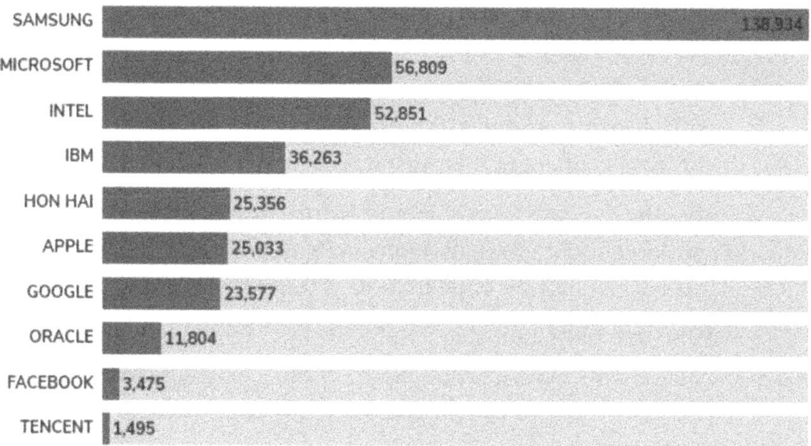

Tech industry patent bragging rights

It's not about *having* the innovation, rather about *delivering that innovation to a market that cares.*

Your IP Value Test

For each item on your IP list, describe the difference this has made for your customers. How have they responded?

I'm going to pause again while you return to the list of innovations you created moments ago and take the IP Value Test.

It matters not whether your list is long or short—simply whether or not your customers have noticed.

Next up, let's spend some time thinking about innovations you could add.

ALL TOGETHER NOW

Time for a reprise of Chapter Four's Miss You Test (**p. 79**). Pull out your answers to that test and repeat the exercise—provided below for your reading convenience.

Why do your customers care about your business again?

I'm serious. What do you do that they could not live without? If "live without" is too strong a term, then what do you provide that they would miss? If you ask this question of any customer—and I hope you ask lots of them all the time—they're likely to say one of three things...

1. **We need you.** We may not admit to this, but we couldn't live without your product. It's removed major pain and would present huge challenges if we lost it.
2. **It's OK**. We have your stuff and we're using it. In fact, we've been thinking about alternative products that could replace you. We just haven't had the time to look at this yet.
3. **Who are you?** Oh, that's right. In fact, my boss (or spouse or parent) was asking whether we could cut some costs. Let me check with my team whether we really need to keep paying for your product.

This is too important to skip over. Reprise the Miss You Test now.

Most robust businesses are still around because enough people are happy to pay them good money for what they provide. And that's the best way I know of defining your version of Newman's Own special sauce.

Let's think about how your customers use your sauce. Odds are they have some job they want to get done—share baby photos with the grandparents, talk about last night's party, run payroll, grow their investment portfolio, take just-in-time delivery on supplies, and so on. These are all jobs that people feel the *need* to get done. As we saw in Chapter Two, we've always been accustomed to using better tools to get more things done in a day (or to get the same things done and have more time to chill. Whatever).

Miss You Test—Reprised

Write a sentence to describe the thing your customer would miss if you shut up shop tonight. If you have more than one, keep writing till you run out.

So you and your business are part of your customer's process.

Everything you do before, during, and after you've delivered your thing will have an impact on your customer's day. If you do something simple, you'd better make the job easier for them. Why is it so hard to renew your driver's license, submit an insurance claim, or correspond with a lawyer (sorry—email not accepted)?

Trusting mantra: You and your business are part of your customer's process.

If you do something difficult, you should still make it easy. Imagine seeing these thank-yous on Twitter, Facebook, or Reddit:

> *"You've diagnosed my IBS—I feel like a new person. That was so easy. I love you."*

> *"It used to take us five days to process payroll, but now it takes an hour. No complaints."*

> *"We were distraught when our house burned down, but your claims department made it fun."*

Maybe that last one is a stretch, but you get the point. What's your version of the above?

I don't ask these questions to prompt you to create a new vision and mission. I ask because I'm assuming you want to define the best way to serve your customers, and you can't do that by looking at the many steps that takes in isolation. If you design your business that way, you'll simply end up with a bunch of more efficient silos.

No more silos anymore

Any business with more than two employees is at risk of silo behavior. Companies spend a lot of time eradicating silos from the culture—only to recreate them next year.

But the real silos today, the ones that present the biggest challenges or opportunities, are the silos at the boundaries of your business. When you talk about business systems that connect the organization, that span silos, you're missing the point.

I ventured in Chapter Four that your business is a machine that serves your community. And that your community spans your customers, colleagues, partners, and suppliers. Since you're still reading several chapters later, I assume you're on board with that idea. So here is the natural extension:

The real system here is the one that connects your community.

Pause.

Still there? Great. Because we're going to talk about systems thinking next, so it's important that we set some boundaries.

Flying a drone through your business

Have you noticed how TV shows feature a lot more flyover shots these days? Some are incredible in their depth and range. I first noticed this a few years ago, and it took me a while to realize that directors had found a killer app for the then-new drone technology. I may have found another killer app, at least by analogy....

Time to reach for your holistic thinking cap. Imagine placing your drone in the office parking lot, turning on the GoPro, and pushing the "up" button. You ascend past Reception, Accounting on the second floor, up past Product Development, Marketing, and the boardroom window (whatever floor that's on). Up above the rooftops, you begin to see your customers on the horizon. Keep going till you have a bird's eye view of your community. That may be a strained technology-related analogy, but I like it.

Returning to your Big-O, divide the company box into the three basic functions of any business—sales, delivery, and support.

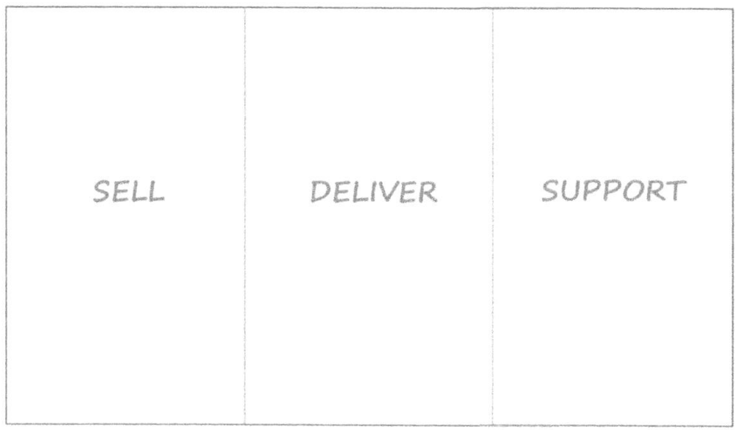

The three basic functions of your business

Place this in context of your business community, and you'll have something like this:

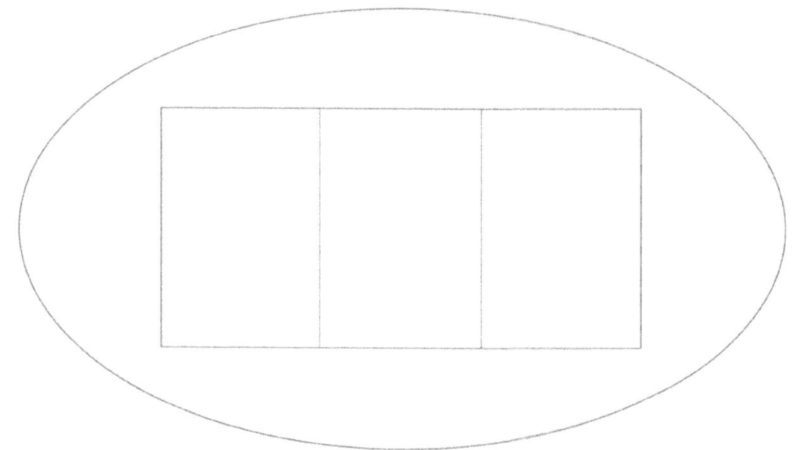

Your market community, holistically speaking

Now let's picture the work that goes on. No doubt, you'll already be most familiar with the activities that go on inside your business. Product Development creates products, Marketing finds prospects, Sales builds relationships that lead to deals, orders are taken, product is delivered and supported, and Accounting keeps tabs on the numbers. Simple. Universal. You'll have your variations, some peccadilloes perhaps, but we're in the ballpark.

If you draw these connections on your Big-O model, it would look something like this: (Remember that there's a template at the booksite if you want to do so, and it will provide a way to label each link. I encourage that, but it's not necessary for now.)

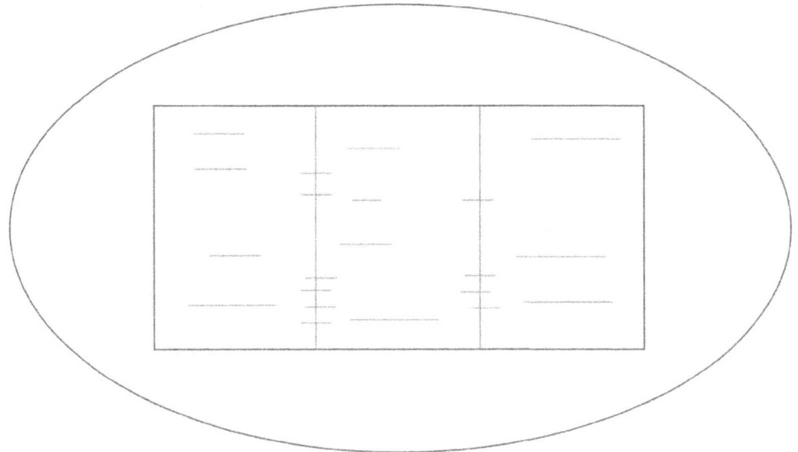

The work inside your business

Are you really solving your customer's puzzle?

Next, turn your attention to the circle that represents the boundary of your community—your market. Some folks in there will already be customers, others will be prospects. When you completed the Miss You Test, you listed the thing(s) they need that you provide. Now it's time to identify how you fulfill that need and how that fits into their process.

Does your customer place a new order every time they need you? If you supply building contractors, they may or may not have an idea of what they'll need from you when a job starts, but construction has a habit of springing surprises. Do they ever call you in a panic, asking for urgent delivery on some stuff they need in order to keep moving on the job? Do they have to jump in their trucks and drive over, or can you deliver within two hours?

Or does your customer buy once and use many times? Maybe they rent some software and pay a year's subscription upfront. Better keep them happy with easy ordering and ultimate support then, right?

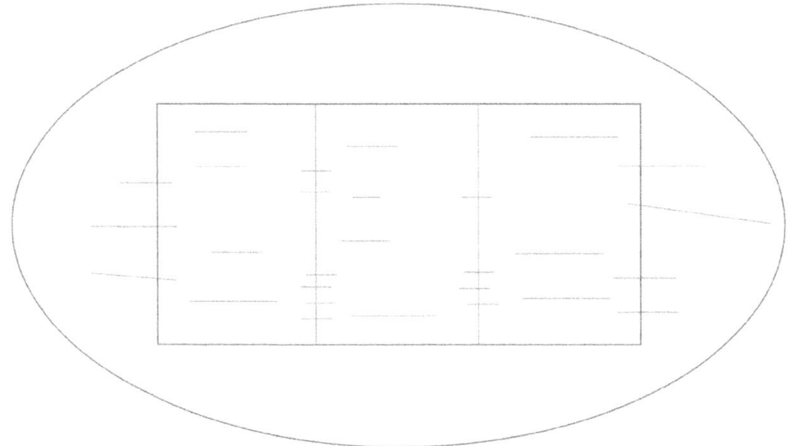

- *Customer checks pricing online*
- *Customer calls to discuss discount*
- *Sales returns customer call*
- *Etc*

The work inside and outside your business

Whatever your customer's process, you can support it better by being the final piece in their puzzle. That means imposing the bare minimum needs on them and giving them the necessary control of their own destiny. As for going the extra mile—delivering those supplies to the contractor—premium services attract the customers who will pay for it.

Rule of thumb: The fewer times the baton is passed,
the less often it is dropped.

I like this rule of thumb—it means that the fewer touches it takes to complete a process from origin (such as a customer with a need) to destination (such as a customer with need resolved) the better. Well-designed ecosystems powered by technology provide a way to reduce touches without losing control.

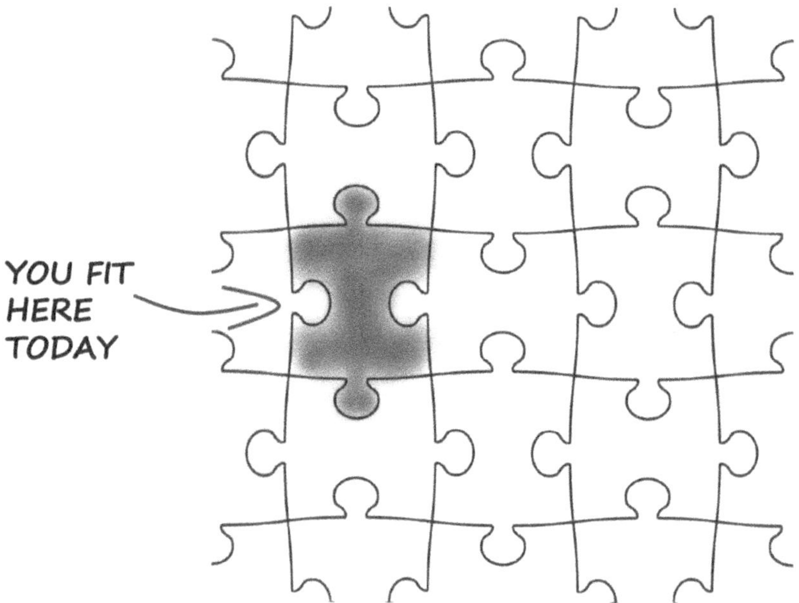

Which piece of your customer's puzzle do you solve today?

We've heard Theodore Levitt's trope that no one really wants a drill—they just want holes. I used to think this analogy was too existential, but having applied it to many businesses, I've seen it spark some remarkable conversations.

FinTech is a living example of this holistic thinking. Banks used to think that we really wanted to travel to their branch, line up, and watch other customers do their thing, step forward and explain what we needed to do, and pay a premium for the privilege of doing something with our own money. That was all well and good when there was no alternative, but it turned out that many of us prefer a better way that allows us to move our money 24/7 from the comfort of wherever we are at the time we feel like doing it. No more braving winter storms or standing in line. And FinTech is developing ways to deliver the service at low cost, which means it's cheaper for us.

At time of writing, $37 billion of Venture Capital money has gone into FinTech, while the top four US banks have invested $25 billion. While we can't measure or compare efficacy on the basis of budget, it's clear that innovation is coming from both disruptor and disruptee.

What is the equivalent in your industry? Pick up your pen—you're going to solve your customer's puzzle right now. I'll see you back here in ten minutes.

Done? Great! Shed your customer's persona, and let's look at what that means from a holistic perspective. You just identified how you would like to interact with your business if you were your customer. You set aside any concerns about your internal processes, Accounting's need for detailed financials, Marketing's hunger for additional customer data. All important to your business—but not to your customer. If you ask me to answer questions that don't benefit me, I'm likely going to be disgruntled.

Copy the template below. Now draw a line that crosses the boundaries of your business for every interaction customer-you would be happy to have in order to do their job. You might draw lines for...

Solve Your Customer's Puzzle Test

Close your eyes and imagine yourself in your customer's shoes. Doing what they do every day. Suddenly, customer-you has a need that they rely on your business to fulfill.

What should happen next? The questions below may help.

Forget the way it works today and consider:

- When does your customer need you?
- What are they trying to do when they need you?
- When does customer-you know you're done and happy?
- For bonus points, what more could you do for them?

- Placing an order online.
- Paying a bill.
- Researching how they can do their job faster, cheaper, with greater confidence.
- Receiving help.
- Calling for a social chat with your support staff.

(It's up to you whether that last one is all part of the service. There are pros and cons to making friends with your customers.)

Label each line. The template provides space for this but do it however you please, as long as someone else could understand your notes.

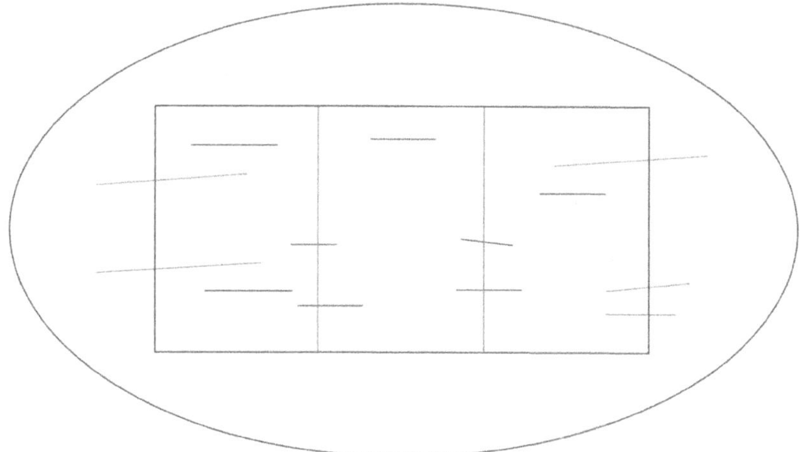

- *Customer checks their pre-assigned discounts online*
- *Customer selects quantity and clicks Buy*
- *Etc*

The work that bridges boundaries faster

I don't want you to boil the ocean, so don't spend more than five minutes to capture every line.

Done? Congratulations—you've just described your view of the best experience customer-you would want. I encourage you to ask a few colleagues to do this exercise in isolation and gather together to compare notes.

Then you can ask some customers and build their ideas in. If you ask them to consider their best experiences and suggest some inspiring examples, I guarantee you'll find a way to improve on what you're doing today.

Who's in control here?

A lot of people have to do a lot of work to deliver the value that you provide to your customers. Taking the drone's-eye view of your business community offers you new insight into *who* is doing *what*, and *when* and *how* they're doing it.

Most businesses evolve from the inside out. The founders (from Edison to Zuckerberg) have an idea (usually in their garage or bedroom, it seems), they test it (in the lab, then in the market), and figure out the operations as the needs of scale dictate. Usually, that means the business is created in a hurry with little time for design thinking. Needs must, but it pays to pause at some points in the evolution of the business to pose a question:

If we were starting out again,

Knowing what we know today,

How would we do this,

And when should we do it that way?

Poetic? OK, I won't give up my day job.

When, you may ask, is the best time to do this?

Or, as soon as you can give the right people some time to think about it. Let's examine where this would land on your priorities list by considering a simple process that is universal to all businesses.

> *"The best time to plant a tree was twenty years ago. The second-best time is now."*
> *—Chinese proverb (allegedly)*

Order, please!

So far, we've focused on your business through a telescope. I'm not going to suggest that you reach for the microscope in this book, but we'd be denying the devil in the details if we didn't spend a little time looking deeper. If you absolutely can't handle the details, skip to the next section, but you might miss something.

If any business were to draw out the work they do, every single one could start with three boxes:

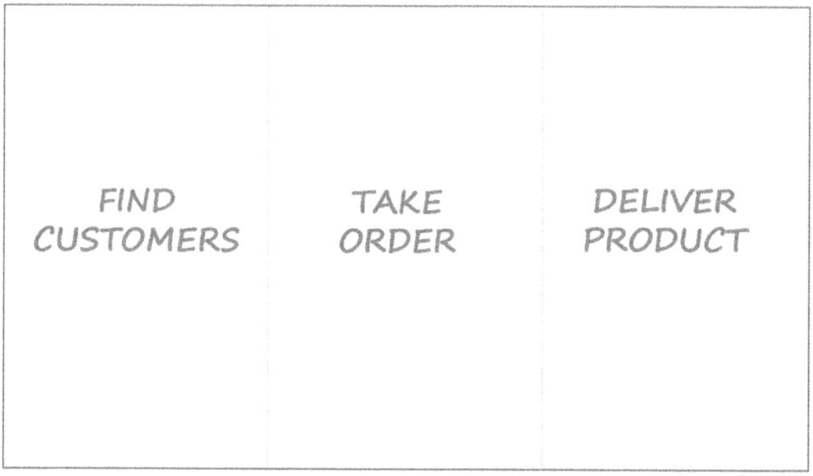

FIND CUSTOMERS	TAKE ORDER	DELIVER PRODUCT

Gimme three steps—find customers—take order—deliver product

Each box begins with some inputs, (information and objects), does some magic, and passes the output (new information and modified objects) along. Many businesses also close the loop.

Let's drill into a pretty mundane example—the order-taking process—to complete the four steps:

1. Receive information of a customer's choice.
2. Capture the order.
3. Arrange for payment.
4. Deliver the product.

If you were to sketch out the way it's done today, that might look like this...

Your order please			
Job to be done	**Customer action**	**Employee action**	**Total effort (hrs)**
1) Receive information of a customer's choice.	Find out that they're running low. Or run out of stock.		30 minutes
2) Capture the order.	Call you during business hours to place their order.	Gather customer's information over the phone and key into the system. May misspell the address.	20 minutes, on average
3) Arrange for payment.		Ask for credit card details.	2 minutes
	Go dig out their card.		5 minutes
		Key card details in (or write them on a sticky if the system's slow)	5 minutes
4) Deliver the product.		Print a shipping request and walk it to the warehouse at the end of the day.	10 minutes
	Open their mail 4 days later.		2 minutes

A pretty mundane example...

If we look at the total effort and consider how we could reduce this, we might end up with the following changes:

- *Put more control in the hands of your customer* by asking them to complete the order details online. They could do this 24/7, and you'll let them know you'll get back to them with a turnaround based on your staffing model. You'll make their job easier by simplifying order options, automating some of the steps, and validating information they provide so their order does not require back and forth later to correct errors.
- Your staff will receive notification of the order. If there are no issues, that notification will let them know that the order has gone through to shipping. If things are more complex, or payment needs to be handled manually, your staff will handle it before confirming. *This ensures that information is shared as efficiently as possible between customer and employee—plumbing insights.*

- Whether the order is straightforward or complex, your shipping team will receive notification and delivery (digital or physical) will commence. *This ensures that information is shared as efficiently as possible between* employee *and employee—more plumbing.*

Anyone who has ordered anything from Amazon in the last twenty years is familiar with this process. They were early adopters of online ordering—they patented 1-Click ordering in the last millennium for goodness' sake—and are the masters of this stuff. Yet many, many businesses have not been able to crack the code on simple ordering—i.e., "being easy to do business with"—decades later.

Last time I ordered a widget from Amazon, it showed up on my doorstep five hours later—one day before the committed date. Have you had that experience? Have you ever *delivered* that experience? You could, you know.

If you were to think about a better way to do this—starting out again knowing what you know today—you might monitor your customer's buying habits and prompt them when you think they're ready to place another order. The distribution of work might look like this.

A better way			
Job to be done	**Customer action**	**Employee action**	**Total effort (hrs)**
1) Receive information of a customer's choice.	Respond to confirm order	Receive notification that customer may be low on stock. Request confirmation.	1 minute
2) Capture the order.		Check a box	1 minute
3) Arrange for payment.		Bill the card on file	1 minute
4) Deliver the product.		Next day shipping is triggered by the system	0 minutes
	Open their mail next day.		2 minutes

...but there's always a better way

In this simple case, we went from a seventy-five-minute project with a four-day delay to a five-minute chore, resolved within twenty-four hours.

When I placed that order, it felt like Amazon could have shipped it to me before I knew I needed it. If you do that already, kudos to you. If that blows your mind, don't scoff before you read Chapter Ten, because that's where we're headed.

If you consider the customer to be part of the system, understand where you could fit into their process, and look at how these pioneers are changing their customer's lives, what ideas come to mind? Complete the Your Order Test to describe how your better way might look.

Your Order Test

Run through the "Order, please!" example yourself by jotting your current steps, leaving room for three more columns to the right. Now use the Customer, Employee, and Effort columns to describe the work that happens today.

Next up, list the changes you could make to increase your customers' control, reduce the migraine work for your employees, and decrease the total effort for all.

This may take some thought, so give it twenty minutes.

Well, what did you come up with?

By these means, you can provide your customer with the tools to do what they need to do, take the tricky work out of their hands, and share all the information they need to do it right first time.

For example, three levels of purchase experience might be:

1. Online self-service—à la Amazon and a gazillion others
2. Confirming your suggested order—"people also bought"
3. Pre-approving your suggested shipment (e.g., Stitchfix)[28]

Before we move on to how you might do that, let's recap:

- Your business exists to do a job that your customer needs to get done.
- Your job is a part of their day. If you slot neatly into their process, they'll be more loyal.

28 Stitch Fix. Stitch Fix Inc. *https://www.stitchfix.com/*, accessed June 30, 2019.

- In order to do your job this way, you'll need to understand their process.
- In order to do this better than your competitors, you'll want to let customers control what they can.
- Consider the job you're sharing with them, and put the work in the hands of the best person to do it. That could be your customer, a colleague, or even a supplier.

Rule of thumb—Moving a problem won't solve the root cause.

This is holistic thinking—draw the boundary of your plans around your business's community, not confined to the walls of your head office.

FORGING YOUR OPERATING SYSTEM

The three little techno-pigs

We build technology like we build houses. We lay foundations, add walls, and place a roof on it. (Actually, technology doesn't really need a roof, but I don't want to spoil the analogy.)

I talked about the technology stack in Chapter Two—the hardware and software bricks that we pile up to build pretty much any technology thing today. Your business's operating system will be no different.

Just about every business out there uses some kind of technology, but many do not have operating systems—a collection of tools that work together to make a business run. Some are built of straw (shaky network connections, crashing systems), some of sticks (systems functioning in isolation), and some of bricks (solid components that connect the enterprise and business community).

Take the Huff and Puff Test to see where you stand.

The point of this deceptively childish exercise is simply to level set your current situation.

Your business can operate in any of the three houses, but a house of straw is no protection from the wolf. A house of sticks is not resilient to the winds of change.

No business needs to excel in every area, but every business would do well to be best in some. We'll come back to this later, but first, let's look at the bricks at your disposal.

The bricks at your disposal

Business systems have been evolving for over half a century. The first wave solved the challenges of departmental functions, and so the available systems mapped quite neatly onto your org chart.

Your business already has some technology bricks. Your accounting system is a brick (several, probably—GL, AR, AP, fixed assets, budgeting, and so forth). Same goes for your CRM sales/support system, and your business would be practically unique if you didn't have several "systems" of spreadsheets. And so forth.

That's all well and good for implementing solutions to make departments function well. While this first wave is still alive and kicking, the second wave has been concerned with connecting, or integrating, departments to create an "enterprise-wide" collection of systems. This has turned out to be a more complex exercise—imagine building a house with bricks of different shapes and sizes—and few organizations have really mastered the complex enterprise system.

Huff and Puff Test

Do your systems go down more than once a month?

- Teams lose productivity due to downtime.
- Bugs create errors and operational rework.

Yes? You're the first little piggy with a house of straw.

No? Then do your systems pass information between each other without manual intervention?

- Customers place their own orders.
- Orders can be shipped with no more than a quick approval.

No? You're the second little piggy in a house of sticks.

Yes? Bingo! You're the third little piggy.

In Essence—Systems Thinking

Systems thinking is about drawing the right boundary and considering the consequences of one's actions throughout the area defined. It's the "butterfly flapping its wings and causing an earthquake" syndrome.

Tracing these consequences requires that you connect the dots within that boundary. If any of those connections cross the boundary, you redraw it or, more likely, just be very clear about that interface—what's needed and what must be given back.

Systems Thinking is an invaluable tool for defining "holistic" and revealing new insights from the broader perspective that follows. Those insights inform your business design and, not coincidentally, the structure of the technology tools you draw upon.

If you'd like a more sophisticated definition, here's one from Donella Meadows:

> *"Systems thinking is a holistic approach to analysis that focuses on the way that a system's constituent parts interrelate and how systems work over time and within the context of larger systems. The systems thinking approach contrasts with traditional analysis, which studies systems by breaking them down into their separate elements. Systems thinking can be used in any area of research and has been applied to the study of medical, environmental, political, economic, human resources, and educational systems, among many others."*[29]

[29] Donella H. Meadows, *Thinking in Systems: A Primer*, (White River Junction, VT: Chelsea Green Publishing, Inc., 2008).

The industry has responded by marketing enterprise-wide systems, often referred to as "enterprise resource planning" systems. That's not a perfect descriptor, but technology marketing isn't a precise science. These systems are centralized, offering the promise of "seamless integration," but that comes at the cost of greater complexity of implementation. Picture building a house with one humungous brick—it looks great when it's in place, but delivery's a bitch. And where is the door, BTW?

The alternative approach is to assemble many smaller bricks into one hole. This places the emphasis on building good connectors—the mortar if you will. It also means lots of smaller projects spread over time. Since you've read my opinions on minimalist change (**p. 150**), you'll know that I see that as an advantage—the approach that enables a truly agile organization to build what you need when you need it and to adjust course as often as your market dictates. No doubt, this approach takes time, but no one who has tried to shoehorn their business into a gargantuan enterprise-wide system in one big-bang project would claim that to be a simpler alternative.

Trusting Mantra: think big, build small.

Bricks as assets

The tech industry offers a gazillion building blocks. Here are some examples for context.

Common Bricks	Specialist Bricks	Unique Bricks
Accounting	Claims (Insurance)	Risk modeling IP
CRM (Sales/ Support)	Health records (Medical)	Combinations
Website	CAD (Engineering)	Embedded software
Email and MS-Office	Parts (Service)	One-click orders
Chat (Slack)	Demand (Manufacturing)	Apply AI to your data
Planning (Project)	Services (Consulting)	Apply AI to customer data
Basic security	Advanced Security	
Phones	Tablets (field staff)	Can you think of more?
Laptops and desktops	M2M (device management)	
Storage	AI (seek sense in big data)	
Networks		

Common, Specialist, and Unique Bricks

Do me a favor—flip back to the notes you made for the Your IP and Miss You Tests. Now scan the lists above and note which bricks might truly distinguish your business from the competition. Of the ones that remain, which would be valuable as a "standard" tool?

What I'm hoping you find is that the common bricks are just that—commodity tools that you could almost lift off the shelf to support processes that you already have. Furthermore, you're not married to your current way of doing these things and are open to what these tools offer. For instance, innovative accounting approaches are generally frowned upon, and selling is selling, right? If my hope is realized, you'll recognize that these are not areas in which to invest your precious innovative thinking and will accept the "standard practice" that these bricks provide.

The quid pro quo for this flexibility is that you can implement out-of-the-box solutions for your basic business functions, focus more attention on your specialist functions, and—if it makes strategic sense—build your own unique bricks.

Build unique bricks and you create assets.

Stacking your bricks

You don't just throw these bricks up in the air and see how they land, of course. There is a structure to your business systems architecture.

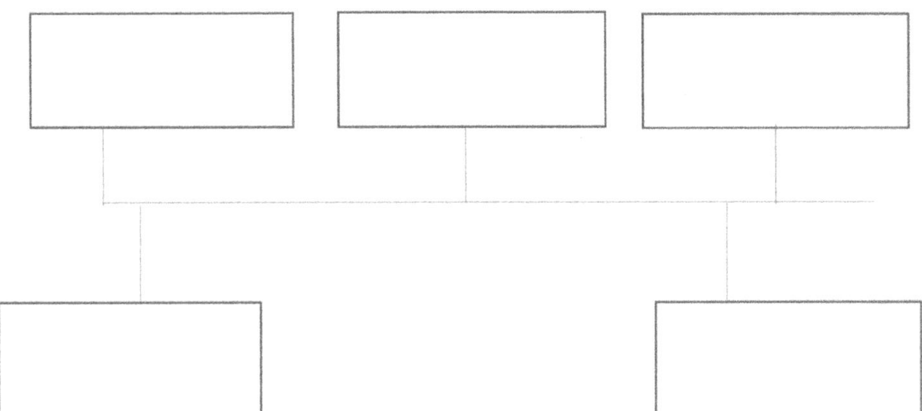

Bricks waiting to be named

The common bricks tend to be mandatory—you need accounting, benefit greatly from an ordered approach to sales, and have to communicate through documents, email, voice, and files.

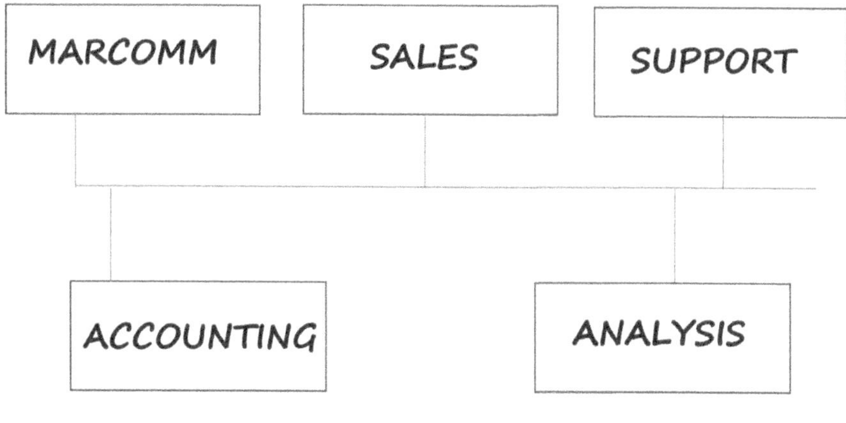

Universal Bricks

These systems provide the foundation of your business technology. Necessary but not sufficient—if you don't already have robust platforms in place, new or upgraded systems should be top of your shopping list.

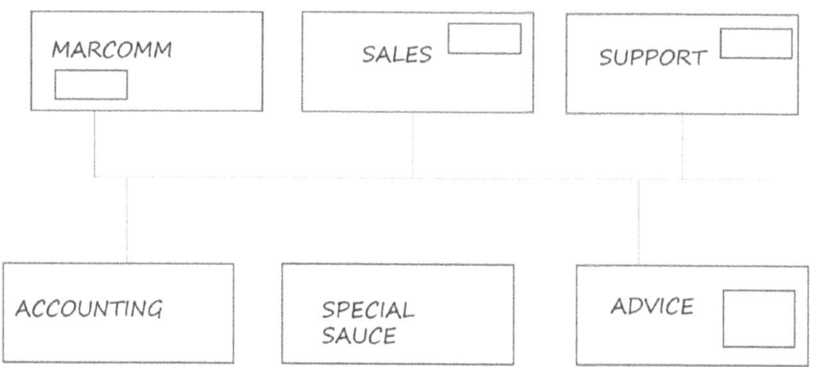

Focus on the bricks with unique value

It will benefit you to implement *some* uniqueness within your platforms, and you'll have entirely unique bricks. We'll talk about ways to place these investments in the next chapter.

One last observation from these simple charts—the lines that join the systems together are the plumbing for your business information—the way you deliver insights. *That's where the information and activities come together to create your best assets.*

The bricks you sell

As you consider your business in context of these bricks, think also about your customer's business. Our mantra—you are part of your customer's process—implies that your systems, or product, are also part of your customer's systems architecture. Consider:

- How well do you plug in to their architecture?
- Where are you on *their* Common—Specialist—Unique list? The further to the right you are, the more value you provide.

Don't panic—a word on upgrades

At this point, you may be panicking at the prospect of upgrading your business systems architecture or rolling your eyes "as if" you'd ever take this on. If either is the case, I'd much rather you felt positive about it, so here's a timely word about how this is done.

The first thing to recognize is…

You can make a lot of progress with the bricks you already have.

Woohoo! That's right. You don't have to throw the baby out with the bathwater.

In fact, I'll go further and say that you need to find a damn good reason before you start changing your existing building bricks. There are several steps before you go there.

So please grab a coffee, meditate a while, and read on.

HOW GOOD IS GOOD ENOUGH?

Reduce, reuse, and re-invent—work to stop, expand, or re-imagine

At risk of flogging a dead horse, there's no new process under the sun. At least, there are very few that are truly unique to your business. That's a relief, because building software from scratch—and being the only business that cares about its upkeep—is the most expensive way.

Before you decide to do that, you need to apply three tests to the job or process under consideration:

1. Reduce—Is this job really necessary? Can I reduce or remove the need for this?
2. Reuse—Is this job like any others? Can I reuse software that someone else has created?
3. Re-invent—Is there anything unique about this job that my customers really care about?

Re-work! Hang this poster-size on your wall

You should build your own software *only* if you answer "yes!" to question three. There are, of course, many businesses that will answer in the affirmative—every successful software business, any business in any industry with a proprietary and valuable way of doing what they do.

The point, though, is that many businesses attempt to roll their own software for non-differentiating jobs. And that's a very long list—anything to do with your accounting, most anything to do with communications—sales, support, and the like. "Rolling your own" encompasses buying business systems and customizing the heck out of them because you need to do things exactly the way you've always done them.

You never *need* to do things exactly the way you've always done them.

So where, exactly, is it ok to write your own software? Here's how you can tell:

If your customer will care when you change the way you do something, you should think about how you do it. If they don't notice, they won't care. Code or customize to:

- Avoid doing it in a way that hurts your customer.
- Do it in a way that will delight your customer.

Customers will see your software when you put it in front of them, but they can also notice the benefits of behind-the-scenes customization. Any production process that involves time-consuming automatable work can be accelerated by proprietary software to allow you to deliver much faster—and at higher margins. Manufacturing, consulting, and configuration can all benefit from accelerators.

	Standard practice	Accelerators	Unique Valuable
Buy vs. Build	Buy/minimal Custom	Buy or Build	Build or Buy/Custom
Examples	Commodity processes Accounting Orders Shipping Communications Tracking sales Tracking support	Consulting efficiency Faster Manufacturing Product configuration On-boarding	IP Customer experience Patentable

Consider build for accelerators and unique value

This may still leave you with a long list of opportunities, and we all love those. Until we have to decide which comes first. There's an additional filter you can apply to narrow this down further, by asking **where you need to be best**.

Where do you need to be best?

Let's take a look at an example within your business. Take the Your Activity Test, and we'll look at the results when you're done.

Your Activity Test

Draw your own version of the Gimme Three Steps figure above, leaving lots of room in each box. Then, for fun, just write down all of the different activities that your business completes within each box, one or two words each. Don't think about it, just write. After five minutes, you'll be surprised how full your page is. If any of the boxes have more whitespace, there could be a gap in your understanding—spend five minutes with a colleague to fill out more details.

Congratulations—you've just created an activity inventory. All—or most—of the work your business does to deliver value to your customers.

Now pick a function—any function will do, but the one you know best will be easiest (and this is meant to be easy). Say that's Sales. Time to make the world a simpler place:

1. Strike out any activities that are not essential to the selling of your product. Could these be dropped?
2. Circle the activities that contribute the most value to the sales process. How could these be optimized?

Congratulations number two—you've taken the first step in improving your operation.

I have a pet hate for "best practices." Not the concept, but the term. There are areas in every business where being the best is valuable. But most often, better is good enough.

Like many tech marketing terms, "best practices" is a well-intentioned cliché. Who says these practices are the best? That's pretty definitive. Best for who? Is *best* the same for every business? I'll let you know whether they're best for me.

Guard against being sucked in by the promise of doing something the best possible way—it's often unnecessary and distracting. I look at four options:

1. **Reduce/Stop**: wind this down—it's no longer relevant to your business.
2. **Good** enough: maintain what you have.
3. **Improve**: should do better—steady improvement is useful.
4. **Excel**: become the best you can—it'll make or break your business.

You already know what distinguishes your organization from your competition—what your customers need in their provider. Getting to *best* for these things is worth the effort. That means not trying to be best at everything. Knowing where to focus makes all the difference.

Take the Where to Excel Test to find your focus.

Where to Excel Test

Find your focus by answering these questions:

1. If your business could improve in five ways this year, which three would your customers appreciate the most?
2. Who in your industry is best at each of these things?
3. How good do you need to be? Write each thing in the appropriate "How good?" box.

Voila! Your mission is clear.

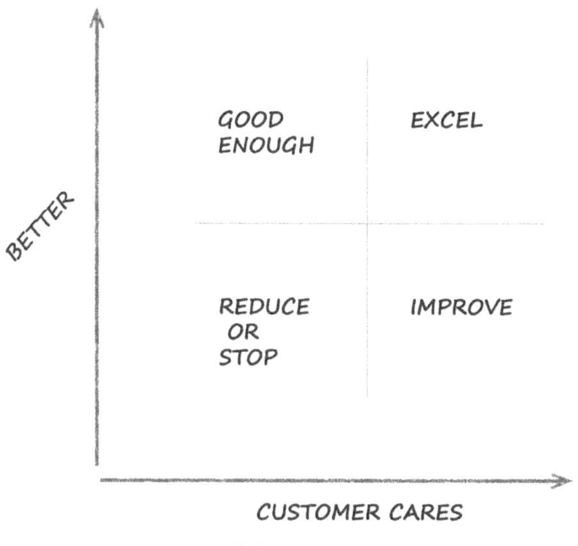

How good does it have to be?

For fun, you can carry on filling out this chart for all your major business functions. Where would you put sales processes, accounting, product design, marketing, distribution, and support? What other specialist functions does your business have, and where would you put them? When you're done, you'll have a sketch that looks something like this.

How good, for instance

Who gets a vote?

Using "Customer Cares" as the only criterion may seem a tad simplistic, but only a tad. You could run the same quick exercise for "Shareholder Cares"; if you're in a regulated industry, you'll need to run it for "Regulator Cares" to stay onside, but who else gets a vote, anyways?

However you proceed, you can easily assemble the results.

Trusting maxim: you don't need great technology. But you may need to be great at something that tech excels at.

If your chart is lopsided—like everything needs to be perfect—go back at it and make some compromises. You can only be great at a few things. What should they be?

Notice, if you will, that I didn't ask you to put technology on this chart. Do you need great technology? No! You need to be able to do some things really well, and if tech can help you do that, it's important.

You're figuring that out as you read this book....

How to be good and how to stand out

Keep this two-by-two handy—here's a sneak preview of how you'll use it in the next chapter:

> **Reduce or stop**: tech can help you automate the migraine work to refocus your team on more valuable work. Keep an eye out for redundant reports that cost time to produce only to be ignored.
>
> **Improve**: tech can help you code your rules, simplify your model, partner with outsourcers.
>
> **Good**: Buy solutions from suitable providers, share their standard practices, and spread the cost of upgrades with the rest of their customers.

Perfect: invest in best in class technology, fast as you need. If it could be your crown jewels, build your own version on top of existing technology to create something unique with built-in barriers to entry for your competition.

Let's get real—"Our business is too complicated."

I've laid out an approach here for holistic design that I hope will generate new thinking for you and your team. Before we move on, I want to say a word about implementation.

Very few businesses are as simple as the examples I've provided. One of the advantages that new businesses have is that they can design their operations for simplicity. That may last for a few years, though any successful business will achieve longevity, and complexity comes with evolution.

Since this is a book about the general techniques for technology success, we don't have time or space to go deeper.

So yes—it's never this simple. Since that deters many businesses from ever stepping back, always pushing for more from their "legacy" model, I'd like to emphasize…

It's not as hard as you may think.

Like everything else, it's not about budget, it's about priorities. The Basecamp team rewrites their product every four years. Each time, it's fresh, new, and better designed—because of all they've learned. Imagine what you could achieve if you were able to channel all your learning into your next-generation business.

Well, you can. All you need is to allow your people the time to get out of their daily routines, follow an efficient process, and generate implementable ideas.

When businesses are held back by their legacy operations, stepping back and punting is the way out.

WHAT IS YOUR PATH FOR CONTINUOUS IMPROVEMENT?

Would you rather go to the gym three times a week for twenty years or have open heart surgery?

Continuous improvement is a long gig—lifelong, I guess. In essence, knowing where you are and where you want to go eventually helps you figure out where to go next. "Eventually" could be next month, next year, or when you retire, but next is always the first step from where you stand.

In that spirit, let's look at one way to think about your business's technology journey that helps you determine what needs to be done now, next, and eventually.

The Innovation Ladder

Picture, if you will, a ladder to your goals. You may be on the first rung, or the second, or even the second from the top—no matter, as long as you know where you are.

On the bottom rung is your Foundation—the necessary underpinnings. In the context of your innovation platform, that would include secure, efficient, and cost-effective access to computing (network, servers, devices), the basic tools of most any trade (phone, email, MS Office), and solid business systems for your basic operating procedures (accounting, sales, and others more specific to your business). These are the table stakes that we all know, the foundation. They don't have to be perfect, but they do have to be reliable—you can't step up the ladder if you're constantly fixing the first rung. If you're good on this, step up. If not, your next step is to put these basics in place—again, in the spirit of good, not perfect.

The next rung is Acceleration. Many operating procedures will be automated, relieving your staff of migraine work, information will be delivered to analytical experts and insights shared. If either of these call for better security or faster computing, they're on the shopping list too—never let great software fail for want of hardware. Depending on the condition of your competitors, you may begin to differentiate yourself on this rung. Faster delivery, better service, efficient advisory, and a higher quality product can all be enabled by these pieces.

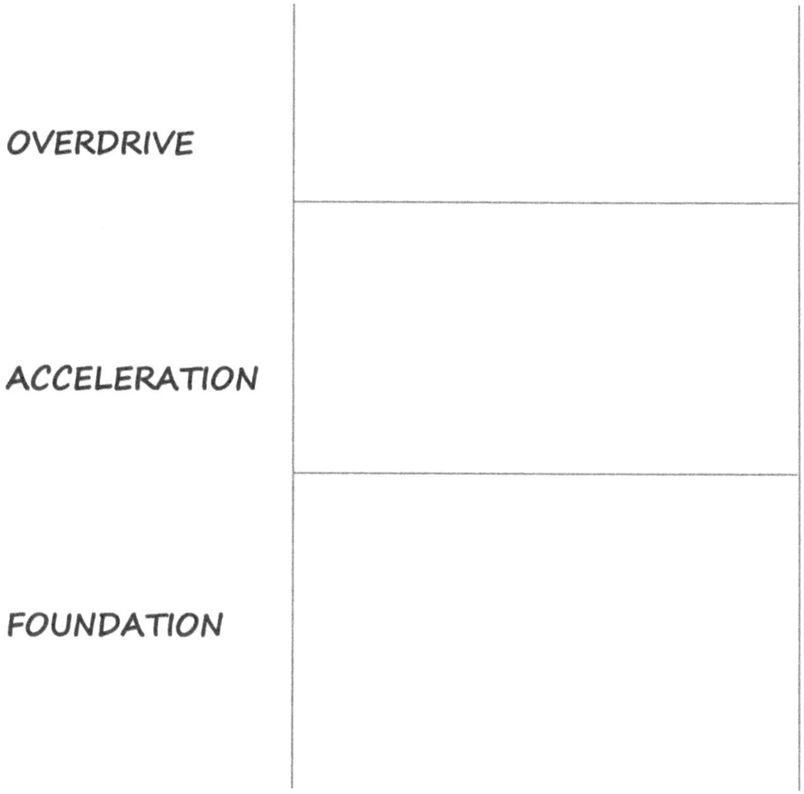

OVERDRIVE

ACCELERATION

FOUNDATION

My three-rung Innovation Ladder framework

The third rung—Overdrive—is the top rung. More of a stepladder than a real ladder, I suppose, but that makes for a shorter climb, right? If your customers don't notice the benefit of your technology stack on the second rung, they'll sure notice now. Here, your technology will connect your business community; your customers will benefit from your insights and have control of their own destinies (well, they'll be able to place their own orders, at least). Any IP that you can describe will be enshrined in software and sold at scale. And if your market requires, you will be passing security audits and have certificates to prove it.

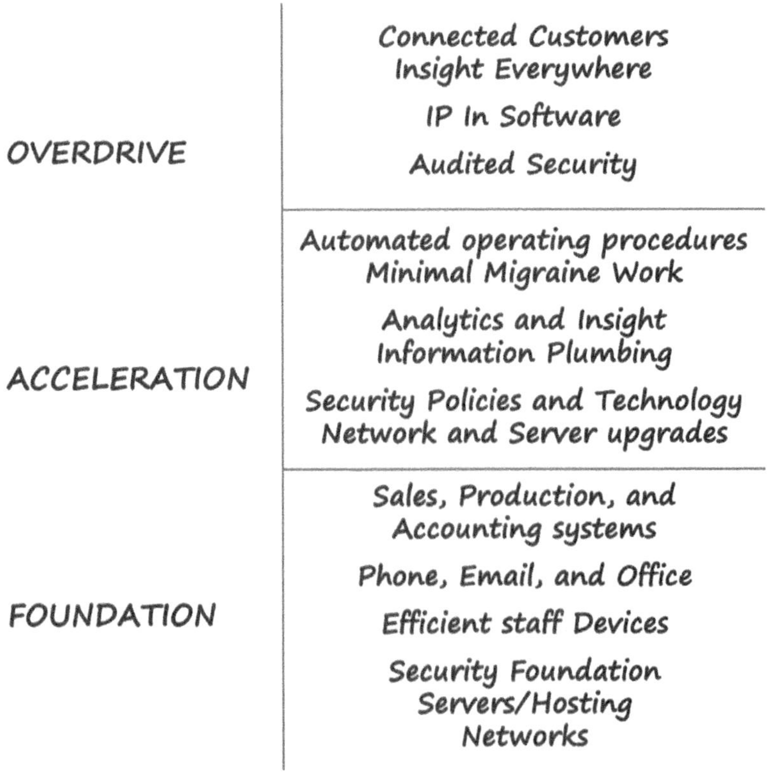

OVERDRIVE	Connected Customers Insight Everywhere IP In Software Audited Security
ACCELERATION	Automated operating procedures Minimal Migraine Work Analytics and Insight Information Plumbing Security Policies and Technology Network and Server upgrades
FOUNDATION	Sales, Production, and Accounting systems Phone, Email, and Office Efficient staff Devices Security Foundation Servers/Hosting Networks

What does your Innovation Ladder look like?

Your innovation portfolio

It will take time to climb your Innovation Ladder, years if you're on the bottom rung.

The trick, of course, is to identify your best bets—the small steps that will provide the biggest leaps toward your goals. These will be dotted up and down the ladder, but finding the next ones and continually reviewing the opportunities beyond—Agile style—will allow you to avoid less-favorable investments.

Consider your innovation portfolio. What path could it follow, and what are your next steps? Because that, my friend, will lead us to the next chapter.

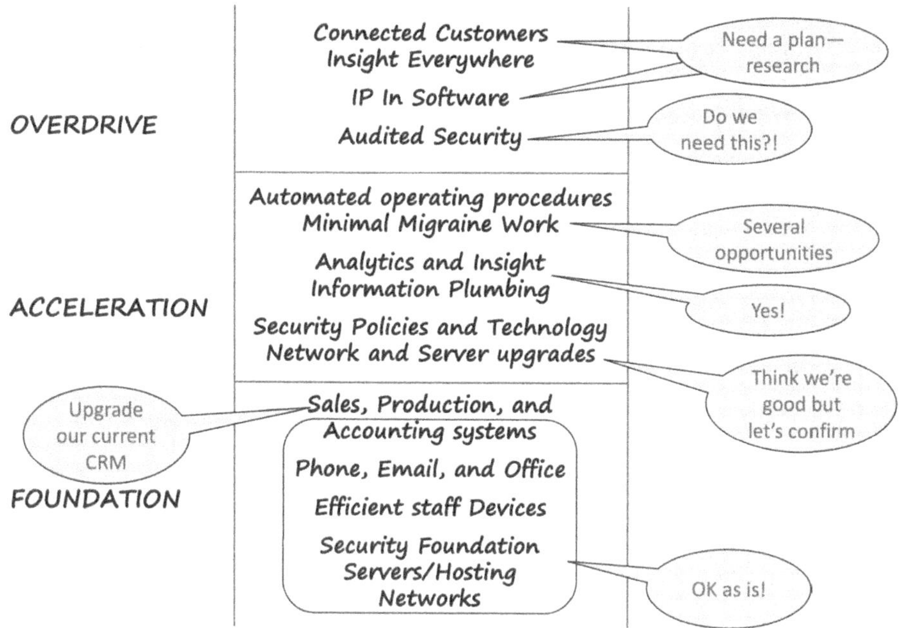

Your Innovation Portfolio best bets

GATHER YOUR THOUGHTS

Chapters Seven and Eight have laid a foundation of design thinking for your business—to be referred to as business design from here on. All the while, you've been considering concepts that are only feasible because we have the technology—plumbing information to feed insights, shifting the work to the best place in your business community, and automating anything we can define rules for.

But we haven't actually talked about technology. In keeping with the thesis of this book, that comes at the end of these two chapters. As in, right now.

If these chapters have helped you to generate some exciting new ideas for your business, you'll doubtless be thinking how the heck you can make these happen.

Your Brainwave Test

Remind yourself of the exercises completed in this chapter and the previous chapter, and list your new insights and ideas here in the order you feel most appropriate:

1. ____________
2. ____________
3. ____________
4. ____________
5. ____________
6. ____________
7. ____________
8. ____________
9. ____________
10. ____________

Let's just level-set here—take a moment to capture those thoughts with the Brainwave Test. (If your thinking has been constrained so far by the concern that none of this may be possible, please set that fear aside and go crazy for this test.)

BOTTLING INNOVATION—IN A NUTSHELL

Technology offers many ways to patch up your business. Faster network here, better email client there. Shiny new phones, an upgrade to the accounting and sales systems. While each of these initiatives may have merit on their own, the greater value comes by beginning with one question:

How can you turn ideas into assets that capture value for your business and community as a whole?

Easy questions often don't have simple answers. This chapter provides one path to answering the question above:

1. What exactly constitutes a valuable asset to your business?
    - What has your business created that is unique or rare?
    - What is the value of those creations?
    - What constitutes a valuable asset to your business community?

2. What role do you fulfill in your business community?
    - Why do your customers care about your business?
    - What problem do you solve for your customer?
    - How do you fit into your customer's process?
    - How can you help your business community work better together?

3. How do you assemble your operating systems?
    - What bricks are at your disposal?
    - How good is good enough?
    - How can you be good, and how do you excel?
    - What is your path for continuous improvement?

4. Gather your brainwaves for the next step.

Rules of thumb:

- If you can describe the way you do a job, someone can code it in software.
- The fewer times the baton is passed, the less often it is dropped.
- Moving a problem won't solve the root cause.

In the two remaining chapters, we will build on this notion of applying technology holistically to extend the value that you offer your business's community.

❑❑

Booksite extras at *www.trustingtechnologybook.com/chapter8* include:

Template for the Big-O model
Template for the work inside your business
Template for your innovation ladder
Workbook for all the exercises

Your Journey to Becoming a Tech Company

In which you will review your business in light of the principles of technology mastery. We'll look at what "mastery" could actually mean—for you. And you'll map the route to wherever that is.

This chapter provides a master plan for bringing together the components of technology-enabled innovation in your business. Your needs are unique, and you'll plot a roadmap here. When done, you'll have a vision, ambition, and a place to begin your journey to becoming a better tech company.

Think of this as a playbook for you to plan your next business upgrade. You can also use it as you begin each subsequent upgrade.

We'll recap the principles provided in the foregoing chapters and summarize the technology superpowers at your disposal.

Then we'll assess where you stand. I'll share the kickoff questions I've developed as a result of working with over 250 businesses. You'll find your current position on the stairway to technology mastery and figure out how this can help you evolve through a clearer understanding of the opportunities and hurdles that lie ahead.

As an added bonus, I've included my down-to-earth perspective on today's headline technologies, some of which could provide useful building blocks for your business. As I mentioned in the introduction, you could begin your read of *Trusting Technology* here and refer back to the previous chapters as you explore this chapter. Your call.

If you've been following along with the exercises these past few chapters, you'll have formed a good picture of the key inputs. It's time to wet your thumb, page through your notes, and dive in.

THE PRINCIPLES OF MASTERY

The principles of technology mastery are the ingredients for your future business: your "new business as usual." Some may already be in place, others may be premature, yet others may not apply. Before you sort that out, let's refresh the things that (I say) are your steps to becoming a great technology company.

The first three principles apply to mastery of any change.

Customer partnership

In Chapter Four, we looked at rooting your business upgrades in your customers' needs. More specifically, to better fulfill your role in their process. Understanding exactly what it is they need you for after you've removed the useless and commodity aspects of what you provide.

We introduced the Big-O model to represent the community of customers and prospects in which your business operates. And we looked at three levels of partnership that will allow you to change with your market by evolving your brand promise, testing better ways to deliver on that promise, and building evergreen customer partnerships. We also asked whether you lead or follow your vanguard customers.

Confidence

Making change is a muscle you need to grow. Despite our innate powers of adaptability, transitioning to new ways of working is uncomfortable. When applied to teams of colleagues, havoc can ensue. The ultimate measure of your team's ability to adapt is confidence. Confidence to move ahead despite uncertainty, confidence that a way will be found, and confidence in each other. The absolute best way for a team to develop this confidence is to overcome challenge changes together. Again and again.

Cadence

We like to know where we're headed, whether that be in the form of a roadmap or plan. No plan, no confidence. But it's important to see fantasy planning for what it is—the pretense that we know exactly how everything will go down weeks, months, or years into the future. Much better to decide on a course of action, identify the things we know how to do based on experience, and call out the things we need to learn, the theories we need to prove or disprove, and the order in which we need to get smarter. We plan what we know (Waterfall) and plan to learn what we don't (Agile).

The remaining principles apply to the two areas where technology can help.

Insight

We act on decisions and decide based on insight. The best insights arise from providing the right people with the right information at the right time. Technology has revolutionized our ability to gather, cleanse, parse, and deliver information. Every technology initiative you conduct should improve your plumbing of information between colleagues, customers, and suppliers.

Assets

Your business is the sum of its experts, the colleagues who know how every job gets done. But experts come and go. If you know how a job is done, you can capture it in software and enshrine it in the intellectual property of your business. In this way, technology allows your company's expertise to be delivered at scale, to be protected, and to be continuously improved.

	Step 1	Step 2	Step 3	Step 4	Good enough
Customer	Goal				
Confidence		Goal			
Cadence			Goal		
Insight				Goal	
Assets					Goal

A roadmap for the principles of technology mastery

These principles provide the basis of your stairway to technology mastery.

Let's go a little deeper into some of these areas.

Your customer's puzzle

In Chapter Four, we asked where you fit in to your customer's process. Let's take a slightly different perspective and ask how you fit into their puzzle. Of all the things they need to get done, which do you help them do?

Which piece of your customer's puzzle do you solve today?

If your customer is a business, what part of their marketing, sales, production, distribution, or service process do you help with? Write that down now.

Now, considering the information you share with customers and the jobs you do for them, which of their other processes could you help with? These may include adjacent activities, an expansion of the same activity into their other product lines, or a host of other ideas. Whatever you come up with, write that down now.

Which piece of your customer's puzzle could you solve tomorrow?

Don't let the moss grow

Your ability to execute is a factor of where you go next and how far you have to travel to get there. It will dictate how quickly you can climb the stairway.

Upgrading business technology is not an undertaking to be taken lightly. Unfortunately, too many businesses tend to push this work off until the legacy systems are falling apart and there's no choice but to act. Running down the clock in this way adds pressure, but that may not be the worst adverse effect. When you come across an opportunity to adopt a compelling new technology, you may be hamstrung by your "legacy" systems. Meaning that you've got to upgrade (a process all its own) before you can do anything and delay the adoption of the thing that produces the real value.

Technology masters do not let the moss grow under their systems. This doesn't mean they upgrade willy-nilly, just for the sake of it, but it does mean that they have a longer list of criteria for "keeping current." For instance, a technology master will focus on the top half of this list, which coincidentally obviates the bottom half.

- We stay within striking distance of leading-edge technologies and implement when the time is right.
- Workarounds for performance and scale are not acceptable.
- We exercise minimalist change and focus on the simplest solutions.
- We seek ways to do more with less.
- We will invest what it takes to maintain our current systems.
- Security patching must be available to us.
- Our systems are not Y2K-compliant.

Which half does your business focus on?

Do you extend your comfort zone or tie your hands?

Confidence is connected with comfort. If you're embarking on work that's comfortable, you'll likely have confidence in the outcome. But remaining comfortable will not grow your confidence.

Comfort zones stretch—they also break.

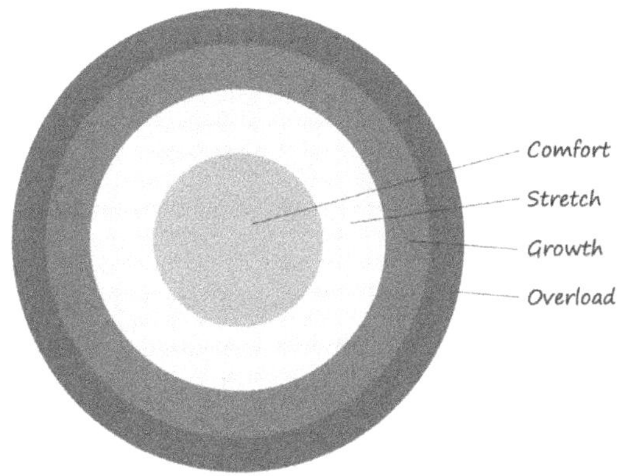

Businesses, teams, and individuals share zones of comfort and discomfort

A confident team performs best at the boundary of their stretch area, just shy of panic and well short of crash. The best way I know of growing the confidence of a team is to unite them in the achievement of stretch goals. This is how you should pace your change objectives:

1. What outcomes does the business need to achieve, and when is the window for that achievement?
2. Who are the best people to make that happen? That's your team.
3. How do they think they can get there? What are the anticipated steps, and which early steps are critical to overall success?
4. How can you, as the leader, sponsor, or general boss, set constraints of time and budget to incite the team to do better than they think possible?

Support them as they go. The more you stretch a team, the more efficiency and coaching they'll need.

The good news is that your organization needs to take on new challenges in order to survive, let alone prosper. If you stay in your comfort zone, you tie your hands and future prospects. At one extreme, this means that you'll never disrupt your own business—a common conundrum, because that means someone else will. At the other end of the scale, this means you'll stagnate.

Once again, you face the same three questions:

1. Where do you need to go?
2. Where are you starting from?
3. Where do you go next?

Your decisions are a) where to move the organization's comfort zones, and b) how. Only you can know what will work best, but here are some alternatives:

Nudge with +1 thinking: incremental improvements are slow and steady—look at what we have, decide what's not yet good enough and add features, tweak processes, or subtract low value steps. +1 thinking is good to kickstart the comfort shift or to fine-tune things that won't move the needle. It's appealing to the risk-averse and fits nicely with our Agile mantra of *think big, act small.* Find and fix that one issue that had the call center phones ringing off the hooks yesterday. Done well, +1 will generate the confidence to take bigger risks.

Blow it up with 10x thinking: when there's no way to get where you need to go by refining the current ways, 10x thinking forces the team to consider radical approaches. Applying tight constraints on budget and timeline can force the issue. For example, healthcare projections suggest that the number of hospital beds required in a decade's time will vastly outstrip the current funding model. It's simply not possible to continue with the current prevention/cure model. So, we need to consider new ways to reduce the need for beds, such as promoting greater health or providing for more scalable home care for those who are unable to avoid sickness. 10x thinking is the best way to find big wins but is challenging for those that haven't experienced success before.

Blend +1 and 10x: thing is, your upgrade portfolio will suit a blend of approaches. The important point is to realize that you're not confined to +1 (our natural default) or 10x (some entrepreneurs' favorite) thinking. If your upgrade can be achieved by tweaking what you have, go +1 a few times. If you need radical, start with 10x.

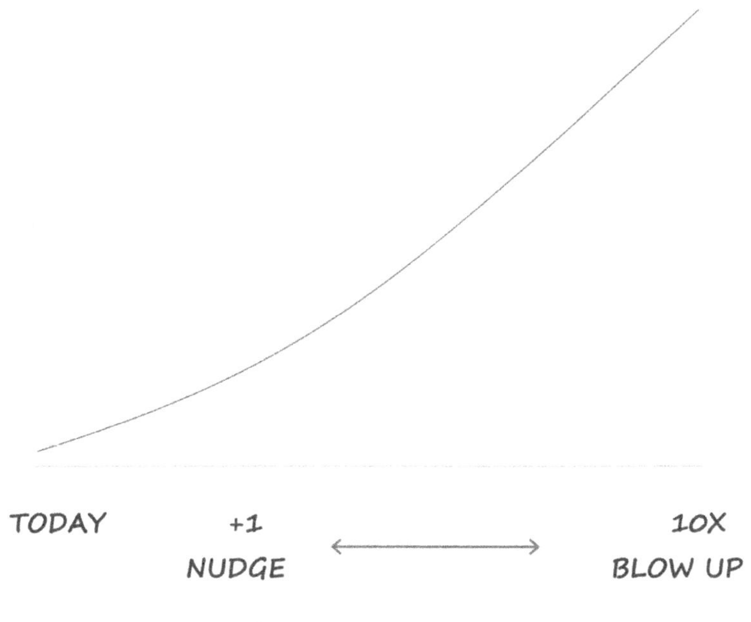

The Uncomfortable Scale

The reality of innovation

The average success rate of Silicon Valley startups is one in twenty—95 percent fail to build a lasting business.

When you read the innovation press, it's easy to form a picture of this rosy culture where everybody's changing the world and embracing failure between rounds of foosball. Whether or not that prospect is a factor in the twenty-to-one ratio, it's a misleading view.

Building a culture to embrace failure sets the wrong tone. The failure has to have a purpose—learning by trial and error. Absent that, it's hard to distinguish failure from incompetence.

Don't believe that nonsense that you have to hire a Marvel team with innovation superpowers. Innovation is our natural state. We're bred to survive in the wild—it takes a very long time for DNA to change—and adapt to changing circumstances every day.

Myth-buster: Don't embrace failure. Embrace learning and accept failure as a means.

Like every skill, some people are better innovators than others, just as some folks are better operators, planners, and the like. But everyone has the innovation gene, and most everyone could exercise it more readily. Innovation is fun, so give people challenges that get them excited. Set 10x goals and they'll come up with something better than you have today.

When we use experimentation to validate our theories about unanswered questions, it's all too easy to lean too far toward the need for validation, to prove we are right. Yet a conclusive experiment is successful regardless of the conclusion. Prove it right, or prove it wrong, just prove it quickly.

We display many biases in our daily routine. A good way to fight the validation bias is to create "kill experiments"—tests that, if successful, will lead us to kill off an idea or approach. If those tests fail, we may have been right all along. It's a no-lose situation.

There's one thing above all else that an innovation culture must have—candor.

Being candid saves time. No wishy-washy feedback. Short and

to the point, with backup if required. That doesn't mean being rude or disrespectful.

So how do you distinguish smart learning/experimentation from incompetence? Retrospectives are an important part of any learning organization's modus operandi. One question to include on any retrospective agenda is:

Could we have foreseen that?

If the answer is yes every once in a while, consider what could have been done differently to foresee the outcome and then do that thing differently in future. If yes comes up all the time, dig deeper for radical changes—there could be a competence issue.

From +1 to 10x thinking in three steps

I've advocated a few criteria for turning ambition into action—think big, act small; always be pragmatic; practice makes better.

When finding your place on the Uncomfortable Scale, consider this approach:

1. Clean up annoyances and simplify
2. Automate parts of what's left
3. Instill a daily routine

Let's look at an example of how this has been done—how would you like to improve your customer turnaround by 10x?

Sometimes your performance will slip. Over time, inefficiencies accumulate. When this impacts your customer experience, it's time to focus on returning to excellence.

In the insurance business, customers care about the turnaround of their claims. A payout is usually the consequence of something bad happening. Your insurer has an opportunity to mitigate that by quickly reimbursing your expenses—or to add to the pain with a long, drawn-out claims process.

When one insurer decided to focus on a return to excellence, they achieved a 10x (as in *ten times*) improvement on their claim reimbursement turnaround time. That meant seventy days of waiting for a claim to be reimbursed down to seven. Not only did this delight the company's loyal customers, it also made their staff's jobs a lot easier. It's a whole lot more fun for call center staff to deliver good news.

They achieved these incredible results by applying the holy trinity of change with "SAS":

> **Simplify**: Firstly, the team documented the process on paper. They looked at the actual day-to-day activities and captured every step, every variation. Filled the walls of four rooms with sticky notes. Most of this stuff was not in the SOP manual. Redundant steps were discarded, inefficient steps were earmarked for improvement, and a phased plan was outlined for the coming year.
>
> **Automate**: Step two was to apply technology to operate the streamlined process with greater speed, accuracy, and at lower cost. Information plumbing was improved—the customer could file claims online rather than submitting a twenty-page fax—and processing rules were defined so that claims could be pre-screened before going to adjusters.
>
> **Support**: Third, and most importantly, programs were developed to enable the whole team to work more effectively. Training, coaching, work-from-home options, and regular scrums to address daily challenges.

The 10x outcome couldn't have happened if any one of these steps had been skipped.

And there's an epilogue. These improvements allowed the insurer to buy new books of business that substantially increased their portfolio.

It speaks to this team's ambitions that they then embarked on version two to achieve further drastic improvements. Confident teams don't rest on their laurels.

Your technology superpowers

If this book was a Marvel comic, we could look at technology as providing your business with superpowers. Not the ordinary powers that you might associate with systems that help you manage the transactions in your business or draw information from those records, but the sum of those parts. If that were the case, here's how I would break those superpowers down:

> **Differentiation**: the opportunity to do things differently than your competitors to the noticeable benefit of your customers and at lower marginal cost. Faster than a speeding bullet—and more scalable with greater accuracy and consistency.
>
> **Agility**: with the right foundations in place and a view to the horizon, your business can leap tall buildings by being responsive, reactive, and explorative.
>
> **Resilience**: when your star players fall ill—or leave the business—you'll be happy when you've invested in coding their expertise.
>
> **Insight**: technology will not have sentient wisdom for some time, but it can generate wisdom by quickly, accurately, and securely plumbing information to the right people at the right time.
>
> **Automation**: remember—if you can describe the way you do what you do, you can code it in software. Whether you automate parts of your work or simply complement your business's wetware with technology tools to handle the grunt work, automation translates to greater speed.

Generating Insights	Supporting the work
Just-in-time need-to-know	Redistribution of control around your community
Monitoring performance indicators	Simplifying the design of your business
Protecting information	Automating the migraine tasks to free your people up for more valuable work
Finding needles in your data haystack	Accelerating work
Focusing attention on trends and exceptions	Scaling—reach more customers at lower cost
	Enshrining your IP in software
	Leveraging others' work through reuse
	Buying commodity infrastructure

Which technology superpowers do you need most?

You can use these superpowers to do as little as you need or as much as you want—from reducing your Accounts Receivable to creating whole new business models. In the next chapter, we'll look at mastering these capabilities, but we're going to wrap up this section with some ways you can innovate with your customers on a daily basis, or as often as makes sense for your business.

At the very least, I hope these powers can help inform your opinion on the role that technology can play in your business and your industry at large.

THE STAIRWAY TO TECHNOLOGY MASTERY

What's wrong with your business?

You picked up this book because you are interested in building a better business. Allow me to ask—better how? What's wrong with your business today? What could be better?

More to the point, what aspects of your business should be best in your industry? This is the place to begin your mastery for one simple reason. It's where your success will be most noticed. It's the way you'll move the needle. And you answered that question in Chapter Eight when you determined where to excel.

Let's pick up from there. Beginning with the impactful end in mind allows you to work back and see all the things you'll have to do to get there. If your foundation systems are creaking, you may need to upgrade them before starting on your big wins. Are the wins still worth it when you take that into account? What other side benefits will that upgrade have that you can throw on the benefits pile?

Vital Signs: The first step is to test your business's vital signs by answering the following:

1. *Are you able to close your monthly books within one week of the following month?* This is a simple test of how much of your business process is handled outside your systems—how many exceptions need to be accounted for in your books.
2. *Do you lose less than four hours a month of employee productivity due to tech issues?* A test of system reliability—or fragility.

3. *Would business survive if your systems went down for a week?* This measures your business's dependence on technology—survival means you have contingencies.

If you answered *yes* to all these questions, your vital signs are good, and you can move on to the next examination. If you answered *no* to any of these, focus on addressing those issues before proceeding.

Migraine Work: Step two is to assess the level of support that your technology provides. Answer the following:

4. Can new hires learn how to use the technology at their disposal in under a month?
5. *Is your cost of administration for each transaction acceptable?* You may have opportunities for efficiency, but unacceptable means fixes are urgent.
6. *Is your IT ticket backlog steady or declining?* If the backlog is increasing, you need to address maintainability.

Again, if you answered *yes*, you can move on. Use any *no*s to guide remediation.

Resilience: How will you fare if something breaks? Consider:

7. *Do you have a business continuity plan in the event that primary systems fail?* Take a more comprehensive perspective than question three.
8. *Does your business have an appropriate security strategy?* Review the security one-pager in Chapter Seven for guidance.
9. *Do you have at least two experts in each area of your business (tech and non-tech)?* This question of organizational resilience—on-boarding, training, succession planning, and so on—is important in any area of your business. The more you trust technology, the more important it is to double up on skills.

Yes-yes-yes? You're looking good. In fact, you're in good shape to consider advanced technology investments. Just one more question before we go there.

Complexity: Diversity may be good for revenue but forces certain investment decisions:

10. *Does all your revenue come from a single line of business?* Focus reduces the complexity that your systems need to support.
11. *If not, are you clear on which line of business will drive the majority of your margin?* This *may* imply a focus for your tech investments.

Diverse revenue sources often mean diverse technology needs, and this confuses the picture as to where best to invest. If you have the resources within each line of business, go for it. If you have any doubts, pick your best bet and hit that one out of the park before you dilute focus on several areas. It doesn't always follow that the best tech opportunities lie in the biggest sector of your business. It's rare, however, that you'd invest first in a low-earning or declining sector unless you anticipate a turnaround.

Renovations and upgrades

If any of the areas above are weak, you may need to renovate your business's technology foundations. If your base systems are sound but have fallen behind over recent years, an upgrade may suffice. As keen as I'm sure you are to get on with the "big win," don't forget those three little pigs. Any steps you take toward greater customer connection, agility, insight, and asset-building will be twice as hard if you build on straw foundations. As we've discussed, people are naturally inclined to resist change anyway; straw foundations that make daily work frustrating will encourage people to dig in their heels and stymie morale.

Solid foundations will provide the conduit for much of this work. Renovate or upgrade, then maintain, and your big wins have a chance of, well, becoming big wins.

The first two steps

Your stairway begins with the foundation you have in place. You may need to evolve this foundation as you progress. In addition, we need to make sure that the stairway you build can be operated with the appropriate efficiency and reliability. We'll complete the stairway by adding a couple of rows to capture these items.

	Step 1	Step 2	Step 3	Step 4	Good enough
Foundation					
Maintenance					
Customer					
Confidence					
Cadence					
Insight					
Assets					

The stairway model—ready for your roadmap

BUILDING YOUR STAIRWAY

What will your plan look like? I've pounded my Think Big, Act Small message enough, so here is a model that breaks down the big goals into manageable steps.

1. **Foundations**: did any challenges emerge from the eleven questions above? If so, remediation goes here—usually to be addressed in step one or two. You'll check back regularly on this as you contemplate more and more ambitious steps later.
2. **Maintenance:** a.k.a. operational efficiency of your foundations. This stuff needs to hum along so you can focus on the ambitious differentiation stuff. That means that your support team is efficient, keeps the backlog of day-to-day issues under control, and has a solid process for delivering the small and medium changes you need for business-as-usual. Hyperactive maintenance is a drain on your ability to deliver innovation.
3. **Customer:** The start and end point for your differentiation. How will each item in your innovation portfolio be noticed by your customers? Who will it impact? How will it improve or expand your role in their process? Which initiative comes next?
4. **Confidence:** What will your organization need to do to make that initiative happen? Is the change inside or outside your team's

comfort zone? How many colleagues will be impacted, and how much will their lives be changed? Are they a flexible bunch or very comfortable in their ways? Are they too busy to do it right? What will you do to lead them through this?

5. **Cadence:** As your team pulls together the steps required for this work, do they have a solid overall approach? Which steps feel familiar—been there, done that—and which have unknowns? What does the team need to learn to find the answer? Has the work been broken up into two-week sprints? Who's on the steering committee?
6. **Insights:** What information will be gathered by this initiative? What insights and actions could that generate for your customers? And for your colleagues? Who should it be distributed to and when? Where will the information reside, and how will it be presented? Are there any security concerns? How can these insights best be monetized?
7. **Assets:** When the work is done, what company assets will be created or enhanced? What new IP will be enshrined in code? How can that be monetized?

Every business begins this journey from a unique position with its own goals and priorities. Before you complete your roadmap, it'll help to consider a few examples.

Example: Technology reset

Let's take a look at a business that installed its basic accounting and order management systems ten years ago and hasn't found the need to improve them since. Things could be better, but they've been able to get by. Technology is a bit of a black box to be honest, and they've been focused on doing whatever it takes to bring in the business.

The problems have mounted up to a point where something must be done. It's also a good time to review opportunities to catch the competition.

Here's the roadmap they cooked up.

	Step 1	Step 2	Step 3	Step 4	Good Enough
Foundation	Review foundation	Implement new system			
Maintenance	Muscle through	Fix persistent niggles	Lower support frees time	30% IT team on support; 70% innovation	25% IT team on support; 75% innovation
Customer		Fewer order corrections; faster resolutions	25% of orders online, 7x24; 20% auto replenished	40% of orders online, 7x24; 25% auto replenished	40% of orders online, 7x24; 25% auto replenished
Confidence		Prove we can do it	Bring it on	Ready for most anything	Ready for most anything
Cadence	Hire project manager	Initiate Steering	Efficient Steering	Shorter Steering	Change comes easy
Insight		Data quality; Clear KPIs	Understand buying habits	Provide customer recommendations	Leverage understanding of buyer habits
Assets			Partner with 5% of customers	10% customers provide active feedback	20% customers provide active feedback

A reset roadmap

You can see in this example how the roadmap begins with some basic retooling. Although "problems had mounted," the opportunity is twofold—address the long-term niggles and lay the foundation for new value. By Step 4, the business is approaching "Good Enough." And maybe the next set of goals.

Example: Upgrading your operation

Remember our insurer that improved their turnaround by ten times, delighted customers, and created confident colleagues? Their approach was to streamline processes, apply technology to plumb information and automate work, and give their team the daily support they needed to succeed.

Their roadmap would have looked something like this:

	Step 1	Step 2	Step 3	Step 4	Good enough
Foundation	Cleanse process		Online claims system	Pre-screening	Optimal process coming soon
Maintenance			Kinks ironed out	Low cost	< 0.5 FTE
Customer	70d claims	60d claims	30d claims	15d claims	7d claims
Confidence		Visible improvement	Further improvement	Take on more business	Let's do this again!
Cadence		Daily issue resolution	Daily issue resolution	Daily issue resolution	Mean time to resolution under two days
Insight		Process KPIs	Online claims	Operational understanding to drive further improvement	Operational understanding to drive further improvement
Assets				Pre-screen claims	Automation

Operational upgrade roadmap

Example: Building on solid foundations

Exciting times. This company invested in a new Enterprise Resource Planning to run their entire operation just a couple years ago. The teething problems have been ironed out, and the team has had a chance to take a breath. Everyone is somewhat relieved that the change is done, but they're ambitious and gained a lot of confidence after pulling through.

It's a good time to build on this success and drive home the value for the customer.

Here's the roadmap they christened "Bring it on!"

	Step 1	Step 2	Step 3	Step 4	Good enough
Foundation	Confirm vendor roadmap in line with needs	Weekly security patching	Upgrade foundation system		Stay no more than one version back. Weekly patching.
Maintenance	Streamline support process	Train additional supper staff	Cut average backlog to 3 days		Average ticket backlog under 3 days
Customer	Establish customer validation group	Market validation to prioritize roadmap	Extend customer validation group	Weekly customer feedback	Weekly customer feedback
Confidence	How can we improve further?	Establish improvement metrics		Tighten improvement metrics	Continuous differentiating improvement
Cadence		Streamline communications Slack and video	Reduce sprints from 4-weeks to 2-weeks	Prepare for weekly upgrades	Weekly upgrades
Insight	Identify redundant data	Fully digitized—paperless	Daily operational dashboard	Sell insights to customers Security audit	Daily dashboard Insight revenue
Assets	Streamline and document process	Automated fulfillment	Automated on-boarding	Patent key IP	Protected IP including in business valuation

Roadmap for building on solid foundations

Example: Your turn

Write a few sentences to describe your big ambitions and starting point. Then fill out the blank template below beginning with the Good Enough column and plotting steps for each row. Better still, share a copy of this book with your team and run the exercise as a group. (Remember that you can find digital templates for all exercises on the booksite).

	Step 1	Step 2	Step 3	Step 4	Good enough
Foundation					
Maintenance					
Customer					
Confidence					
Cadence					
Insight					
Assets					

What does *your* roadmap look like?

There are as many stairways to technology mastery as there are businesses. I hope these examples illustrate how you can apply this process to your entire business or to a business unit of significant size. There's nothing wrong with having multiple stairways within your business as long as you ensure they are aligned, that any synergies are exploited, and that every team is set up for success with the resources and focus required.

Ask yourself how many plates your business can spin at one time. Think about reducing that number whenever you smash a plate.

TWENTY QUESTIONS FOR THE NEW INNOVATION OFFICER

In the course of working with over 250 businesses over the last three decades, I've developed a list of questions to assess the appetite and readiness of a business for the kind of breakthroughs that technology can afford. I've taken care to curate the list to keep it short and usable.

If you are charged with looking at your business this way—whether you've been newly appointed or founded the business years ago—I urge you to answer these questions as a starting point for your new plans.

I've found the best answers come from asking about "upgrades" rather than technology. I introduced the topic at the beginning of Chapter Five, but this is worth a moment of clarification. Below I use the term "upgrade" to connote a significant improvement in the way a business operates. This could include a better customer experience, doing more with less in operations, the successful launch of a new product, innovations that garnered interest from press or public, or gaining new insights that created value. "Upgrade" does *not* include major new deals, over-budget profits, or revenue, no matter how happy those events made your shareholders.

Although this is a "self-assessment," you'll get the best results if you allow a third party to judge "significant improvement." A customer group or candid partners are well-positioned to weigh in. Feel free to answer the questions yourself, but don't count your chickens until you've collected answers from several others whose opinions you would stake your reputation on.

Need

1. What upgrades could move the needle for your business? Consider:
    - Customer experience
    - Scalable IP
    - Operations
    - Pace of change
2. Check off the things that work well enough today. What upgrades are left?
3. Who does these things better than anyone else? (Don't limit your answer to competitors.)
4. How much do you need to improve to move the needle 5 percent? 10 percent? More?
5. Write a sentence for each area that describes what should change and how it will move your needle. (Don't think about the *how* yet.)
   Congratulations—you've just created your upgrade portfolio!

Appetite

6. How many times has your business been upgraded over the last five years? When was the last upgrade? Are your colleagues anxious to repeat the experience?
7. Is the CEO convinced that the upgrades you've listed will move the needle? (If that's you, you'll know the answer; if it's not, share your portfolio with the CEO and ask her.)
8. Is anyone on the management team prepared to put their reputation on the line for any of those portfolio initiatives?
9. If they succeed, would any other members of the team jump in with more?
10. When new ideas do not meet expected targets, are they judged as successes?

This section tells you how fertile your business will be for innovative upgrades.

Readiness

11. Can your business execute on major new ideas within one year?
12. Name the colleagues that would be on the team assigned to each upgrade on your portfolio. Park any upgrades that don't have a complete team.
13. Add the names of trusted partners and known consultants for each upgrade where you think their contribution will help. Also, look hard at any teams that include the same names. You'll need to rank priorities for these people.
14. Rate your teams' experience from one (low) to three (high) for each of the upgrades in your portfolio. Favor upgrades where you've rated experience to be higher than two. Park any with a rating near one.
15. Assess the confidence of your teams in their success. Ideally, they should be just outside their comfort zones. And they should remain there if you need them to grow.

This section tells you how much you can plan to do and how much you must *plan to learn.*

Ambition

16. For each item in the portfolio, write down one or more existing activities that could be stopped (ditched—replaced—halted—verboten) to free up resources.
17. How much resource will be freed up by stopping these activities? How soon can they be stopped? Will new capabilities need to be developed before each can be stopped? Are these capabilities addressed by the portfolio? Should some be added?
18. Having taken into account what resources—people, time, and budget—can be freed up in this way, plot your high-level view on the resources you'll need to deliver your innovation portfolio. Write a sticky for each initiative in the portfolio, and shuffle the

stickies around until you're comfortable that you can resource the peaks and valleys of the work.

19. You should be forming a good high-level picture of the order of the work. Does this reflect dependencies and prerequisites? If you moved Initiative B before Initiative A, would that make A easier to do (always streamlining a process before automating it, for example)?
20. Step back and look at your sheet of stickies. Does this configuration:
    - Deliver early wins that will build confidence?
    - Continue to inject wins to remind people that the program is working?
    - Ultimately leave your business better off (10x better in some areas) in terms of customer experience, scalability, increased IP, efficiency, and any other important measures that you have identified?

    If so, get started and shuffle your stickies around whenever new information suggests you should. If not, consider what you could remove without reducing the ultimate benefits.

The ambition section provides your roadmap to a better operation and helps you shuffle the portfolio to fit within the best resourcing plan.

It's important to note that what you produce is a living, breathing document. You should return to it whenever you feel the need, at least every quarter. The world changes, and you don't want to be left behind.

TECHNOLOGIES—IN PLAIN LANGUAGE

In the last chapter, we talked about using building bricks to forge your business's operating system. Now that you have your roadmap, it's time to get serious about finding the best bricks to build with. There are, of course, a gazillion choices, many of which you'll already be familiar with. In this section, I debunk some myths and give you the skinny on some of the more talked-about technologies.

AI

Alan Turing led the team of scientists that invented the Enigma Machine in the early days of World War II. Enigma was a computer—a room-sized box of cogs and valves—that decoded thousands of Axis radio messages. In so doing, Turing's team saved millions of lives. Enigma hastened the end of the war by making D-Day possible.

But Turing didn't stop there. When he published "Computing Machinery and Intelligence" in 1950, he couldn't have imagined how seminal his paper (and its "imitation game" thought experiment) would be, nor how misused his term "artificial intelligence" would become.

AI is a technology concerned with finding needles in haystacks of information. The more data, the bigger the mystery and the less likely we are to know where the answers lie. If we think there are answers to our questions in that haystack, we can use AI to seek them out. No guarantees, but you never know till you try.

I first dabbled with AI while creating a route-planning solution. AI turned out to be the wrong approach, and we found a better way. The reason, we learned, was that we lacked for data. When Google launched their free version—Google Maps—over a decade later, they thrived. Because they had the data.

AI's been around a long time, and we now have more data than ever before—more than we know what to do with. The technology has moved on from *2001: A Space Odyssey*'s and *Blade Runner's* androids to become mainstream. You can use AI yourself today. In fact, you do—every time you do a Google search, scan Amazon's catalogue, or read a job posting suggested by LinkedIn.

The term has been co-opted by the tech press to describe practically every novel use of computing that's been released in the last decade. If we're to avoid another cliché, we should distinguish between AI for machine learning and good old-fashioned software engineering.

Many problems have known solutions, established rules and formulae that we can instruct a computer to follow. That's what programmers have been doing since Turing's day. It's how your insurance premiums are calculated, your bank balance updated, your salary is paid—99 percent of the things you use a computer for. If we know a good enough way to solve these problems, we simply program it.

If, on the other hand, the problem is more complex than contemporary math can address, or the number of variables is too massive to brute force, we can program our computers to attempt a solution, understand the difference between success and failure, and keep adjusting the formula till they get it right. That's the exact same process by which humans have tried and learned for, like, ever. But you see, computers can simply do this much, much faster. This speed of trial, error, and learning brings many new solutions into the realm of possibility.

So please apply a pinch of salt the next time you read an article on AI. Ask yourself whether the solution is being learned or was already known by its developers.

Consider AI when you know the questions you need to answer and have access to a haystack of information in which you have good reason to believe those answers lie.

Big data

What do you call a haystack of information? That's right—big data.

Digital storage used to be a premium technology. Hard drives were expensive, slow, and sounded as though you'd released a bag of bolts inside a laundry dryer. But that all changed in the late aughts when new approaches allowed massive amounts of data to be stored at low cost. Then flash storage increased access speeds significantly.

At the same time, a billion people were busy acquiring pocket cameras that could actually make phone calls. And wi-fi technology provided avenues for remote devices of all kinds to send data to some big disk.

If this data had been stored as atoms, it would have made for the biggest slag heap on the planet. Instead, we just built data centers.

Big data was born.

Great! Now we can store information about practically everything we do and choose to share, anywhere we go, and what we spend. What's more, we've got all kinds of sensors measuring other stuff.

But what to do with it?

Progress is a process of convergence. It's rare that a single technology makes for major change. But when several technologies emerge at the same time, you get the printing press, YouTube, and the iPhone. In this case, the convergence of massive, inexpensive high-speed storage, pocket computing, and ubiquitous urban networking gave birth to big data.

And we had AI to help us make sense of all that stuff we stored up—just in case it might be useful.

Big data and AI is a marriage made in heaven (perhaps). Like a horse and carriage, as Sinatra would say.

We're still discovering problems for this solution to solve. Likely always will be.

Consider big data if you believe that there are hidden secrets that will give you a jump on the market, or if you manage a very large number of devices and can achieve real economies by increasing fault tolerance.

Blockchain

Blockchain is a technology that offers unimpeachable shared data.

It does this by capturing a ledger of events and storing them in a database that is replicated across many database servers.

The promise of blockchain is to make faking, tampering, or other deceit impossible. Since many people own copies of the same data, no individual or minority group is able to fabricate history by changing the ledger.

Its many supporters are excited by the potential for blockchain to provide the "Internet of Truth." Whenever a vote is cast, a unit of currency changes hands, a property transaction completed, or a product is passed on to the next phase of the supply chain, that change is recorded forever.

The technology is synonymous with cryptocurrency, but that is just one of many use cases, albeit the one that has hit the headlines. Cryptocurrency is somewhat tainted in the public's eyes, but do not make the mistake of applying that taint to the underlying technology.

The underlying technical approach to sharing the data relies on the trustees' ability to invest in significant computing costs, a model that will likely not scale to fulfill the "Internet of Truth" ideal. But if the appeal of this promise is as attractive as many people think, someone somewhere will solve the technical challenges.

Blockchain doesn't have to deliver this nirvana to be useful. IBM, Walmart, and J.P. Morgan have invested significant amounts in recent years to test the value of "private" blockchains.

Consider blockchain when you have an opportunity to share data with a consortium for mutual benefit. Your supply chain may be a perfect example.

The Cloud

You know what the cloud is, right? It's a bunch of servers in someone else's big data center facility. You've no idea what those people do about security, so there's no way you'd put your data on one of those servers.

Think again.

The means to generate affordable electricity, source natural gas, and pipe water to our homes have been beyond the individual consumer. So infrastructure has been created to do this for us—at massive economies of scale—and we receive the bill every so often for what we use. No matter that governments often fund these services out of our taxes. What's more important than keeping warm (or cool) and hydrated?

The cloud is computing from a faucet.

Computing began this way. Even big business could not afford to own the early room-sized computers. Everyone rented time from IBM *et al.* or paid for payroll services. Computing power was a utility of sorts. Then another generation got used to having a big clunker in front of them. Desks got bigger.

Now we have all the computing power in our pockets. Except it isn't. Speech recognition, for example, takes a lot of computing horsepower, so Siri and Alexa live up in the clouds. Many apps (taking their cue from Salesforce[30]) are hosted up there too. And if you want to build your own software, you simply rent a server at pennies a day, start her up in the morning, and shut her down at night.

It's much more economical to manage one giant computer than thousands of small ones. Some of those economies are passed on to the customer, and cloud margins are the industry's way of overcoming the consumerization of computers and the consequent erosion of hardware margins to near zero. And just like your July A/C bill, you'll need to monitor your use of "unlimited computing."

Computing from a faucet then. Or a fire hose when you need it.

Some—and I'm one of them—argue that the convenience and variable expense model is worth paying for. Utility computing—combined with the galaxy of cloud services now available—has lowered barriers to entry into the software industry. When you build in the cloud, you're building on the shoulders of a giant stack, which means you only need

30 Salesforce. Salesforce Inc. *https://www.salesforce.com/, accessed June 30, 2019.*

to build the part at the top of your solution. Time savings and risk avoidance galore.

That's the biggest single reason there's never been a better time for innovation.

Consider the cloud for every computing need—after you've gotten comfortable with your security strategy.

If you're sold on the cloud—congratulations.

If you're not, I'm guessing it's a trust issue? Are you simply not comfortable with placing your data, your crown jewels, in someone else's building? If so, I strongly urge you to research the matter. Fact is that you'll never get close to the physical security of a data center if you house your servers on-premise. And digital security is your responsibility whether you're on-premise, at home, or on a data center.

I covered security at length in Chapter Seven, but for now, here are some highlights:

1. Develop a robust security posture.
2. Get comfortable that this posture will be safe, probably safer, in a data center.
3. Understand the leverage for your software that comes with using cloud-only services.
4. Begin some work—low data risk if you prefer—in the cloud.
5. Respond to the lessons you learn.

Wherever you compute, compute well!

Cloud services

Remember the technology stack, that pile of software and hardware bricks that makes every application possible? When you embark on any software development, you need to know what bricks you will need to assemble to get the job done. Many of the bricks will already exist—either built by your organization or, more likely, by a third party. Creating new bricks is more costly than reusing existing, tested, proven bricks, and the more you can reuse, the less you have to create. Reuse is the single biggest driver of the software revolution of the last thirty-five years.

Reuse before you reinvent.

The cloud provides two advantages. We discussed the first above—utility computing at the turn of a faucet. Reuse is the second.

The cloud offers a bewildering variety of software and hardware for you to reuse—if you are building software in the cloud. This is important to understand as it may be the factor that helps you overcome your cloud objections.

The cloud allows computing services to be built in layers. If you're building an Internet of Things (IoT) solution, sensors and their data may already be available. If you're building a web or smartphone app, you will be able to call upon existing user interface components and programming frameworks (approaches that make coding much more efficient). All this in addition to the computing and storage provided by the cloud utility.

You may have heard the terms IaaS, PaaS and, SaaS. These are simply layers in the cloud stack that build on each other to offer a more complete solution.

You can use any of these elements whenever your software has a connection to the cloud.

SaaS	Software as a Service Fully functioning application Customers: Business application users
PaaS	Platform as a Service O/S and dev environment included and managed Customers: Developers
IaaS	Infrastructure as a Service Virtual hardware Includes storage Customers: want to manage; alternative to on-premise

Each level in the cloud stack serves different customers

Bottom line is that you should be comfortable that you fully understand the implications of your decision on whether or not to build in the cloud—weigh any concerns with security against the connectivity and productivity benefits the cloud offers. Then make the compromise you're comfortable with.

Consider when you want to do the bare minimum work to build new technologies.

Databases come in many flavors

Databases are places for storing information for a specific purpose.

If it's that simple, why are there so many names—data warehouses, data lakes, data this, that, and the other? Unless you're seeking to become a data guru, the next few paragraphs will tell you all you need to know about data storage.

We impose structure on information to make it more useful. Standard layouts speed up storage and retrieval; aggregation and pre-calculation speeds up reporting and analysis. To do this, we just need to know how the information is to be used in general terms.

Text documents, databases, digital music, and images are the most common data structures. They enable software to better present the contents for our interpretation. That software could be a database system, the file system on your device, a photo app, a video player, or any number of other things. We introduced the stack in Chapter Two and looked deeper into its use in Chapter Eight. Since any useful software needs data, some of the elements in any given stack will be concerned with the management and display of data.

Transaction databases are used by most business systems to store events. What happened, when it happened, and how much it was worth. Orders, customer calls, website visits, IoT device events, security penetration attempts—they're all transactions. These databases should be optimized for fast storage and retrieval of event records. They can also support basic reporting—lists of information. If you're into more advanced analysis, you'll need something else....

Data warehouses are places where data goes to be analyzed. The data is brought over from somewhere else—a transaction system, files, or the internet—and pre-processed to make it more amenable to analysis. Then it sits and waits. It doesn't change. It just waits until somebody has a question.

A **data lake** is a data warehouse of raw—unstructured—data. Most information does not come ready structured. Unstructured data is a way to gather and store that information in its natural state before we know what to do with it. Pseudo-AI algorithms can help discover patterns and, perhaps, create valuable insight.

When you have an idea of what you're looking for but not exactly where it is, you go **data mining**. Algorithms exist to support this (back to those AI-ish pattern-matching things again) but mining is usually an iterative process involving as much wetware as software.

And that's it—data storage in a box.

Encryption

Digitization means we can instantly share information with one or a billion people for free. That's been the heart of the digital revolution. Whether it's Facebook, YouTube, Twitter, or a hundred *cc*s on your emails, it costs us nothing to pass information along.

Mostly this is great, but there are, of course, times when it's a bad thing. When we need to be comfortable that our information is reaching those—and only those—we intend. Hence information security.

Encryption is one of the basic tools we deploy to reduce the risk of information falling into unintended hands. It's a set of techniques that make it harder for someone to interpret data that they're not authorized to have.

When you push send on an encrypted email, your text is converted into a mishmash of digits that's only readable by folks who have a special "key," usually a number with 256 digits. When your email is received, that key is used to unscramble your message. The reader is not even aware that it was scrambled.

The most critical data relates to security access itself—usernames, and particularly passwords, that allow the holders to access systems. Any confidential data can be encrypted at rest or in transit—when stored in memory or disk or when travelling across any network. That means that if someone does hack into your network and escapes with some data, it will be of no use to them unless they can "crack the code" and decrypt it.

Simple and brilliant, encryption has been around for 2500 years—invented by the Spartans—and those unintended hands have been trying to unscramble information ever since. That's what Turing's Enigma machine did. Computing encryption began in the early '70s as a response to the potential theft of digitized data. Encryption technology has been racing neck-and-neck with unscrambling technology ever since.

And here's something you need to know. Brute-force techniques allow computers to "guess" at that magic number, the 256-digit key. The more computing power you have, the more guesses you can make in a given time. And quantum computing is about to unleash massively greater amounts of computing power into the market.

In other words, encryption may not survive as a robust defense mechanism. Watch this space.

Information security

I've covered information security earlier in the book—see "In essence: All a business leader needs to know about security." **(p. 193)**

You may also want to check the "encryption" and "quantum computing" sections above and below.

Internet of Things (IoT)/ M2M

IoT—the Internet of Things—offers insight through connectivity. We know the internet as an entity that has connected our devices—computers and phones—for decades. IoT was enabled by the massive growth in network infrastructure that occurred during the aughts and by miniaturized network technology. This combination allows us to connect with equipment far beyond personal devices. Simple, compact computing hardware now enables monitoring and remote control of billions of devices, from activating your car or your furnace to performing diagnostics on laundry equipment to monitoring the health of crops and livestock.

If your business has anything to do with things that require monitoring or maintenance of any kind, IoT may offer significant benefits. Those things could be equipment—photocopiers, laundry machines, vehicles—or agricultural—health of livestock or crops. They could be people—smartphones offer health monitoring for all ages.

All you need is the right device and a network connection. Reliable and affordable backend infrastructure—collection points, data capture, and analysis—is at the near-commodity level so you don't have to build this yourself.

What are the "things" in your business—equipment, assets and, yes, people?

Consider IoT if a better understanding of real live events in your customer base or asset base would allow you to radically improve service, predict and preempt problems, or repair failures faster.

Be aware that many IoT projects will take several years to pay back the initial costs, especially if you are upgrading equipment that is already in the field. For this reason, it's extra important to understand the outcomes you are pursuing and how the investment will pay back.

M2M is, essentially, a component technology of IoT. Not surprisingly, it describes any two (or more) machines that communicate with each other over any network (not only the internet). There are other subtleties you can research if you want to become an expert.

Quantum computing

The original computers were mechanical, from the abacus to the Enigma machine. The second generation of computers was electronic, built on the storage and processing of information as zeroes and ones. Quantum computing uses zeroes and ones…and twos and threes. That's way more dramatic than it sounds.

The technology has been in the lab for decades as scientists have solved problems from cooling to basic physics challenges that are way above my pay grade.

While the performance of binary technology has improved at the rate Gordon Moore predicted in 1965—doubling every eighteen months—quantum computing is predicted to be *one thousand times* as efficient.

That kind of sea change offers the ability to solve whole new classes of problems that require computing power way beyond the fastest binary computers.

We've all heard of super computers. Think of quantum computers as super-duper computers. You're unlikely to buy one any time soon, but keep an eye out for radically more powerful computing services from IBM, Google, Amazon, and others over the next five to ten years.

Three things you can keep an eye out for:

- New classes of solution for your innovation portfolio to contemplate.
- Lower cost of computing services.
- The need for an entirely new approach to computer security—see my blurb on encryption for more on this.

More Technologies—In Plain Language

If these were helpful, check the booksite for more.

STAIRWAY TO WHERE?

Your stairway to technology mastery demonstrates a path to building new superpowers for your business. Capabilities that offer new strategic and tactical tools for you to fix what's broken today and optimize areas of your business that will differentiate you in the eyes of your customers.

If technology has felt more like free soloing in the past, your stairway should feel like a breeze. I could suggest that you stop reading right here and go off and begin the climb.

But one more thing before you do that. Our final chapter offers up some examples of companies that have already climbed that stairway. Most importantly, they have achieved things that might be helpful to your business.

Continue reading if you're interested in answering the question, "What if we could do that?"

MASTERING TECHNOLOGY—IN A NUTSHELL

Mastering technology is about embracing six key principles:

- Customer partnership, confident teams, and appropriate pacing in pursuit of generating insights and assets to get work done across your business's community.
- Relentless focus on the puzzle you help your customer to solve. What they need to get done, how you help them today, and how you could expand that help tomorrow—with increased insight and automation.
- Don't less the moss grow—stay within striking distance of the leading technologies in your space.
- Extending comfort zones—essential if your business and colleagues are to grow.
- Embracing failure—but only as a means to learning.
- Mastery of selected technology superpowers—ranking the importance of differentiation, agility, resilience, insight, and automation.

The first step on your stairway to tech mastery is to establish what's wrong—aspects of your business that need to improve, perhaps to become the best in your industry. You can diagnose your business by asking questions about your vital signs, migraine work, resilience, and complexity.

The stairway model provides a simple tool with which you can map out goals for each of the key areas—foundation, maintenance, customer, confidence, cadence, insight, and assets. Every business operates in a specific context—reset or turnaround, operational upgrade, and building on existing foundations to name but three. Your roadmap will be uniquely your own, and it'll likely change before you're done building.

I've offered a couple of additional resources to help you figure this out.

My twenty questions for the new innovation officer have been developed in the course of working with over 250 businesses. Since I regularly cull questions, the list is a top-twenty, designed for any leader approaching a renewal challenge—joining a new business or team, or adjusting to a new strategy.

And in the no-BS spirit in which this book is written, I also offer my view on topical technologies—in plain language, of course. The list includes AI, big data, blockchain, the cloud, cloud services, databases, encryption, information security, IoT, and quantum computing.

❐❐

Booksite extras at *www.trustingtechnologybook.com/chapter9* include more Technologies—In Plain Language and the workbook for all tests.

CHAPTER TEN

YOUR NEXT BUSINESS

Picture Your Business in a Future of Technology Mastery

In which you'll envision your business boldly going where others have gone before.

If you're like me, you read business books to help you picture a better future. Where can you go and how might you get there? What thinking patterns, techniques, and processes could you apply? What inspirational paragons might you consider? If you could only model their success, then bingo—you, too, could be featured in a business book!

Yet we all know that these paragons boil down to the same twenty-five businesses. Apple, Google, Facebook, and Amazon have hogged the limelight in this century. If you go back forty years it was Toyota, Xerox, and 3M; Bell Labs and AT&T in the '50s.

The scale, reach, and budget of these companies make them unlike 99.9 percent of businesses. And your business is probably in that 99.9 percent. So I decided to draw upon less famous examples.

The problem with these cases is that we go into areas that the cases themselves are reluctant to be associated with. For two good reasons—either the stories began with failures, or success was based on some secret sauce best not shared with competition.

For these reasons, most of this chapter's paragons are anonymous. I hope you find their stories no less valuable.

I've been honored to participate in some of these stories. As a result, I've been privy to many details and can testify to the passion of the teams responsible for their outcomes. Expertise was important in all cases, but the paramount quality of these folks was a determination to solve the puzzles, a readiness to be wrong, and a passion for learning their way to success. In every case, this success created confident teams that have gone on to even greater achievements.

If I've been able to convince you to master technology, consider these stories to be inspiration. If you're still on the fence, consider them to be evidence for my case. Either way, I'm going to share achievements that you could replicate.

I hope this helps you form a better picture of your business of the future. Most importantly, I hope these examples inspire you to take the next step, to get started, ramp up, or finish the job.

TECHNOLOGY AND SHAREHOLDER RETURNS

Let's start at the top. The ten best stocks between 2007–2017 yielded returns in the 17-50x range. One hundred dollars invested in this basket of stocks in 2007 became $2846 in 2017. I wish I'd had this list in December 2006.

Stock	10-yr Return	Industry
Netflix	4948%	Media Services
EnviroStar	4395%	Commercial laundry and dry-cleaning equipment; industrial boilers
GTT Communications	4371%	Telecom and internet provider
Trex	2447%	Wood-alternative decking and railing
Tucows	2438%	Internet and telecom provider
ZAGG	2360%	Consumer electronics
Mitek Systems	2195%	Sound equipment
National Beverage	1834%	Soft drinks
XPO Logistics	1762%	Transportation and logistics
MarketAxess Holdings	1707%	Electronic trading platform

The ten best stocks between 2007-2017

It's a refreshingly diverse collection—three are technology product or service providers, two are in consumer electronics, and the balance range between media services, construction materials, commercial laundry and heating equipment, soft drinks, and logistics.

Some of these companies were near start-ups, newly listed in 2007. Some had been around for decades. It's comforting to note that rapid growth can happen at any age.

Netflix delivered the biggest return—almost fifty times—with a business that has invested around one third of its profits in technology every year. In other words, they have generated around $2.80 in profit for every $1 invested in tech. In Netflix's case, the investment has been in infrastructure and applications. The have also massively leveraged OPT (Other People's Technology)—by some estimates, 15–20 percent of total internet traffic worldwide is used by Netflix customers.

In most cases, growth for these stocks was not evenly distributed throughout the ten-year period. There was a flat phase—perhaps preparatory in hindsight—followed by a steep acceleration. Then a period of stabilization, even decline.

SEC filings disclose some clues about their paths to success. We're interested here in the role technology use played in that success:

- MarketAxess enshrined their intellectual property in software.
- Netflix differentiated themselves from Blockbuster, cable, and satellite with digital distribution of their product. The fact that they leveraged OPT meant that they didn't have to carry the investment their competitors had made in infrastructure.
- GTT and Tucows implemented that same infrastructure—the internet.
- Mitek, ZAGG, and XPO equipped their employees with the best technology to share insights and automate work.
- Envirostar and Trex were technology leaders in their space.
- National Beverage is the only business in the top ten that did not highlight the role of technology in their growth.

Typically, these businesses generated several dollars of profit for each dollar invested in technology.

Clearly, no business performs at these levels without a strong workforce and excellent leadership. What's clear is that these businesses all placed prudent bets on technology in supporting and, in some cases, driving the collective performance.

PARABLES OF TECH

Bringing the future closer

Three months is a long time in the fashion industry. When you're one of the world's largest footwear manufacturers, you have to bring lots of new designs to market every season. And when you are building the most advanced footwear technology, your design team can churn out thousands of designs every year.

But you can only ship 10 percent of those designs. How do you decide?

"Faster" is how. The industry took around eighteen months to move a shoe design from concept to the retail shelf. That means the design team had to anticipate the fashion a year and a half out. Any way to cut three or more months off that interlude would create competitive advantage.

Faster manufacturing could help, but the real opportunity was in the design process.

Design is a visceral art. You have to see an object, feel it, rotate it in your hands. In some cases, you have to smell it (shoes excepted). The traditional design process was to sketch a concept, decide whether to progress the idea, create colorful images of said ideas, lay out hundreds on a large table and decide which to progress further. Only a few reached the physical prototype touchy-feely stage.

The opportunity to accelerate design lay in this decision-making process. Digital design had already revolutionized the car industry. Sketching technologies had matured, 2-D to 3-D was proven, and manufacturing was adopting digital blueprints. Once designs were digital, they could be visualized earlier and more conveniently.

Could these new techniques be applied to the footwear industry? Our heroes decided to find out.

Fast forward a year or so to 2006 and picture the footwear design team sitting in a room looking at the retail shelves stocked with their product line—for 2007. The wall was a digital illusion but had all of the fidelity of the real thing—more than enough to experiment with hundreds of scenarios in a day. Choices made, prototypes could be delivered within a few weeks.

This work succeeded because it applied practices that had been developed and proven in other industries. It delivered new insights by bringing the future forward.

The thinking room—making everything visible

Consider that life-size digital simulation of the retail footwear environment again.

Imagine walking up and tapping a virtual shoe to see the marketing plan and sales history for that product line. Dragging the shoe to a more prominent position in the store. Then bringing in the retail buyer and wowing them with the product placement potential.

If you have the data to generate insight, we have the technology to build your very own minority report.

The concept of the visualization room, or space, has been around for a while. We built the Alias Visualization Studio in the early aughts to experiment with—and demonstrate—the power of digital visualization for decision-making. Essentially, it was an 1800-square-foot meeting space packed with projectors, projection walls, and interactive SMART devices. The combination of full-size, rotatable 3-D images, digital whiteboarding, and visual facilitation proved to be a remarkable accelerant for decision-making.

The practices we developed owed much to the pioneering work of David Sibbet and Tom Wujec. The Studio attracted a number of business celebrities and prompted many organizations to build their own.

Technology has advanced dramatically since we built the Viz Studio—you could build a visualization room today with ease.

The Alias Visualization Studio, c. 2004

Masters of the fast follow

I've advocated following in the shoes of others in this book—leveraging their experiments and building something even better. No one does this better than Samsung—masters of the fast follow.

When you look at their catalog of patents, it seems disrespectful to call Samsung the best followers, though I regard that as a compliment. But when you check out their market cap, I doubt they care what we call them.

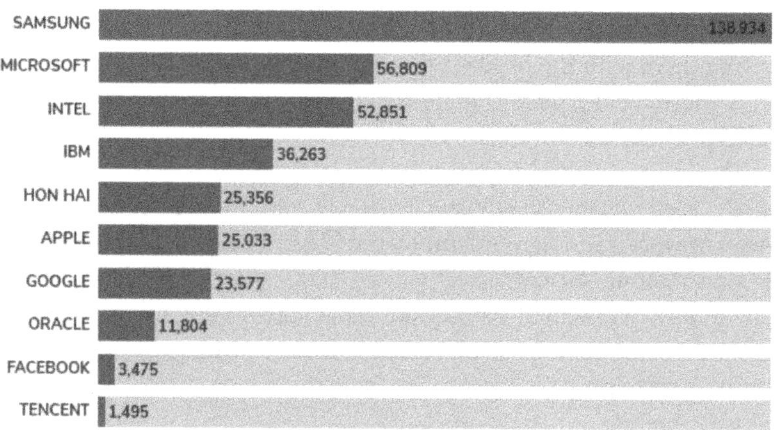

Tech industry patent bragging rights

Samsung was founded in 1938 as an insurance company and dabbled in food exporting on their way to becoming and electronics manufacturer in 1969. They've been pivoting for nearly a century.

The company's recent secret sauce has been to outsource market risk. They've watched their competition create new products, pick the best horses, and bet big on improving on those original designs. "Improve" could mean cheaper, faster, or smaller (remember that small wins in electronics). Bigger unit sales are the result.

Samsung's patent catalog is testimony to another secret sauce—they innovate lower down the stack at the component level. This gives them the bricks to assemble into new products at lightning speed. Their first smartphone was on the market within a year of the iPhone—which was a well-kept secret until Jobs announced its launch. Samsung may have had a head start on the other fast followers—they are one of Apple's biggest component suppliers.

Samsung is not alone in the world of fast-follow winners—I've already cited Facebook, Google, and Microsoft in that category.

Intriguingly, the Korean giant is now being threatened at its own game by Huawei and other Chinese competitors—so much so that Samsung's CEO has been quoted as saying it's time for them to become a first mover. Sounds like another pivot is on the horizon.

Becoming software—transforming the economics of your business

There are two ways to create a software business. The first is to speculate on building the product you think will fly, then finding enough actual buyers to thrive. You'll often give it away—metaphorically or actually—to remove early resistance to the sale. Once you have a viable product, you can price it for the market and launch a business. Before that time, you'll need to beg or borrow (don't steal) to keep your experiment afloat.

The second way is to deliver your solution with consulting. You find customers that pay for the value you provide, deliver your solution, and make profit to launch your business. As you deliver to more customers, you'll learn how to improve your solution, how to market it, and how to describe the tricky parts. Since your startup is funded by customer revenue, we call this bootstrapping.

And if you can describe the way you do something, it can be captured in software, remember?

At some point, you'll face a decision. If, as I'd hope, you've built a profitable consulting business, you may choose to hold. But I'd urge you to consider the next level of growth—capturing your IP in code and becoming a software business.

Consulting and software are both information businesses; the economics for both involve salary, some overhead, and profit. But the ratios vary. A robust services business should achieve gross margins of 35–45 percent[31] while a well-run, mature software business comes in at around 75–85 percent.

In short, software is more profitable than consulting for the simple reason that the software enshrines expertise in process and data. Once that's done, you can deliver that expertise at massive scale with near-zero

31 This ignores strategic work where the big brands like McKinsey and Bain pull in over 60 percent

marginal cost. To scale a consultancy, you need to hire more consultants, at significant marginal cost.

Consulting to software is a proven path to success. Some founders set out with this intent, other consulting leaders stumble across the option. Very few businesses achieve 100 percent software revenues—most complex tasks will continue to need some level of consulting for software integration, customization, and training. But whether you develop software to sell or simply provide your consultants with software tools to handle the time-consuming grunt work, I urge any consultancy to consider becoming software.

Information—monetized

Big data came about when we began digitizing massively more information and it became practical to capture and store that information. In other words, big data happened because we could.

Just as technology history is strewn with solutions looking for problems, we've run the risk of creating vast stores of data that's looking for a purpose. I'd advocate that you should know that purpose before you buy the storage.

Data records events. Business orders, your weight on a given day, photos and videos of families and friends.

Your business no doubt uses data to maintain your ledger of transactions. The new frontier lies in your ability to monitor—and therefore understand and analyze—many more types of events. Beyond sales, deliveries, and support tickets, IoT captures state changes from sensors in the field and CTV captures security video.

The question is what to do with it all? Specifically, how can your business get a return on prospective data initiatives?

There are three principal ways to monetize data:

1. Reduce expense: understand more and make better decisions that save costs.
2. Generate sales: track customers' buying patterns and entice them to buy more.
3. Create revenue streams: curate and sell data to help others do either of the above.

The finance industry was the first IT business. Since the early '60s, it's really been about moving numbers around and providing analysts with information that helps them make profitable decisions.

Information monetization has taken hold in other industries. Energy and utilities manage vast arrays of assets spread across states and countries. Better information reduces risk and maintenance cost. For instance, pharmaceuticals must be stored within a given temperature range if they are to maintain their efficacy. By deploying IoT in their supply chains, pharma distributors are able to monitor the temperature of products in transit to reduce waste.

Tech is, of course, born digital with an embarrassment of built-in data. Some tech companies use this data in the design and improvement of their products. If software plays no role in your product today, consider whether the inherent traceability could provide another reason to adopt.

Data monetization doesn't happen as a side effect. It is a matter of strategy and deliberate intent. GFNorte, a Mexican bank, achieved over 200 percent ROI when they created a data monetization business with its own profit and loss statement.[32]

Creating a cyclone—the patience of an innovator

James Dyson built 5,127 prototypes before he learned how to create and control a cyclone. And it only took him five years. That's three experiments a day, every day. Four a day if you take a little time off. Dyson calls this kind of patience the serendipity of persistence.

What Apple did for the personal computer and phone, Dyson did for the vacuum, hand dryer, and household heating and cooling. His DS100 had the design feel of Jobs's '97 iMac re-launch, yet Dyson shipped in '93.

And Dyson shares Jobs's approach to asking the customer. He resisted distributor opposition to the transparent "basket" because he thought it neat that the user could see all the gunk the vacuum's collected. Five billion dollars in revenues with over five thousand engineers and scientists suggests he was right.

32 Jose A. Murillo, Yuri Levin, Mikhail Nediak, and Ivan A. Sergienko, "How One Company Made Its Analytics Investment Pay Off," *Harvard Business Review*, last modified January 22, 2018, *https://hbr.org/2018/01/how-one-company-made-its-analytics-investment-pay-off.*

He talks freely about the company's approaches. The company hires engineers and upskills them to be designers. Combining both skills speeds up the product creation process. You can find that process here:

https://www.jamesdysonfoundation.com/content/dam/pdf/Standalone_DesignProcess.pdf

After launching his business, Dyson hired a CEO and went back to the lab to indulge his love of invention. His foundation funds research into cancer and meningitis.

You might say he cleaned up.

Changing industries

Sometimes you happen upon an opportunity to create or change an industry.

For a century, the UK transit industry was built on a city-by-city basis. Large corporations with thousands of double-decker buses moved commuters to and from work, shoppers to and from High Street, and students to school. When the industry was deregulated, start-up companies were given a chance to compete with these massive incumbents. The barrier to entry was the capital cost of the vehicles, but the key to survival was in the planning and scheduling of the bus routes. New entrants needed insight into which parts of the city were underserved by the existing services, and how their new service could build a loyal passenger following.

Scheduling vehicles was an expertise. Skilled planners would sit with massive sheets of paper, pencil, and eraser and use their decades of experience to trial-and-error their way to a new schedule. You can imagine that once planned, the routes would not change without good reason, often for decades.

The start-ups needed agility. And that's where Wootton Jeffreys's BUSMAN came in. We had bus-planning software that the schedulers could run on their desktop PC. It was fast enough that they could experiment with several plans before locking in. And they could modify those routes after a few months on the road. It's gratifying to have customers tell you that they could not have survived without you.

Eventually, the large city companies jumped on board. They were harder to convince because they'd operated with paper and pencil for a century. But convince them we did.

The UK transit industry was changed forever. Services improved, competition kept fares down, and the passenger won.

These massive changes were brought about by packaging our route-planning and vehicle-scheduling IP in software that was specifically designed to be accessible to computer newbies.

The style you drive

Your car is a metal box containing hundreds of products—radios, navigation systems, phones, seats, DVD players. Oh, and the engine and other mechanics to move the box from A to B.

The automotive industry competes on technology and design. New models every year with new features to entice you to upgrade. Major redesigns every few years for every line in the catalog—and it costs around $1 billion to launch each redesign.

Try this—pick your favorite vehicle and spend a few minutes on Google to place photos of the last ten models side by side. You have a snapshot of the design stretching back a couple of decades. Now check out how that design has evolved. Notice the sleeker lines?

Sure, this reflects changing fashions. But you won't be surprised when I say that this manufacturable sleekness was enabled by technology. The car design process used to require hundreds of iterations—dozens of hand-sculpted clay models from tabletop to life-size, thousands of design decisions, followed by endless rancor between designer and engineer as they compromised on a shape that could actually be mass-produced.

At Alias, we were able to revolutionize this industry by providing 2-D and 3-D design technology that shaved months and many millions of dollars off this design process. By creating software around the way the designers worked, we were able to support their process, complement their skills with a host of convenient tools, and create digital representations of complete car designs. These were ready for downstream use in decision-making, manufacturing, and early marketing—it helps to put a concept car on the road before it even exists.

The approaches pioneered in the automotive industry have been adopted across the panorama of industrial design. I'll bet dollars to donuts that your car was designed with Alias (now Autodesk) technology, and you likely own a hundred products that were styled with the same tools.

Those were exciting, industry-changing times.

The 10x-ers

If you skipped over Chapter Nine's "From +1 to 10x thinking in three steps," go back and read it. If not, it still bears rereading.

So much of what we have to achieve has to do with the goals we set. Set conservatively and you can rely on limited success. Set ambitiously and you remove the artificial constraints that impose those limits. You get to choose where you sit in that range. Maybe you begin with a couple of 10x initiatives in your innovation portfolio. If they materialize, you can up the ante.

To be candid, 10x-ing is not achievable in most cases. And if it was easy, everyone would be doing it. But the mindset of asking how you can dramatically improve the way something gets done is at polar opposites to the "fix the next bug" approach. With 10x thinking, you can conjure up new ways that can easily be two times easier, faster, or cheaper. And what's so bad about 2x?

Here's another simple example of how a software company 10x-ed the value that came out of their development shop in five steps:

1. Assess the usage of product features that had been newly released in the prior year.
2. Establish how much of the associated development time was spent solving problems that the customers didn't care about—on features that customers didn't use.
3. Invest some of the time saved in validating next year's features to cull the roadmap.
4. Invest more of that time in coding, testing, and diagnosis tools to speed up the dev process.
5. Build and ship next year's roadmap.

Simple, eh?

Yet look at the numbers gathered—65 percent of last year's dev effort was wasted on features that customers didn't use. Coincidentally, the validation process culled the roadmap to around one third of its original length. What's more, the new dev tools saved so much time that code could be churned out at over three times the previous rate.

One-third dev effort at over three times the speed is nearly a 10x improvement. Bingo!

Upskilling

James Dyson trained as an architect, became an engineer, and developed a designer ethic. He now trains his engineers to become designers.

Just as a technology's adoption progresses along the Rogers curve, its use quickly grows beyond the techie community. As more and more people adopt, diverse perspectives engage in sculpting the technology. When Adobe pioneered design tools, designers brought an eye for style and usability to the original engineers' perspective.

Marketing creatives have taken hold of the look and feel of the internet. If you have any doubt of the aesthetic value of this, hop over to the Wayback Machine[33] and remind yourself what a few '90s websites looked like.

For these reasons, business technology has extended beyond the walls of the IT department. Just as James Dyson trains his engineers to become designers, it's important that your colleagues put their stamp on the role of technology in your business.

But there's a bigger point here. The potential for technology has always outstripped the supply of "skilled" technicians. The schools simply can't churn out enough techies to do all the work. This leaves you with two options:

1. Move at the pace you can hire staff with "proven experience" in tech.
2. Create expertise in the people you already have.

Before you decide to do anything, I encourage you to shed any stigma about technology, recognize the ambitious talent you already have on staff and create an environment where they can practice, fail, and learn.

I'm also a big believer in giving "business" people tech experience and tech people business experience. Choose your mechanism—project assignment, secondment (a more formal kind of job rotation), career change—but propagating the marriage of business and technology skills is essential if we're to develop multi-disciplinary leaders and close the "skills gap."

OK—I'll step away from the soapbox now.

33 "Wayback Machine," *https://web.archive.org/*, accessed July 1, 2019.

Employee experience

I've been beating the customer experience drum throughout this book, but there's another side to this coin.

Employee experience hasn't really been a thing in the tech world until quite recently. While consumer tech needed to adopt a lightweight "user friendly" design, business systems were things we used at work, not for pleasure. This has excused much criminally bad design. That's why we get screens that look like database dumps, forms that require three days in a classroom to comprehend, and processes that take fifteen mouse clicks when two should suffice. Software that's not designed for people to use.

If a business is to serve its community of customers and colleagues, those people will communicate through the same technology. That means they should share the same experience. Usability equals.

When PwC surveyed twelve thousand employees,[34] they found that 73 percent felt they knew of tools that could help them do their jobs better. Yet while 90 percent of C-Suite members think they pay attention to employees' needs with new tech, 47 percent of the employees couldn't see that. That's a 40 percent miss. Worth thinking about?

Furthermore, most employees are eager to learn more tech. Two-thirds associate improving their tech skills with career advancement, and most would be prepared to spend 10 percent of their time learning the stuff.

Glint is one of the new generations of enterprise software providers that designs their product with user ease and insight in mind.

Glint's mission is to help employees be happier and more successful at work. The software consults employees and helps managers to uncover insights and take action to improve engagement and transform their business. The business was founded in 2013 and acquired by Microsoft—through LinkedIn—five years later for $400 million. Not a bad path, and testament to the importance of connecting colleagues and improving engagement.

CCO Mary Poppen is passionate about the link between employee and customer experience. She says:

---

34 "Our status with tech at work: It's complicated," PwC Consumer Intelligence Series, October 2018, *https://www.pwc.com/us/en/services/consulting/library/consumer-intelligence-series/tech-at-work.html.*

> *"With attrition 12 times more likely for disengaged employees within one year (Glint, 2017) and NPS for customers significantly lower (statistically speaking) for companies with lower employee engagement (Aon Hewitt Manager Survey), it behoves all organizations to step back and take a look at the intersection of employee engagement and customer satisfaction."*[35]

Whether you're buying technology for your colleagues or designing for customers, you cannot deliver the best without regard for the experience of using your technology. This comes from a deep understanding of the job to be done, empathy for the people doing it, engagement with these folks when making design decisions, and a commitment to continual learning on everyone's part.

WHERE DO YOU SEE YOUR BUSINESS IN FIVE YEARS?

My purpose in providing these parables has been to illuminate further ideas for technology in your business. Let's see if I succeeded.

Flip back in your notes and review the roadmap you created in the last chapter. By way of reminder, the blank slate looked like this:

	Step 1	Step 2	Step 3	Step 4	Good enough
Foundation					
Maintenance					
Customer					
Confidence					
Cadence					
Insight					
Assets					

What does *your* roadmap look like?

Look down the Good Enough column and consider whether any of these parables inspire loftier goals. Scan a few of the rows and consider any takeaways. For example:

35 Mary Poppen, "Happy Employees + Happy Customers = Better Business Results," LinkedIn Pulse, July 14, 2017, *https://www.linkedin.com/pulse/happy-employees-customers-better-business-results-mary-poppen.*

Customer: Changing industries, driving your own style, creating a cyclone, monetizing information

Confidence: Upskilling, employee experience

Insight: Bringing the future closer, the thinking room, monetizing information

Assets: Becoming software, mastering the fast follow

Edit your sheet accordingly. Step back and decide whether the overall feel is ambitious enough. Is there enough 10x thinking?

This chapter can only provide a glimpse of what's possible—what you could do by building on the success of others. This roadmap should be a living, breathing document, but I hope you've reached a point where it's ready enough for you to start creating.

THE NEXT STEP ON YOUR STAIRWAY

Much of this book talks about your business, your customers, and your colleagues, but I don't want to wrap up without talking about you.

Ultimately, this book is only as useful as you say it is. The lessons you learn, the people you tell, the recommendations you give.

How can I leave you in the best position to take advantage? I figure I'll be happy if I can help you lock down your next steps to a career of technology mastery. Make sense?

About those reservations

Good. Let's start with me keeping a promise.

Way back in Chapter Three I asked you to review your Great and Good to-do list then take the Reservations Test. Remember? That was before you were a tech master. Here's that chance I promised to revisit those reservations.

What do you see?

Now that you've completed the book, you could go back and take any number of the tests. Your answers to questions like *What if We Could?* may be quite different second time around. You may see different needs when you *Name Your Squad*, new potential for *Where Are You Headed.*

Whatever your conclusions, I hope you've answered the questions in your *Vote of Confidence.*

If you have, then my job is done!

Reservations Revisited Test

Take another look at your Great and Good list. *Before* you look at your old reservations list, write down reasons why you can't make that work.

____

____

____

____

____

Mark the top three reasons with an *X*.

Now compare the new list with your original reservations.

YOUR NEXT BUSINESS—IN A NUTSHELL

Are you tired of reading the same old success stories? In this final chapter, we'll look for inspiration elsewhere. Everyday companies that have gained advantages with technology, from foundation and re-birth to thriving.

We began at the top. The ten best stocks between 2007–2017 yielded returns in the 17-50x range, with an average of 2846 percent.

- Some companies were near-startups, newly listed in 2007. Others had been around for many decades. Rapid growth can happen at any age.
- SEC filings disclose some clues about how these firms leveraged technology. Every single company referred to tech investments in their annual reports.
- Typically, these businesses generate several dollars of profit for each dollar invested in tech.
- Some leverage other people's tech (OPT) to reduce the capital expense required to build their business. Netflix customers, for instance, consume over 15 percent of the world's internet capacity—at no cost to Netflix.

- Many businesses equipped their employees with the best technology to share insights and automate work. Mitek, ZAGG, and XPO.

As for the rest of us, you read tech parables on:

- **10x-ers**—examples of successful 10x thinking
- **Bringing the future closer**—accelerating design decisions
- **The thinking room**—making everything visible
- **Masters of the fast follow**—building on the experiments of others
- **Becoming software**—the benefits of enshrining IP in software
- **Information, monetized**—making data pay
- **Creating a cyclone**—the patience of an innovator
- **Changing industries**—enabling competition in a deregulated world
- **The style you drive**—tech's unseen impact on one hundred things you own
- **Upskilling**—overcoming the skills shortage

Inspiration:

- Which of these parables could apply to you?
- Your final homework is to review and revise the roadmap you created in the last chapter.

Booksite extras at www.trustingtechnologybook.com/chapter10 include the workbook for all tests.

Enough About Your Business—What About You?

FOR THE CEO AND GM

When I've led organizations, I've seen my job as finding the best people, pointing them in the right direction, getting out of their way, and being there to help when they need it. Tough decisions, coaching, resources, and emotional support—that sort of thing. And owning the outcome, good or bad.

If that's how you see your role, allow me to venture that you need to be informed enough to know the direction, flexible enough to encourage experimentation, connected enough to know who you need on the team, and tough enough to stay out of the way.

A few habits to develop and hold on to are:

1. Check what's going on in tech, both inside and outside your industry.
2. Cut some slack when the occasional setback occurs, and instill retrospectives to share what was learned.
3. Build a network of business technology experts that you admire.
4. Enjoy the successes.

This book has focused on helping you become better informed. My intent has been to prompt you to look at your business in a new light.* This new perspective might set you on a course with ambitious goals. Of course, the planning and preparation is the easiest part, and when the rubber hits the road is when the first setbacks occur.

That's the time when you need to be confident that you have all the right people on the bus to do the job at hand. That, in fact, is the single biggest difference I've seen between technology masters and also-rans. Make sure you recognize who else could help and never be afraid to seek another opinion.

* Incidentally, if you are interested in looking at your business in a new light, you might find my 10-Minute Reflections series of interest.[36]

FOR THE AMBITIOUS TECHNOLOGY LEADER

I've coached many technology leaders, and the challenge for most is to marry the needs of business to the capabilities of the technology in their charge. This may manifest itself in difficult communications, lack of clear of goals, over-commitment of resources (especially yourself), or a host of other symptoms.

Becoming a tech leader means taking on much broader scope, and that typically means a bigger team and the associated challenges of organization, delegation, and plate-spinning required to deliver what's needed. If you have followed a technical career path, odds are you got into technology to write code, configure complex networks, or fine-tune massive databases—in other words, some expertise that didn't involve personnel management, recruitment, or delegation.

If you are struggling with these activities, your next step is people mastery. Rounding out the core skills of Learning, Simplifying, Communicating, Changing, Planning, Focusing, Delegating, and Decision-making. The best technology leaders average a four out of five across the board on these skills (no one would be a five anyways). When you get there, you'll be in the "excellent" category.

36 Graham Binks, *10-Minute Reflections: One Month Of Daily Exercises That Will Spark Growth In Your Business* (Scotts Valley, CA: CreateSpace Independent Publishing Platform, May 25, 2017) ; Graham Binks, *10 Minute Reflections: Volume 2: Another Month Of Daily Exercises That Will Spark Growth In Your Business* (Scotts Valley, CA: CreateSpace Independent Publishing Platform, November 25, 2017).

Don't put your audience in a tech coma. This happens when you respond to a simple question with too much information, yet strangely not enough to answer your inquisitor. Here's a test you can try and repeat until perfect:

1. Pick a complex technical topic, such as security strategy or why it takes so long to build good software.
2. Find a non-tech colleague. Your CEO or GM is ideal.
3. Ask for five minutes of their time for them to give you a coaching moment.
4. Explain the topic to them.
5. Ask how you could make that clearer.
6. If it's already clear, ask them how you could make it more interesting.

I'm serious. If you can perfect the art of explaining a complex topic in under five minutes and in terms your non-technical colleagues can understand, you'll be a top 10 percent tech leader.

There isn't room in this book to provide all the advice I'd like to give—I refer you to my *Technology Leaders Handbook*[37] for that—but you're best served in knowing what kind of leader you want to become. Are you jazzed by delivering a hundred projects in a year? Or do you prefer a quiet environment where you can go deep and wrestle a complex problem to the ground? Do you prefer to be called an expert or a leader?

If "expert" is you, think hard before you take on responsibility for a team. If you want to make a broader impact, ask colleagues and customers for help with a 360-degree assessment of your soft skills and decide where you can commit to excelling.

The soft skills are the hardest. They're also the biggest factor in your success as a technology leader.

And if you're interested in shaving years off your learning curve, find a great coach. It'll make your development process a whole lot easier.

37 Graham Binks, "Technology Leader's Handbook," GrahamBinks.com, accessed July 1, 2019, *https://www.grahambinks.com/technology-leaders-handbook/*.

FOR ANY AMBITIOUS BUSINESS LEADER

You just need stuff to work so you can get on with your job, right?

If you'd only known what it was going to take to get the tech do what you needed, you'd never have built your annual plan around it before you saw it working with your own eyes.

Am I wrong?

It's a matter of trust and enlightened self-interest. Your best path to make everyone's job easier is no different from the (non-tech) CEO. Becoming—and staying—aware of the technology vanguard in your field will inspire ideas and give confidence that you can adapt their successes.

The single biggest difference I've seen between tech success and failure has been the alignment between business and tech contributors. Alignment on expectations—what's needed versus what's possible, sharing your business vision with your techie colleagues and partners, and collaborating in compromise as the work plays out.

Clarity is the best investment you will make. Miscommunication is a killer. Fortunately, that's a match made in heaven.

We've all seen the consequences of miscommunication way too often—lots of wasted time and work. It's painful to observe and costly to fix.

Life's potential for ambiguity seems unlimited. You speak—I hear. But did you convey your intent clearly enough? Did I comprehend fully and have an opportunity to challenge the approach and enrich the outcome?

The best way I know to close the communication gap is to make a simple request:

Play that back to me.

Begin with a clear, shared path and you'll be set up for success. As for the rest, you've read the book!

CIAO

That's it—we're done. I said earlier that the challenging part of writing a book is that you never actually meet your reader. You do your best to provide as much value as you can for a huge range of readers and their very distinct circumstances.

All the time I've been writing this book, I've done my best to picture you—my reader—and write as if we were meeting face to face. I hope we get a chance to do that one day.

For now, how about you write a press release that you will issue in five or ten years' time. Write about your current or future business.

Say what you did, then go do it.

Trusting Technology is about adapting to new ways of life and work. Technology merely provides the platform.

When we talk about the challenges of technology, we're really talking about the challenges of improvement; the ways we change and the lessons we learn on our path to making things better.

The problem is that technology offers us so many options. It's bemusing. What areas of our business do we focus on? How can we make them better?

Trusting Technology is a handbook to help business leaders become centered in their focus, approach, and resilience with adopting and adapting technology. You will learn how to:

- Forge rapid communications across your community of customers and staff.
- Feed insights with the information that matters to your colleagues and customers.
- Describe your security strategy in five minutes.
- Capture your business's special sauce to create new assets.
- Navigate a course to your business future with rapid learning and minimalist change.
- Master the art of estimation.
- See your business in a new light and uncover opportunities for improvement.
- Benchmark your organization—any organization—as a tech business.
- Build a platform to keep pace with the innovation needs of your business.

The vital conversation is not really about technology but about the connections it enables and the change it imposes on our comfortably imperfect routine and environment.

The means are not software code and hardware bits, rather systems thinking, empathetic change, rapid learning, and adaptive planning.

This book is about the humanity of advancement feeding the advancement of humanity.

ACKNOWLEDGMENTS

We all embark on intense endeavors at some point in our life. When we do, we should be grateful to those around us for their support, tolerance, and advice.

Writing this book was just such an endeavor for me. In that vein, I am grateful to Ken for his agency, Debra and Elena for their affirming reviews, and Heather for her expert shepherding. My gratitude goes out to my CEO Book Club for their feedback on the drafts—you know who you are. I must also thank Alan, Noah, and Roberta for nudging and cajoling me into taking this on.

I'm especially grateful to Mike for his help in the closing stages, and to Maddie and Hayley for their youthful insight.

And to Dana for her constant encouragement and support.

Thank you all.

ABOUT THE AUTHOR

Graham Binks is an expert in helping businesses get the best out of their technology investments.

Over the course of more than five hundred career projects conducted in a wide range of industries, he has helped countless small, medium, and large organizations to quickly achieve their technology goals under budget and with low risk. His work is focused on helping formulate the best technology roadmap to support business strategy, guiding teams through delivery and assisting leadership to deliver on the plan.

Graham is the CEO of primeFusion Inc and has over thirty years of technology leadership experience in Europe, North America, and Asia. He's spent a decade in CTO and support roles for several software companies, and another decade as CIO in a number of international businesses. Graham's client list spans four continents and includes Nike, Procter & Gamble, Citigroup, JP Morgan, and Eurotunnel.

He writes and speaks as often as he can on the union of business and technology—with a particular interest in the human side of change through technology.

Graham lives in Toronto, Canada.